D1599495

The Options Trading Body of Knowledge

The Definitive Source for Information

About the Options Industry

Michael C. Thomsett

Vice President, Publisher: Tim Moore
Associate Publisher and Director of Marketing: Amy Neidlinger
Executive Editor: Jim Boyd
Editorial Assistants: Myesha Graham and Pamela Boland
Operations Manager: Gina Kanouse
Digital Marketing Manager: Julie Phifer
Publicity Manager: Laura Czaja
Assistant Marketing Manager: Megan Colvin
Cover Designer: Chuti Prasertsith
Managing Editor: Kristy Hart
Project Editor: Betsy Harris
Copy Editor: Water Crest Publishing
Proofreader: Language Logistics, LLC
Senior Compositor: Gloria Schurick
Manufacturing Buyer: Dan Uhrig

ISBN-10: 0-13-714293-5
ISBN-13: 978-0-13-714293-4
Pearson Education LTD.
Pearson Education Australia PTY, Limited.
Pearson Education Singapore, Pte. Ltd.
Pearson Education North Asia, Ltd.
Pearson Education Canada, Ltd.
Pearson Educación de Mexico, S.A. de C.V.
Pearson Education—Japan
Pearson Education Malaysia, Pte. Ltd.
           Library of Congress Cataloging-in-Publication Data

Thomsett, Michael C.
  The options trading body of knowledge : the definitive source for information about the options industry / Michael Thomsett.
      p. cm.
  Includes index.
  ISBN 978-0-13-714293-4 (hardback : alk. paper)
  1. Options (Finance) 2. Stock options. I. Title.
  HG6024.A3T476 2010
   332.64'53—dc22
                         2008053241

For George C. Huff,
mentor and friend, who opened so many doors for me.

Contents

Acknowledgments

Thanks to the many options industry folks who have shared information generously and provided support for this and many other projects. Notably, I want to thank Marty Kearney of The Options Institute and CBOE, who is always ready to share information and to provide support; Paul Ronan, who has provided so many people with a paper-trading platform for advanced options strategies; Guy Cohen, fellow author and friend; and Virginia Gerhart, CFP, whose insights have always been invaluable.

Thanks also to Jim Boyd of FT Press, who, as executive editor, provided editorial guidance and support of this project.

Finally, thanks to my wife Lulu for her objective critique and willingness to review my work and help me to remove many typos and other errors before sending work forward, and for willingly providing a first edit of my work.

About the Author

Michael C. Thomsett has authored dozens of financial books, notably on the topics of options. These include *Options Trading for the Conservative Investor* (FT Press); *Winning with Options* (Amacom Books); *The LEAPS Strategist* (Marketplace Books); and the best-selling *Getting Started in Options* (John Wiley & Sons), now in its 8th edition with over 250,000 copies sold.

Thomsett is also author of *The Investment and Securities Dictionary* (McFarland), named by *Choice Magazine* as an Outstanding Academic Book for 1988, and many other investment and trading books. Before starting his professional writing career in 1978, Thomsett was an accountant. He also spent seven years as a consultant in the financial services industry with clients including securities broker/dealers, insurance master agencies, and insurance companies. He has been an active options trader since the mid-1970s.

Thomsett lives in Nashville, Tennessee, and writes full time.

Introduction

Enhancing profits is a goal for every stock investor. The options market is one avenue to achieving this goal, but it is complex; within the market itself, there are many ways to trade. This makes the options market both exciting and potentially risky.

The scope of possible strategies can be overwhelming for an options trader. The basic trades—buying calls or puts for speculation—are only the most obvious uses of options. They can be used in a broad range of expanded strategic applications. Some are very high-risk, and others are very conservative.

One of the most popular strategies is the *covered call*, which involves selling one call against 100 shares of stock owned. A covered call seller (also called a writer) receives a premium when the option is sold, and that premium is profit if the call ends up expiring worthless. The short position can also be closed at any time or held until exercise. In any of these outcomes, the trader continues to earn dividends on the stock and has a lot of control over the outcome. A properly selected covered call can easily create double-digit profits in any of the possible outcomes. This makes the strategy practical for most people.

On the far side of the spectrum is the practice of selling naked options. When traders do this, they receive premium income, but they also risk exercise and potentially large losses. Many variations of naked writes might be used to mitigate the market risk. In between the very conservative and the very high risk are numerous other strategies. Options can also be used to hedge stock positions, reduce risk, and enhance profits in many ways.

This book is designed to provide readers with a comprehensive reference for the entire options market. Most people prefer to focus on the listed options available on individual stocks, and this is the focus of the examples provided in the "Option Strategies" chapters. However, options are also available on futures, indices, and mutual funds, and the options market has expanded beyond its original limited scope and size. In the 1970s, when publicly traded options first became available, only a few traders even knew about options. Today, the entire options market has become mainstream, and a growing number of people are recognizing that options can provide many roles within a market portfolio and can serve a broad range of risks.

The one change in technology that has made the options market so widely accessible has been the Internet. Two developments have significantly affected the way that traders are able to trade and can afford to be in the market at all. First is access itself. With the Internet, anyone can go directly to current option listings and track their holdings or identify opportunities. Only a few short decades ago, before the Internet existed, options traders had to rely on stockbrokers, which meant having to visit or telephone an office, wait for the stockbroker to look up listings, and then decide on whether to make a trade. Any stockbroker who was not physically on the floor of an exchange had a considerable time lag as part of this process, making active trading impossible.

The second major change is cost. In the "old days" when you could only trade through a broker, commission costs were quite high compared to today's cost. With widespread use of online discount brokerage services, options trades cost as little as a few dollars, with the average ranging between seven and ten dollars each way. So a round trip (buy and sell) can be accomplished for less than quarter of one point, which is a huge discount over commission costs of the past.

Do you need a broker? This is the question that every trader has to deal with when thinking about moving to a discount service, where trade execution is offered without advice. Ironically, the answer for options trading is that you not only do not need a broker, but using one means you probably should not be trading options. By definition, any trader who has enough experience or knowledge to actively trade options should be using a discount broker. The concept of asking a broker's advice for an options trade is nonsensical for three reasons. First, stockbrokers are not necessarily skilled within the options market, even if they are licensed to execute options trades. Second, options trading demands on-going tracking of both options and the stocks they refer to. Third, paying a high commission to a full-service brokerage firm erodes profits from options trades, making many strategies marginal or impractical.

This book is designed for the options trader, whether a novice or skilled pro, who understands and appreciates the market issues. They are going to be more likely than average to employ a discount brokerage service, to make their own decisions, and to monitor their investments. Full-commission brokerage is appropriate only for clients who are worried about risk, who are less knowledgeable about markets, and who trust their broker to give them sound advice. This is a large market, although it is not growing. In comparison, the options market is growing and expanding. Not only are options available today on more products than ever before, but the volume of trading has also grown at incredible speed. In 1973, slightly more than one million contracts were traded. In 2007, more than 944 million traded. In the 34 years between 1973 and 2007, the annual volume declined only seven times. But the recent explosion of the options market has been impressive. For example, between 2006 and 2007, total volume grew by 40 percent; the previous year, growth was 44 percent. The future of this market is going to be even bigger, and a growing number of investors will use options in some form as an integral feature of their portfolio. This alone is a substantial change in the options market.

In the past, options have been viewed by "the crowd" of Wall Street as an oddity, a side-bet, or an entirely separate market, appropriate only for speculators. But as new products and new strategies have been developed, this outlook has evolved. Today, retail and institutional investors use options to (a) insure long portfolio positions, (b) hedge short risks, (c) play short-term market price swings, and (d) enhance profits. Even in the most basic of portfolios, all these applications of options make them valuable management and risk-reduction tools. The most basic speculation in options is an entry strategy for many options traders, but it is becoming less important over time. Today, the options market has grown into a means for taking a lot of risk out of the investment equation.

This book provides a market overview and discussion of risks, in addition to a comprehensive listing of strategies. Most of these strategies are accompanied by tables and illustrations identifying profit and loss zones, as well as breakeven points. The strategy section uses companies for examples. These are based on actual option values for three publicly listed companies; however, their names have been changed due to the ever-evolving share prices of each. All the stock prices and option premium values are based on the closing values of those stocks and options as of December 31, 2007. By using this fixed moment in time, all examples are based on the same data. However, even though stock and option valuation changes constantly no matter when you analyze relative values, the approximate option risks and opportunities remain identical. As long as time to expiration is the same as that in the examples, and proximity between strike price and current market value remains within the same range, the values of options and the likely outcome of strategies will work in the same manner.

This book also provides a very comprehensive explanation of how option premium develops based on various elements of value; calculation of returns from options and stock trading; federal taxation works in the options market; how stocks are picked for options trading; online and print resources; and a very complete glossary of terms that options traders will find valuable.

chapter 1

Market Overview

The realm of options is a highly specialized, intricate, and often-misunderstood market. The reputation of options as high risk is only partially deserved. In fact, you can find option products to suit any investment profile, from very high risk to very conservative. This market has grown tremendously since 1973, when the modern era of options trading officially began. Since that first year when options trading began in the U.S., annual volume has grown from 1.1 million contracts (in 1973) up to over 3 billion (in 2008).[1]

Today, options are more popular than ever and have become portfolio tools used to enhance profits, diversify, and reduce risks. Only a few years ago, a few insiders and speculators used options, and the mainstream investor did not have access to trading. Most stockbrokers were not equipped to help their customers make options trades in a timely manner, placing the individual investor at a great disadvantage. With today's Internet access and widespread discount brokerage services, virtually anyone with an online hook-up can track the markets and trade options.

The History of Options Trading

There really is nothing new about options. They can be traced back at least to the mid-fourth century B.C. Aristotle wrote in 350 B.C. in *Politics* about Thales, a philosopher who anticipated an exceptionally abundant olive harvest in the coming year and put down deposits to tie up all of the local olive presses. When his harvest prediction came true, he was able to rent out the presses at a greatly appreciated rate.[2]

In this example, the deposits created a contract for future use. When that contract gained value, the option owner (Thales) proved to be a shrewd investor. Options enable traders to leverage relatively small amounts of capital to create future profits or, at least, to accept risks in the hope that those options will become profitable later. This all relies on the movement of prices in the underlying security. Thales relied on supply and demand for olive presses, and the same strategic rule applies today. Options are popularly used to estimate future movement in the prices of stocks or indexes. The concept is the same, and only the product is different.

A similar event occurred in seventeenth century Holland with a much different outcome, when interest in tulips sparked a mania. The tulip had become a symbol of wealth and prestige, and the prices of tulip bulb options went off the charts. By 1637, prices had risen in these options to the point that people were investing their life savings to control options in single tulip bulbs. The craze ended suddenly, and many people lost everything overnight. Banks failed, and a selling panic took the high level of prices down into a fast crash. There is a valuable lesson in this "tulipmania" for everyone trading options today. In an orderly market, prices of stocks and options rise and fall logically. The reasoning is sound because tangible supply and demand factors make sense. In a market craze, prices change quickly and irrationally. In the tulipmania example, there was no rational reason for anyone to invest everything in tulip bulb options—other than the fact that everyone else was doing it, and it seemed that they were getting rich in the process.

The difference between Thales and the Dutch was one of common sense. Thales saw an opportunity and invested with a clear vision of how profits would follow. He was correct, and he made a profit. In the tulipmania example, greed blinded people, and the reckless actions brought about the crash. Symptoms included the rapidly growing prices, expansion of the market, and the failure to realize that the prices were simply too high.

For many decades after the Dutch experience, public sentiment about speculation was unfavorable. Of course, there were numerous examples of market speculation, which never seems to disappear altogether. However, in the U.S., nothing really took place in any form of options trading in the public markets until 1872. That year, a businessman named Russell Sage developed the first modern examples of call and put options. He made money on the venture and bought a seat on the New York Stock Exchange two years later. His career was successful, but was spotted with occasional scandals. In 1869, he was convicted under New York usury laws and was later associated with Jay Gould, an infamous market manipulator. Gould had tried to corner the gold market at one point and later invested in the railroad industry, along with Sage and many others.

The Sage options lacked standardized terms (rules making option features identical in each case), making it difficult to expand the market beyond the initial buyer and seller. Standardized terms in use today include the number of shares of stock each option controls, the day the option will expire, the stock on which an option is being offered, and the stock price pegged to each specific option.

The Sage options started a trend that never ended. These contracts remained largely limited to a few insiders in the exchanges and were traded over the counter (any form of trading when a specific exchange is not involved in the trade). This trading format remained the same, without any reliable trading rules or valuation, until the 1970s.

The Chicago Board of Trade (CBOT) was interested in diversifying the options market as a means for bolstering trading in the larger investment market. CBOT established a new organization in 1973, the Chicago Board Options Exchange (CBOE). On April 26, 1973, CBOE initiated the first options market with guaranteed settlement (ensuring every buyer and seller that the market would promise execution) and standardization of price, expiration, and contract size for all listed call options. The Options Clearing Corporation (OCC) was also created to act as guarantor of all option contracts. (This means that the OCC acts as buyer to each seller and as seller to each buyer, guaranteeing performing on every option contract.) Trading was initially available on 16 listed companies.[3]

By 1977, when put options trading was first allowed, the market had grown to over 39 million contracts traded (in 1973, only 1.1 million traded). Trading began taking place not only through the CBOE system, but on the American, Pacific, and Philadelphia Exchanges as well. Today, volume is higher than ever before and spread among the CBOE as well as the American, Philadelphia, New York, International, and Boston Exchanges. A breakdown of 2007's record 2.86 *billion* contracts traded is provided in Figure 1.1.

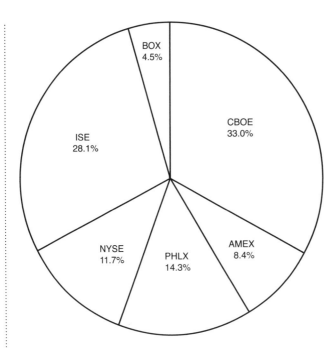

Figure 1.1   Option contract volume by Exchange, 2007

Source: CBOE 2007 Market Statistics

Growth in the markets over 35 years has been impressive. This is summarized in Figure 1.2.

In 1982, a new concept was introduced beyond the use of calls and puts on stocks. Index options were originated by the Kansas City Board of Trade with options on the Value Line stocks. This Value Line Index option was followed in 1983 with CBOE's introduction of the OEX (comprised of 100 large stocks, all with options on the CBOE), which is now known as the S&P 100 Index. The Chicago Mercantile Exchange introduced S&P 500 futures trading, which began a trend in trading of futures indexes as well as options. In 1976, CBOT began trading in Government National Mortgage Association (GNMA, also known as Ginnie Mae) futures, which was the first interest rate futures product. Many more options and futures indexes have since followed. By 1984, after years of futures trading on agricultural commodities, options were first listed on soybeans. This began an expansion of both options and futures markets. Today, you can write *options* on *futures*, which is a form of exponential leverage. A futures option is a derivative on a derivative.

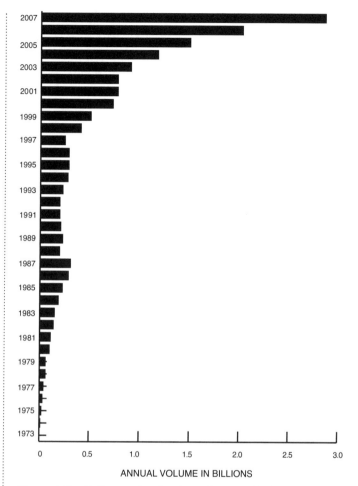

Figure 1.2 Option contract volume by year, 1973–2007

Source: CBOE 2007 Market Statistics

In 1990, the CBOE introduced a new type of options, the long-term equity anticipation securities option, or LEAPS. The LEAPS option is exactly the same as the listed call or put, but its lifespan is much longer. The traditional option lasts only eight months or so at the most before it expires, but the LEAPS option extends out as far as 30 months. This longer-term option makes strategic planning much more interesting and flexible, allowing traders and investors to use the LEAPS option in many ways that are not practical with a shorter-term call or put.

Today's options market looks much different than the market of a few decades ago. It has expanded and continues to expand every month. You can buy and sell options on stocks, futures, indexes, and even exchange-traded funds (ETFs). In the future, additional forms of expansion will broaden the influence of options into many more markets, with the introduction of new and potentially profitable option tools.

Basics of Options—Standardized Terms

Today, all listed options include standardized terms. These are the type of option (call or put), the underlying security on which options are bought or sold, the strike price, and the expiration date.

Calls and Puts

A Call Is the Right to Buy 100 Shares

A *call* is an intangible contract that grants its owner the right, but not the obligation, to buy 100 shares of a specific underlying stock at a fixed strike price per share and on or before a specific expiration date. The owner of the call acquires these rights in exchange for a premium paid for the option. The value of the option rises if the terms become more attractive before expiration, meaning the market price of the stock rises. If the current market value of the call is higher than the fixed strike price, the option value rises; if it remains at or below the fixed strike price, the premium value falls.

The call buyer is not obligated to exercise the option; there are three choices. The option may be allowed to expire worthless, which occurs if the current market value remains below the strike price. The contract can also be closed at a profit and sold on the open exchange. The sale might also occur at a small loss; the options trader may realize that the position is unlikely to become profitable, and taking a partial loss then becomes preferable to letting the contract expire. Finally, the options owner can exercise that option and buy 100 shares at the fixed strike price. For example, if the strike is 50 and current value per share is $56, exercise of the option enables its owner to buy 100 shares at the fixed price of $50 per share, or six dollars per share lower than current market value.

The call seller does not pay a premium, but receives one. When a trader sells an option, or goes short, the trading sequence is reversed from the sequence most people understand. Rather than the well-known *long* position of buy-hold-sell, a *short* position has the sequence sell-hold-buy. When a trader sells a call, this grants the rights under the option contract to someone else: a buyer. The seller and buyer do not meet face to face because all options trading is done through the Options Clearing Corporation (OCC), which facilitates the market (acting as seller to each buyer and as buyer to each seller). When exercise does occur, the OCC matches the transaction and assigns the shares of stock to an options writer. In the case of a short call, the seller is obligated to sell 100 shares of the underlying stock at the fixed strike price. For example, if the strike is 50 and current market value per share is $56, a seller is obligated to sell shares at the fixed strike of $50 per share, even if that means having to buy the same shares at $56 per share, or for a loss of six dollars ($600 for 100 shares).

A Put Is the Right to Sell 100 Shares

A put is the opposite of a call. This option grants its owner the right, but not the obligation, to *sell* 100 shares of stock at a fixed strike price, on or before a specific expiration date. Just as a call owner hopes the value of the stock will rise, a put owner hopes the value of the stock will fall. The more the price falls, the more valuable the put becomes.

A put buyer might take one of three actions before expiration. The put can be closed at its premium value and a profit or loss taken. The put can also be allowed to expire worthless, which occurs if the underlying stock is at or above the strike price at the time of expiration. Finally, the put can be exercised. This means the owner is allowed to sell 100 shares of the underlying stock at the fixed strike price. For example, if a trader owns 100 shares purchased at $50 per share and also buys a 50 put, exercise will occur at that price. If the stock's value falls to $41 per share before expiration, the put owner can exercise the put and sell 100 shares for $50 per share, even though current market value is far lower. The put protects the stock investor from the decline by offsetting the stock loss in the appreciated value of the put.

A put seller grants the option rights to a buyer. So if a trader sells a put, it means that he might be obligated to accept 100 shares of the underlying stock at the fixed strike. If the strike is 50 and the current market value of the stock falls to $41 per share, the put will be exercised. The put seller will have 100 shares put to them at the fixed price of $50 per share, or nine points above current market value.

The Underlying Security

The underlying security in an option contract is fixed and cannot be changed. Options are traded only on a single security, which may be a stock or an index, future, currency, commodity, or exchange-traded fund (ETF). Many creative expansions and variations of the options market have been developed and continue to be introduced. Examples in this book focus on options on stock, as the best-understood and most popular form of listed options trading.

Every option refers to the rights on 100 shares of stock. A single option grants rights to those 100 shares, either to buy (call) or sell (put). The option's current premium value is expressed on a per-share basis, however. For example, if an option is currently valued at 4.60, that means it is worth $4.60 per share, or $460.00 (per 100 shares).

Strike Price

The value at which options can be exercised is called the *strike price* (also known as striking price and exercise price). For example, if the strike is 50, it means the option will be exercised at $50 per share if and when exercise does occur. The proximity between strike price and current market value determines the option's value, along with the amount of time remaining until expiration.

When the underlying stock's current value is higher than a call, the call is in the money (ITM). When the price is lower than the strike, the call is out of the money (OTM). When it is exactly equal to the strike, the call is at the money (ATM).

For puts, this is opposite. When the stock's price is higher than the put strike, it is out of the money (OTM); when the stock price is lower than the fixed strike, that put is in the money (ITM). These distinctions are very important; a strategy for buying or selling options relies on stock moving in a desired direction to create profits.

Expiration

Every option is scheduled to expire in the future. The farther away the expiration date, the higher the option's value. With options, traders coordinate time with proximity of price. The closer the strike to current market value of the underlying stock, the more the price of the option reacts to price changes in the underlying stock; the closer the expiration date, the more the option's premium value reacts to the stock's price movement.

When a trader opens an option, the time remaining until expiration affects the decision about which specific contract to buy or to sell. Time to expiration affects the value of the option and defines risk. For options sellers, the longer the time until expiration, the greater the risk of exercise. Exposure to this risk is one of the most important factors in comparing option prices. Exercise is most likely to occur on the last trading day, but it can occur at any time during the life of the option. For options buyers, a long time until expiration is positive because with more time, there is an increased chance of movement in the price of the underlying stock. A desirable change in value (upward for call buyers or downward for put buyers) defines whether options will be profitable or not. But a negative to this expanded time is higher cost. The more a trader pays to buy an option, the more difficult it will be to create future profits.

The Option Premium and Its Components

The *premium*—the cost of the option—is going to vary over time based on three factors: time to expiration, volatility, and intrinsic value.

Time to Expiration

The longer the time until expiration, the higher the "time value" of the option. Time value tends to change very little for exceptionally long-term options. For example, for a LEAPS (long-term equity anticipation securities) option, which may have as much as 30 months to expiration, changes in the underlying stock's price have little or no effect on the time value. As time approaches expiration, however, the rate of decline in time value premium accelerates. At the point of expiration, time value will have declined to zero.

The tendency for time value to accelerate as expiration approaches affects the decision about when to buy or sell an option, especially for those trading short positions (selling options). The majority of long options are not going to become profitable, mainly due to the declining time value. However, short options traders know that time value creates profits. As time value evaporates, the option loses premium value. And because short traders go through the sequences of sell-buy-hold instead of the opposite, reduction in value equals profits. So the short trader sells to open, and then when value has fallen, buys to close at a lower premium level. This is where time value works for the seller.

Volatility

The most elusive and hard to understand part of premium value is due to the level of volatility in the underlying stock. This volatility is an expression of market risk. Stocks with relatively narrow trading ranges (the distance between highest and lowest price levels) are less risky, but they also offer less opportunity for profits in the stock or in options. Stocks with broad trading ranges and rapid changes in price are high-risk but also offer greater profit opportunities. The option premium level is directly affected by this price volatility. The level of unpredictability in a stock's current and future price level defines an option's premium value.

Some analysts include this volatility effect as part of time value, but this only confuses the analysis of options. Time value by itself is quite predictable and, if it could be isolated, would be easily predicted over the course of time. Simply put, time value tends to change very little with many months to go, but as expiration nears, the rate of decline in time value accelerates and ends up at zero on the day of expiration. But time value cannot be separated from the other elements of value, so it is often seen as part of the same price feature. Time/volatility value is often described as a single version of "time value premium." If these two elements are separated, option analysis is much more logical.

The portion attributed to volatility might be accurately named "extrinsic value." This is the portion of an option's OTM premium beyond pure time value. Extrinsic value can be tracked and estimated based on a comparison between option premium trends and stock volatility.

To understand how volatility works for the underlying stock, a few technical tools are required. The trading range is easily quantified for most stocks. If you study and compare stocks, you discover that trading ranges vary considerably. The greater the breadth of the range, the more extrinsic value you find in option premium. Even so, the most popular version of price volatility is far from accurate. To accurately track and predict extrinsic value, you need to adjust the method for calculating volatility for the underlying stock.

In its most common definition, price volatility is calculated by mathematically reviewing the price range over the past 52 weeks and then assigning a percentage to the range. For example, if the stock's range has been between 27 and 34 points, volatility is 26 percent. The calculation requires dividing the net price difference by the low, as follows:

$$(34 - 27) \div 27 = 26\%$$

This seven-point price range is really quite narrow when you consider what can happen over a period of 52 weeks. Now consider how those seven points change in terms of volatility when the price range is between 85 and 92:

$$(92 - 85) \div 85 = 8\%$$

The same seven-point price spread has been reduced to an eight percent volatility level, even though the price range is the same.

Another problem with volatility is that it does not distinguish between rising and falling price trends. One stock might experience a 52-week range but currently reside at the low end. Another with an identical price range might currently be valued at or near the top of that range. This price trend also affects the value of options at various strikes.

Finally, the price range does not allow for the occasional price spike. In statistics, one principle required to arrive at an accurate average is to exclude any unusual spikes in a field of values. This should apply to stock prices as well, but the adjustment is rarely made. For example, a review of Yahoo! (YHOO) at the end of August 2008 showed a 52-week price range from 18.58 to 34.08. The volatility was 83%, as follows:

$$(34.08 - 18.58) \div 18.58 = 83\%$$

However, this price range includes a spike up to the top of 34.08 when Yahoo! was negotiating with Microsoft, and rumors were that the Microsoft offer might be made at that highest level. Negotiations fell apart, and the price retreated. If you exclude this one-time price spike, the trading range was closer to 18.58-30.00. In this situation, volatility is reduced considerably:

$$(30.00 - 18.58) \div 18.58 = 61\%$$

Applying a basic statistical rule that spikes should be removed, the volatility for this company would be far lower than with the spike included. The definition of a spike is that it takes price above or below the trading range *and* that following the spike, prices return to the normal range without repeating the spike again.

The unreliability of the typical method for computing volatility should be discounted. To select options based on volatility, it is first necessary to develop a more comprehensive method for the basic calculation. This includes consideration of the following:

1. Price spikes, requiring adjustment of the 52-week range.

2. Changes in the breadth of the trading range over time (a changing trading range implies increases in volatility, which is likely to affect future premium value).

3. The number of points in the range compared to the stock price itself. For example, a seven-point trading range for a stock trading in the mid-20s is more significant than a seven-point trading range for a stock trading in the high 80s. Although this point spread varies in significance based on stock price, its effect on option premium is what really matters. Thus, the analysis of the point count should also track the trend from the beginning to the end of the one-year range.

Determining the level of extrinsic value (or, volatility value) requires considerable technical analysis of the stock's price *and* its trend. No current value should ever be studied as fixed in time, but rather takes on meaning when its change is part of the analysis. The trend affects recent changes in option extrinsic value and may also point to how that trend is going to continue to change in the future.

Intrinsic Value

The final portion of the option's premium is the most easily explained and understood. *Intrinsic value* is that portion of the premium attributed to in the money (ITM) status of the option. When an option is at the money (ATM), meaning strike is equal to stock price, there is no intrinsic value. When the option is OTM, meaning call strike is higher than current stock price or put strike is lower than current stock price, there is no intrinsic value. The only time intrinsic value exists is when the option is in the money (ITM).

For example, a call has a strike of 60 and the current stock price is 62. This option has two points of intrinsic value, worth $200. Each change in the stock's price will be matched by change in intrinsic value, down to the strike and upward indefinitely.

For a put, the movement is opposite. For example, a put has a strike of 45, and the stock price is currently at 42. There are three points of intrinsic value. So if this put's premium is reported today at 4.50, that consists of 3.00 points in intrinsic value and 1.50 points in some combination of time and extrinsic value. Like the call, the put's intrinsic value moves point for point with the stock. As the stock's price declines, the put's intrinsic value rises; and as the stock's price rises, the put's intrinsic value falls.

A Range of Strategies

Within the options market, a broad range of strategies can be employed to control risk, enhance profits, or to create combinations between stock and options or between related option contracts.

The range of strategies can be distinguished as bullish, bearish, or neutral. A *bullish strategy* produces profits if the price of the underlying stock rises. A *bearish strategy* becomes profitable when the stock price falls. And a *neutral strategy* does best when the underlying stock's price remains within a narrow price range. The types of strategies can also be broken down into a few broad classifications, as follows:

1. *Single-option speculative strategies.* The speculator uses options simply as an estimation of how the underlying stock price is going to move in the future and leverages that movement. This means the option cost is far

lower than the cost of buying 100 shares; so, a portfolio of speculative options controls far more stock than trading in the stock itself. Long option positions benefit when the price of the stock rises (for long calls) or falls (for long puts). Short speculative strategies, also called uncovered or naked writes, assume higher risk positions. Although the holder of a long position will never lose more than the cost of opening the position, naked short selling includes potentially higher risks. A naked call writer has potentially unlimited risk based on the possibility that a stock's price could rise indefinitely. A naked put writer faces a downside risk; if the stock value falls, the put will be exercised at the fixed strike price, and the writer will be required to buy shares at a price above market value.

Speculative strategies serve a purpose in many circumstances and can be efficiently used for swing trading. This is an approach to the market in which trades are timed to the top or bottom of short-term price swings. Rather than using shares of stock for swing trading, using long options provides three major advantages. First, it requires less capital, so a swing trading strategy can be expanded. Second, risk is limited to the cost of the long option, which is significantly lower than buying or selling shares of stock. Third, using long puts at the top of a short-term price range is easier and less risky than shorting stock.

Single options are also used to insure other positions. For example, traders may buy one put to protect current paper profits in 100 shares of long stock. They might also buy calls to mitigate the risks of being short on stock. Insurance of other positions, or hedging those positions, has become one of the most important ways to manage portfolio risk.

2. *Covered calls.* The most conservative options strategy is the covered call. When a trader owns 100 shares of the underlying stock and sells a call, the market risk faced by the naked writer is eliminated. If the call is exercised, the writer is required to deliver those 100 shares of stock at the strike price. Although the market value at that time will be higher, the covered call writer received a premium and continues earning dividends until the position is exercised, closed, or expired. A variation of covered call writing that varies the risk level is the ratio write. This strategy involves selling more calls than full coverage allows. For example, a trader who owns 200 shares and sells three calls has entered a 3:2 ratio write.

3. *Spreads.* The *spread* involves buying or selling options at different strikes, with different expirations, or both, on the same underlying stock. Variations include calendar, butterfly, ratio, and reverse spreads. These are among the most popular of options strategies because profits and losses can be controlled and limited in the structure of the spread.

4. *Straddles.* The *straddle* involves buying or selling dissimilar options with the same strike prices and on the same underlying stock. Risks might be greater, and creating profits is often more difficult than with spreads, but many variations make straddles interesting and appealing. Because one of the two sides can be closed profitably at any time, straddle risks can be reduced over time, especially for short positions or for the strangle, a variety of straddle.

5. *Combinations.* Some strategies involve the combined positions in options with related positions in other options, often with weight favoring bullish or bearish movement in the underlying stock. Any position with both calls and puts that is not a straddle is classified as a combination.

6. *Synthetic positions.* Some strategies are designed to create profit and risk profiles equal to other positions; these are called *synthetics*. For example, opening a long call and a short put creates synthetic long stock (an options position whose price will react in the same way as buying 100 shares of stock). A long put with a short call creates the opposite: synthetic short stock. The appeal to synthetic positions is that they can be opened for less capital than the mirrored position and often with identical or lower risk.

Anyone embarking on the use of options in their portfolio needs to appreciate the various levels of risk to a particular strategy as a primary consideration. The next chapter explains how risk varies among the different options strategies.

Endnotes

1. Source: Chicago Board Options Exchange (CBOE), *2008 Market Statistics.*

2. Aristotle, *Politics*, Book One, Part XI, c. 350 B.C.

3. The original 16 companies on which call options were traded in 1973 were AT&T, Atlantic Richfield, Brunswick, Eastman Kodak, Ford, Gulf & Western, Loews, McDonald's, Merck, Northwest Airlines, Pennzoil, Polaroid, Sperry Rand, Texas Instruments, Upjohn, and Xerox.

chapter 2

Market Risks

The real value of an investment and of its potential for profits can be compared and evaluated only when reviewed in terms of how much risk is involved. This important qualifying fact is too often overlooked by investors.

Options traders face the same risks as all investors, and these risks are caused by the same market forces, both within the market and outside the market. Risks come from economic causes as well as market-driven ones, such as supply and demand or the more complex investor and consumer sentiment indicators. The domestic political cycle and geopolitical changes all affect markets. Today, with improved communications and global Internet access, markets have become global in a real sense. In the past, references to a global economy or global market were often forward-looking but not practical. Today, the markets around the world are universal, and anyone can trade in foreign stock, futures, currency, precious metals, and other markets, all online. In the past, investing in a foreign-listed stock was both cumbersome and expensive. Today, the lines of international trade have blurred, and investors are no longer held to investing only in companies listed on domestic exchanges.

This new reality has also increased profit potential *and* risk. These two—profit potential and risk exposure—cannot be separated because they are different aspects of the same feature of all investing. The connection applies whether in a particular market sector, economic cycle, or type of product. Options, as a type of product, have greater risks of some kinds and less than others. For example, there is less market risk in taking positions in options simply because less money is required to open a position. You can control 100 shares of stock by buying a single call, and its cost will be a fraction (somewhere around 10 percent) of the cost of buying shares directly.

At the same time, this leverage creates a different, equally serious risk. Leverage itself might create greater potential for profits and for losses. For example, if you spend $10,000 in buying stock, the market risk is isolated to the risk of a declining value. However, if you place the same $10,000 into long option positions, that is full leverage. You might acquire up to 10 times more positions, which means much greater profit potential. It also means the position is exposed to greater risks. So you cannot escape risk entirely. When you exchange one risk for another, it may also mean changing the risk *level*. If a position creates greater opportunity for profit, the risk level will invariably be greater as well.

The wise management of risk requires a thorough appreciation of which levels apply to a particular position or mix of positions in a portfolio. Options can be used to reduce the common portfolio risks; however, the appropriate use of options should be designed as portfolio management tools and with an understanding of option risks as well.

Market and Volatility Risk

Stock investors normally think about market risk in terms of how stock prices rise and fall. Focus on overall markets and indices most often defines the market mood at any given time and, as a result, also defines levels of market risk.

Options traders consider market risk in two aspects. First is the market risk of options trading itself; second is the variation of risk levels among different option-trading strategies.

Market Risk of Options Trading

Option-based market risk is most often called *volatility risk*. The likelihood of acceleration or deceleration in option value is invariably the result of changing volatility in the underlying stock. Many speculators and traders employ volatility as the means for identifying entry and exit points in swing trading and similar programs. Using options in place of shares of stock provides many advantages, including limited risk, high leverage, and the ability to maximize sell signals with the use of long puts rather than with short stock. In addition, trading on volatility instead of trading only on price provides additional advantages, especially when the underlying stock is exceptionally volatile. The combination of volatility trading and advantageous use of time value premium near to expiration makes volatility trading a practical method for using market risk (volatility) effectively.

Implied volatility, or an option's prediction about the volatility of the underlying stock, is in a sense the opposite of option selection based on the stock's market risk. In other words, implied volatility predicts near-term stock price trends. If trading begins with observation of the stock's historical volatility, it might lead to timing and selection of options trades. If trading begins with an observation of the option's implied volatility, option trends mandate the timing of stock trades. Few trades employ one approach or the other; it is more likely that volatility trading involves analysis of both historical and implied volatility. However, a growing number of market analysts have begun to realize that an option's implied volatility often precedes stock price changes and that this can be used with other predictive tools to time trades in stocks.

So the total option premium is broken down into three distinct parts, two of which are very predictable, as follows:

1. *Intrinsic value* is always equal to the degree the option is in the money (ITM). If the stock is two points above a call's strike, there is a two-point intrinsic value; if the stock is three points below a put's strike, there is a three-point intrinsic value. In all cases, intrinsic value exists only when the option is ITM.

2. *Time value* is related solely to the time remaining until expiration. As the expiration date approaches, the deterioration in time value accelerates, and on the day of expiration, it drops to zero.

3. *Extrinsic value* is the only unknown portion of an option's premium. It varies based on volatility in the stock but also is affected by the length of time remaining until expiration.

Implied volatility is the isolated, unknown portion of an option's market risk. The intrinsic value (in the money, ITM value) of the option premium is the easiest to calculate because that value is equal to a specific number of points. Time value (that portion attributable solely to time) is also quite predictable if it is considered completely in isolation, and the loss of time value is known to evaporate with increasing speed as expiration approaches. Time value is known to decline, and that rate of decline accelerates as expiration approaches. So it is no surprise when time value acts as it does.

Both intrinsic value and time value are very predictable, but the unknown portion of the premium—extrinsic value—is where all the unknown elements come into play. The extrinsic portion of the premium is specifically related to implied volatility. A side-by-side analysis of two stocks demonstrates how this variable works. Given the same price level of the underlying stock, option strike level, dividend, and time until expiration, options traders will observe differences in total option premium. Why? This is the non-intrinsic, non-time value portion of premium, or the *value* of the option's implied volatility. Some otherwise unexplained spikes in implied volatility can be understood by insider trading or by the publicly known strength of rumors. Potential mergers, delayed filings of SEC financial statements, changes in management, or impending missed dividends are only a few examples of the rumors or events that tend to aggravate implied volatility.

Even in highly volatile underlying stocks, the longer the time until expiration, the less volatility the option premium reveals. As a consequence, the LEAPS implied volatility when expiration is more than two years away is likely to be close to zero—even when the underlying stock is quite volatile. The tendency is for long-term options to have quite low implied volatility, with those levels increasing to more predictable implied volatility levels as expiration approaches. Implied volatility of the LEAPS is influenced by time, which partly explains why it is often included with and described as part of time value. The two influences on premium value are vastly different, but the degree of volatility is going to be less responsive when a lot of time remains until expiration. This facet of implied volatility might be thought of as the "time value" of volatility, although it has nothing to do with the more predictable decay associated with approaching the expiration date. The fact remains that time does influence implied volatility, but in ways that are far less predictable than actual time value premium.

One risk involving volatility is in how well options traders predict the change over time—in other words, the question should be: "Do implied and historical volatility merge as expiration nears?" In practice, some backward-looking analysis reveals that a two-part analysis is a good predictor of implied/historical merge in these volatility factors. But this is not universal. In some cases, predicting a merge between volatility levels is not reliable at all. Implied volatility does tend to become more reactive to the underlying as the time horizon shortens. Implied volatility is probably for judging the relative risk of options. Using historical volatility in the same manner is less reliable, though, because stock pricing tends to be highly chaotic in the short term, and over-reactive to the very latest news, rumor, or market perceptions. So the evened-out moving averages of historical volatility are sound indicators, but historical volatility in the short term (that is, the last three months of an option's life cycle) is more problematic.

Variation of Option Strategy Risk Levels

The analysis of options based on implied or historical volatility is elusive and often intangible. In comparison, the other type of market risk is more easily quantified. When the various option strategies are studied and compared in terms of market risk, it is not difficult to identify strategies in terms of risk/reward levels.

On the highly conservative side, the covered call is the safest and most profitable of all option strategies. A study of possible outcomes reveals that a properly structured covered call is going to yield double-digit returns even in the worst-case scenario, when return is calculated on an annualized basis. A "properly structured" covered call contains specific attributes, as follows:

1. *Built-in capital gains if and when the call is exercised.* A call should be written on stock whose net basis is below the strike price of the short call. This creates a net capital gain in stock if and when the short call is exercised. At the same time, the short call should be out of the money to maximize the advantageous position regarding decline in time value premium.

2. *Yield is part of the overall equation.* Dividend yield should be higher than average to increase overall net return when all sources are considered in the equation (dividend yield, capital gains, and option premium). Dividend yield is often a significant part of the overall yield from the covered call, although it is easily overlooked or ignored. When you limit stock candidates for covered calls to those with exceptional dividend yield, overall covered call profits are increased.

3. *Exposure time is limited to maximize time value advantage.* The turnover rate is high, meaning that selection of shorter-term covered calls will experience accelerated decay in time value, increasing the changes for expiration or, in the alternative, for rapidly declining premium value so that the position can be closed at a profit. Time value falls most rapidly when expiration is close, so the short-term short call loses value more rapidly during this close-to-expiration term.

4. *Rolling to avoid exercise.* You want to have the ability to roll forward and up to avoid exercise if the call moves in the money (ITM) as expiration becomes close. This roll should create a net credit in the exchange of the two positions while also increasing the exercise price by one increment (thus increasing capital gain in the underlying when exercise does occur).

The covered call is popular among conservative traders for the simple reason that it consistently produces profits with a fairly low risk of exercise. Covered call writers profit from loss of intrinsic value when they write ITM short calls. However, it is more conservative and potentially more profitable to seek positions between two and five points out of the money (OTM). This maximizes the chances of declining premium value in the short option even when the underlying price rises and approaches or even surpasses the strike.

Covered call writers avoid exercise by rolling forward if and when the call moves ITM. This not only defers the expiration date and avoids exercise; it also creates an additional credit in the position. The extended period of exposure is a disadvantage; however, if you roll the covered call position forward and up to a higher strike, this achieves two benefits. First, it avoids exercise, and second, it replaces the strike price so that if and when exercise does occur later, additional profits will be earned equal to the difference between original and rolled strike prices.

One danger of rolling occurs when tax consequences are not included in the decision to roll forward. This can be especially costly for anyone who has owned the underlying stock for more than one year with the original basis far below current market value. The assumption is that if the covered call is exercised, the profit on the underlying will be taxed at long-term capital gains rates. That is true only if you write a call that is at the money, out of the money, or within a very limited range in the money. If the call is too deep in the money (see Chapter 6, "Option Taxation," for a discussion of "qualified" covered calls), the long-term counting period might be tolled and, in some cases, started over. The original covered call may be qualified under this rule, only to roll out of the money to a deeper level, creating an unqualified call unintentionally. So the original covered call might have been out of the money, but given today's underlying market value, a rolled call complicates the tax consequences. The forward roll is merely a strategic replacement of one call with another. But from the tax point of view, each short call will be treated as a separate position. So the original, closed at a loss, results in a current-year short-term capital loss, and the new call may be treated as a new and unqualified covered call. If that is exercised, the underlying stock might be taxed at higher short-term rates.

The tax risk of rolling covered calls makes it essential that any rolling for covered calls should keep the tax rules in mind. Ignoring this could result in much greater tax liabilities due to loss of the favorable long-term tax rate on the underlying stock.

Other conservative positions include the use of puts to insure long portfolio positions or long calls to hedge short stock risks. These insurance trades reduce or eliminate risk at and beyond the long option's strike. Ratio writes, or the use of partially uncovered short calls against a long stock position, are relatively conservative. Even though risk cannot be avoided in this variation, it remains relatively low as long as the ratio itself is not extreme. For example, a 2:1 ratio write is actually one covered plus one naked call, and the risk in this position has to be acknowledged. However, 3:2 to 4:3 ratios (three calls against 200 shares or, even safer, four calls against 300 shares) are increasingly less risky. The ratio write is a sensible method for using multiple option contracts to increase cash flow without greatly increasing market risk.

Moderate strategies include those programmed to guarantee limited profit in exchange for limited risk. Any outcome will be minimal in either event. So positions like the butterfly spread can be used when you expect short-term price movement or volatility in the stock. If volatility estimates are low, positions are appropriate that will become profitable within a narrow price range (with losses minimally fixed and to occur either above or below the profit zone). If volatility is expected to be high, the opposite position can be designed to provide a narrow mid-range fixed or narrow-range loss, with fixed profits either above or below.

Slightly greater risks occur in positions with fixed middle-zone losses and increasing profit ranges either above or below that middle zone. These positions might be synthetic because they reproduce price action in the underlying stock, but with a highly leveraged cost structure.

A greater level of risk occurs in the fairly simple but widely practiced single-option long position. Ironically, long option positions are normally the entry level allowed by brokerage firms for new options traders. Three-quarters of these positions will expire worthless or be closed at a loss. However, the advantage of buying calls or puts is that the dollar amount is quite small compared to the purchase of stock, and losses are always limited to the dollar value paid for premium at the time positions are opened. Considering the need to overcome time value decay while building intrinsic value in a long position, long options are speculative. As a long position trader, you rely on a combination of profitable volatility plus rapid price change in the underlying before expiration.

High-risk strategies include naked options, especially when positions involve multiple contracts. The naked put has limited risk because a stock's price can only fall so far. This risk is usually described as between strike price and zero. It is more accurate to define risk of a short put as between strike price and tangible book value per share. When a naked put is in the money, exercise can be avoided by rolling forward. A roll forward and down also reduces potential losses by lowering the eventual price of stock. The ideal forward-down roll creates a net credit while exchanging an in-the-money short put for an out-of-the-money short put. Exercise can occur at any time, but it is most likely to occur right before expiration or on the last trading day. So the short put writer has an advantage in the majority of instances because exercise can be avoided through the forward roll.

The short call is higher-risk than the short put because a stock's price can rise indefinitely, at least in theory. The unknown future high price of a stock is potentially an expensive problem because the short seller has to make up the difference between strike and market value at exercise. Naked call risks are considerable, but they can be mitigated or limited by purchasing higher-strike calls or purchasing shares of the underlying; both of these cover the short call and limit or eliminate risk.

Short call writers avoid exercise with a forward roll. Rolling to the same strike avoids most exercise while creating a net credit in the exchange. However, rolling forward and up reduces the potential loss if and when exercised. In theory, exercise can be avoided indefinitely through a series of forward rolls. However, margin requirements should also be considered. The higher the potential exercise cost (growing as underlying market value moves farther from the fixed strike), the higher the margin requirement will be; traders with limited funds might need to sell other holdings simply to maintain the short call position. The ideal roll forward and up creates a net credit while also replacing an in-the-money short call with an out-of-the-money short call position. This represents an exchange of intrinsic value for time value, which can be profitable as long as the underlying eventually remains at or below the strike. When that occurs, the premium value will decay rapidly as expiration approaches; but the short call position remains high-risk as long as the underlying stock is volatile or when the situation is evolving.

The greatest option market risks occur in short positions involving multiple contracts. Even if margin requirements can be met to keep these positions in good status with both brokerage and federal requirements, the market risk can change rapidly as the price of the underlying stock evolves. Rolling achieves a delay in exercise and, in many cases, can even escape exercise altogether. However, some short options traders have been taken by surprise when early exercise creates losses far greater than their premium income or when the price performance of the underlying maintains option premium value due to implied volatility trends. Depending solely on time value decay is not adequate. If options writers tend toward the more volatile issues, the decay in time value may be offset easily with extrinsic value premium, even as expiration approaches.

Inflation and Tax Risk

In many respects, inflation and tax risks are quite distinct and separate. You face inflation risk whenever price trends impact your purchasing power, and you face tax risk in any situation when income is taxed and the government takes a portion away from you. As serious as each of these risks is by itself, when you consider them together as a combined risk, you immediately realize that it takes a lot just to maintain the value of your capital before making any profit at all. For this reason, options are one of the few alternatives for offsetting the inflation and tax risk combination without violating your own risk tolerance level.

Inflation Risk

One way to look at inflation is as a loss of purchasing power. Inflation is more often thought of as the phenomenon of rising prices, which is the opposite side of the same price trend. One investment and trading goal is to offset lost purchasing power from inflation. To understand how this affects capital value, a highly conservative and risk-sensitive approach might be to make no trades at all; but this only gives way to the eroding force of declining purchasing power.

For example, over a 30-year period, purchasing power eroded in the U.S. to the point that you need $3.67 (as of 2008) to equal the purchasing power of one dollar in 1978. You can calculate purchasing power over any period of years at the Bureau of Labor Statistics website, www.bls.gov/data/inflation_calculator.htm. So in order for a 1978 portfolio to maintain its value for 30 years, it would have needed to grow to $3.67 just to break even after inflation, before any taxes were calculated.

Tax Risk

A closely related problem for any investor or trader arises from taxes. For options traders, there are two types of tax risk. Chapter 6 describes the tax rules for options traders, including how long-term capital gains rates might be lost with the wrong kind of trading activity. The following explains how tax planning may reduce liabilities by timing current-year losses versus gains in future years.

The first tax consideration for options involves the timing of net profits and losses. A short seller (that is, covered call, writer) receives the premium income in the tax year that the position is opened. But the profit is not taxed until the tax year when the position is closed, meaning a purchase-to-close trade, exercise, or expiration of the option. Similar advantages are gained by opening synthetic positions such as the sale of a put at the same time stock is sold. The sale of stock can be timed to create a tax loss in the current year, and the put used to create a synthetic replacement position. From the tax point of view, this will be treated as a wash sale if the short put is exercised within 30 days and the desired current-year tax loss will not be allowed. So as part of a planning and timing system, tax risk has to include a complete understanding of tax rules and penalties under some circumstances.

Another version of tax risk has to include discounting of profits based on tax liabilities. For example, if your combined federal and state effective tax rate (the rate charged on taxable income) is 40 percent, only 60 percent of pretax profits can be counted as after-tax net gains.

Considering that profits may be churned many times during the year, the tax consequence alone might not seem to be a very serious consequence. However, when the tax effect is taken into account along with inflation, the situation can be much more serious—not only for options trading, but for all forms of investing and trading.

The Double Hit—Inflation *and* Taxes

When you take a profit on a trade, the immediate tendency is to mentally count it at its full value. It is surprising to discover that when both taxes and inflation are calculated, some profits may actually be net losses.

To determine how much you need to earn to break even after taxes and inflation, you need to calculate after-tax income and then discount that by the rate of inflation. This requires an estimate, but you can easily calculate it based on recent rates of inflation. These current rates are calculated and published by the Bureau of Labor Statistics, with quarterly updates available online (www.bls.gov).

The formula for calculating your required breakeven rate of return is the following:

$$I \div (100 - T)$$
when I = inflation rate
    T = effective tax rate

For example, if the current inflation rate is 3 percent and your effective tax rate (combining both federal and state) is 40 percent, your breakeven is as follows:

$$3\% \div (100 - 40) = 5\%$$

You need to earn 5 percent on your portfolio just to break even after taxes and inflation. That rate of return preserves your purchasing power but creates zero profit. So you have to exceed 5 percent overall rate of return to earn any real profits.

This is where option returns become so valuable. Many traders discover that they cannot earn their breakeven rate in their portfolio without raising their acceptable risk level. However, with options strategies such as covered calls, this double-risk can be overcome. The returns from covered call writing, which are low-risk but high-yield, can be used to enhance an otherwise average rate of return in a portfolio.

To calculate a breakeven requirement in your portfolio, see Table 2.1.

The higher your effective tax rate and the higher the rate of inflation, the higher your breakeven rate is going to be. If you earn less than the breakeven, you are losing money on a post-inflation and post-tax basis. This is the essential problem with inflation and tax risk. In combination, it is a difficult risk to overcome. However, options are an effective means for overcoming this obstacle. A conservative strategy like covered calls can be structured to outpace the net breakeven level, while remaining a conservative strategy at the same time.

Table 2.1 Breakeven Rates

Effective Tax Rate	INFLATION RATE					
	1%	2%	3%	4%	5%	6%
14%	1.2%	2.3%	3.5%	4.7%	5.8%	7.0%
16%	1.2	2.4	3.6	4.8	6.0	7.1
18%	1.2	2.4	3.7	4.9	6.1	7.3
20%	1.3	2.5	3.8	5.0	6.3	7.5
22%	1.3	2.6	3.8	5.1	6.4	7.7
24%	1.3%	2.6%	3.9%	5.3%	6.6%	7.9%
26%	1.4	2.7	4.1	5.4	6.8	8.1
28%	1.4	2.8	4.2	5.6	6.9	8.3
30%	1.4	2.9	4.3	5.7	7.1	8.6
32%	1.5	2.9	4.4	5.9	7.4	8.8
34%	1.5%	3.0%	4.5%	6.1%	7.6%	9.1%
36%	1.6	3.1	4.7	6.3	7.8	9.4
38%	1.6	3.2	4.8	6.5	8.1	9.7
40%	1.7	3.3	5.0	6.7	8.3	10.0
42%	1.7	3.4	5.2	6.9	8.6	10.3
44%	1.8%	3.6%	5.4%	7.1%	8.9%	10.7%
46%	1.9	3.7	5.6	7.4	9.3	11.1
48%	1.9	3.8	5.8	7.7	9.6	11.5
50%	2.0	4.0	6.0	8.0	10.0	12.0
52%	2.1	4.2	6.3	8.3	10.4	12.5

Portfolio and Knowledge/Experience Risks

Stock investors spend considerable time and energy in trying to allocate their portfolio exposure, reduce losses, and anticipate future trends within the market. Emphasis is placed on specific methods of diversification and asset allocation and on managing leverage risk. Within these risk areas, options are valuable for reducing and managing the risk itself. However, the use of options as portfolio management tools also brings up the problems of two other kinds of risk: portfolio risk and knowledge/experience risk. Many attractive strategies are inappropriate for a trader whose knowledge and experience levels make those strategies unsuitable.

Portfolio Risk

Every trader needs to determine when and why to execute trades. One of the great risks for the stock portfolio is easily resolved with the use of options. This portfolio risk arises when stockholders decide to take profits.

The tendency in this scenario is to sell holdings as soon as profits are earned. These paper profits might disappear if prices reverse, so the profits are taken. Applied throughout the portfolio, this decision has the result of selling off all the winners and keeping all the laggards. This risk, which may also be called *liquidity risk*, is one in which all investment capital ends up in under-performing issues. Money cannot be transferred out without taking losses. Thus, liquidity risk can also be called lost opportunity risk. With capital committed in this manner, it is impossible to move capital quickly when market conditions present bargains.

An options-based solution eliminates or reduces this risk. Assuming that you would prefer to hold stock for the long term, it is illogical to take profits early and dispose of stock. However, with the use of options, you can maintain your portfolio *and* take profits without selling shares of stock. When prices rise rapidly, creating an unexpected higher value, you can take those profits by writing covered calls or by buying long puts. If the stock's price retreats, either of these positions will become profitable.

The advantage to the covered call is that in a short position, you receive the premium at the time the position is opened. Time favors the short position so that the chances of a profitable outcome are quite high. The advantage in the long put is that shares cannot be called away. The disadvantage is that as a long position, the premium must be paid. Secondly, it will require movement in the underlying stock's price to create a profit. The purpose of the long put may be only partially to create profits. The larger purpose is to create potential profits if and when the underlying stock's price does decline.

A related version of liquidity risk is experienced when you select covered calls that end up in the money, producing too little net return. If you have to hold short positions open in this scenario until expiration, it also means the underlying stock cannot be sold, as it has to be kept intact to cover the risk of the short call. The solution to this problem is to limit covered call writing to fairly short-term positions (three months or less) so that time value evaporates at its greatest speed. In addition, although exercise may be acceptable as one possible outcome, conditions often change. It might be worthwhile in some conditions to close short option positions at a loss and replace them with other short calls, sell the stock, or wait and see how the stock acts. If the prospects for stock appreciation have evolved in recent weeks, selling covered calls may no longer be the best strategy.

Knowledge/Experience Risk

Brokerage firms are required to determine that a trader has adequate knowledge and experience before allowing an options trading account to be opened. This usually is limited, however, to filling out an application form and funding a margin account. Approval consists mainly of ensuring that adequate funds are available to cover initial margin and that the individual has at least made a claim to having some knowledge and experience in options trading. Brokerage firms further impose varying trading levels to control investor and trader risks.

The initial, lowest level normally is restricted to taking up long positions only. As each level is advanced, more complex trades and strategies (and greater risk levels) are allowed. In the highest level, traders are allowed to write short straddles and spreads or to sell naked options. This all assumes that adequate available cash and securities are on hand for margin requirements.

Any complex market requires both knowledge and experience. You cannot fully appreciate the levels of risk you are entering without these attributes, and knowledge and experience is often gained in an expensive manner. Knowledge is acquired through extensive reading, research, and observation of how markets work. Many websites (notably the Chicago Board Options Exchange, or CBOE) offer free paper-trading links. This enables less experienced traders to try out their abilities in trading options without real money being put at risk. A paper trade is quite different from a trade with real money, but it provides you with some insight about how a trade actually works and, perhaps of greater value, what can go wrong.

Experience is usually gained by losing money in the market. In some respects, a stock portfolio can be nicely enhanced with a well-chosen range of options strategies; to gain experience in these, you need to move cautiously and slowly. Some basic trading guidelines need to be defined and followed. For example, as conservative a strategy as a covered call is, you need to understand exactly what happens when a call is exercised. For each exercise, 100 shares of stock are called away at the strike price. The covered call writer will see 100 shares taken from the portfolio and paid for at the strike price at a time when the market value is considerably higher. This has to be an acceptable outcome in order for covered call writing to make sense.

As you gain experience, your trading techniques and timing improve as well. Picking the best possible call in terms of strike proximity to current market value, time to expiration, and premium income levels are learned with experience. Covered call writers learn, for example, that with higher implied volatility, the return is higher, but market risks for the stock are higher as well. It becomes quite important to ensure that options are selected on appropriate portfolio stocks and not that stocks are selected based on how rich the option premium is at the moment. Experienced covered call writers also gain skill at the timing of rolling forward to avoid exercise and in the selection of appropriate replacement calls in a forward roll.

Diversification and Asset Allocation Risk

The focus on diversification easily overlooks the importance of ensuring that its application is effective. Options provide one form of diversification in portfolios with many different risk profiles. However, diversification itself is often misunderstood.

For many people, diversification simply means spreading capital among several different stocks. This is a very basic and initial type of diversification, but it might not be enough. If all the stocks in your portfolio react to market trends in the same way, this level of diversification is not effective. Owning stocks in the same industry sector is one common problem; but even owning stocks subject to the same economic cycles presents the same kind of problem. Diversification should extend far beyond the effective spreading of money among different stocks.

It also makes sense to diversify in terms of risk exposure. Buying insurance puts to offset possible losses in long stock positions is a form of diversification, as well as an effective hedging strategy. Using options to hedge a range of risks while limiting capital exposure is also effective.

You may also want to allocate your portfolio among different types of investments, a form of diversification called *asset allocation*. Some percentage of capital is placed in stocks, debt securities, highly liquid accounts, real estate, and futures as an example of broad asset allocation.

Just as a portfolio can be under-diversified, it can also be over-diversified. If investment capital is spread too thin, the overall rate of return is going to perform at average rates of return, at best. This usually means that considering inflation and taxes, the portfolio will not even reach your breakeven point. To out-perform the market in a broadly diversified portfolio, you need to either raise your acceptable risk level or find an alternative. Safe options strategies, notably the covered call, solve many of these over-diversification problems while beating the breakeven point. It is more profitable to limit diversification and to use options to improve net return.

Leverage Risk

The methods you employ in the use of capital define your overall rate of return. Leverage models often claim great potential but fail to address the risks involved in a particular approach. So over-leverage invariably involves serious cash flow risks, such as the need to fund borrowings on margin; margin calls when values decline in long positions or increase in short positions; and potentially higher losses than your risk tolerance finds acceptable.

Leverage risk is especially severe when you speculate with stock. Using margin accounts to maximum allowable trading levels in order to swing trade is not necessary negative in terms of market risk but can be severely high-risk in terms of leverage. Borrowed funds have to be repaid from profits or, if losses occur, from additional funds needed just to maintain minimum margin requirements. This presents special risks for stock investors.

A solution to the common leverage problems speculators face is to not use stock in strategies like day trading or swing trading, but to use options instead. The leverage value of using options in place of stock is considerable, and for a small fraction of the cost of buying 100 shares, a single option enables you to control 100 shares with much lower risk. Swing trading involves buying at the bottom and selling at the top; thus, a sell set-up for swing trading is risky if it involves going short on stock. However, instead of buying and selling shares, swing traders may buy calls at the bottom and buy puts at the top of the swing cycle. This reduces market risk exposure while employing option-based leverage to minimize and replace margin-based leverage.

Options traders also need to manage specific risks inherent in the options market itself. Options can also be used to mitigate, reduce, or completely eliminate many of the common stock-based market and portfolio risks. When used appropriately, options are effective portfolio and risk management tools, in addition to allowing more speculative and short-term trading. If you are a conservative, long-term value investor, you can also use options to improve current cash income, take profits without needing to sell stock, and reduce the risks of swing trading speculation as part of your stock portfolio.

The next chapter examines the elements of value in options in greater detail. Keeping varying risk levels in mind, your understanding of option value can be better coordinated with your personal risk profile.

chapter 3

Elements of Value

The cause and effect of option premium value is elusive to many traders. Many factors come into play, and no simple formula can predict how premium values will change. The influencing factors defining and affecting value include the following:

- Time to expiration
- Proximity between option strike price and underlying stock current market value
- Direction of change in price (in or out of the money)
- Volatility of the underlying stock (historical volatility)
- Implied volatility of the option

The current premium of any option involves three distinct parts: intrinsic, time, and extrinsic value. Each of these values contains specific attributes and behaviors that can be predicted to a degree. But the formulation of change and the weight of that change in option premium is a great variable. Not only do some options react more than others to underlying volatility (the feature known as *implied volatility* of the option), but the attributes of this volatility are constantly changing.

A stock investor knows that the current status of stock in terms of trading range, technical strength or weakness, and fundamental attributes (earnings, for example) are always evolving from past to future, and this evolution creates a continuum of changing market attitudes and perceptions concerning that company. The same is true for options but on an accelerated plane (especially when close to expiration). The looming reality of expiration—during the last month, for example—tends to bring option price variables into focus, but in the period prior to this (estimated one to five months), many changes in the factors affecting value are in play.

Proximity and Price

Traders observe that the closer the price of the underlying stock to the strike price of the option, the greater the responsiveness of that option. When the option is deep in the money or deep out of the money (underlying price is farther away from the strike), price movement tends to be far less responsive. Deep-in-the-money options display the expected point-for-point changes in intrinsic value, which might be offset by movement opposing intrinsic price. For example, an option 12 points in the money might not always be expected to change in value for every point of movement in the stock (especially with a lengthy time until expiration). In this situation, a two-point increase in the underlying might be matched with little or no movement in the option.

This phenomenon contradicts the simplified observation concerning intrinsic value. It is supposed to change exactly with the stock's price change. In reality, there is often a trade-off between intrinsic and extrinsic value. Although intrinsic value increases or decreases exactly with changes in the underlying price, extrinsic value may check actual changes in total option premium. It occurs because implied volatility has to be observed as a predictive force. Every trader who has bought a long option only to see it lose value in spite of favorable underlying price movement knows this occurs. So as a predictive feature of value, intrinsic movement is checked by extrinsic adjustment when the price movement of the stock is not accepted as a permanent trend. A multi-point price movement is not mirrored in overall premium change because the prediction includes the possibility of a price correction in coming sessions. Long traders know that growth in intrinsic value is offset by decline in time value; however, the adjustment made in extrinsic value exceeds even the predictable effects of time value decay.

For this reason, analysis of options strategies (see Chapters 7, 8, and 9) always compares possible outcomes on the assumption that positions are going to remain open until the day of expiration. That is the only time that intrinsic value is likely to move at or close to the movement of the underlying stock.

The three proximity levels of the option—in, at, and out of the money—further influence how this interaction between intrinsic and extrinsic value works. In the money (ITM) options contain intrinsic value equal to the number of points of difference between strike price and current value of the underlying. For example, when stock is at 47 and the strike of a call is 45, there are two points worth of intrinsic value (47 – 45). So the call will always be worth at least 2 ($200) at this moment. Value above 2 is a mixture of time and extrinsic value. For puts, ITM is the opposite; the current value must be below the strike in order for any intrinsic value to occur, and when this occurs, the put is ITM. For example, if the strike is at 47, and the strike of the put is 50, that put is three points ITM (50 – 47). The put will be worth at least 3 ($300) at this moment, with any additional premium value consisting of time and/or extrinsic value.

The price movement of intrinsic value tracks the underlying point for point. This only means that the option will always be worth its intrinsic value at the very least. However, it may also occur that intrinsic and extrinsic exchange offsets this, but rarely to the point that premium is going to fall below intrinsic value (this does occur when options are deep in the money, but only marginally). As expiration nears, the delta of the ITM option increases. When options are deep ITM, the intrinsic value is going to be equal to the ITM points, but extrinsic value may include little or no additional premium. In some cases, extrinsic and time value may even be negative so that the deep ITM option's value is *lower* than its intrinsic value.

For example, check the stock listings in the Appendix, "Options Listings," for an example of premium value reported below intrinsic value. JCN's closing price on December 31 was 108.10, so the intrinsic value of the January 55 call was 53.10 (108.10 – 55). However, the last trade on the January 55 was 48.90. The last trade on this option was 4.20 negative. What is not shown on these charts is the current big and ask. If you were to trade the JCN January 55 based on the disparity of premium versus intrinsic value, the margin would be much smaller. Bid was 52.90 (0.20 below intrinsic), and ask was 53.40 (0.30 above intrinsic). A buyer would pay that 0.30 in extrinsic value, and a seller would receive 0.20 below intrinsic based on these adjustments in the actual spread of premium. The "last" trade is useful for comparison, but actual trades are not going to track those levels precisely. This example demonstrates how this actually works for deep ITM options. The last trade might be less than intrinsic value, but bid and ask are invariably going to straddle that price. The spread is minimal, but it is going to be improbable that traders will be able to actually execute trades that produce easy profits from negative extrinsic value.

Calls and puts are both at the money (ATM) when the underlying stock value is exactly at the option strike. In practice, whenever the proximity is close (within one point in either direction, for example), it is considered to be ATM. A casual observation of the option's delta might lead to the assumption that delta will always be at 0.50 when ATM, but this is not the case. It is usually somewhat above 0.50 for calls and somewhat below for puts because upward price movement, in theory at least, has greater potential than the more finite downward movement. This recognition as a risk factor defines the difference between a naked call and a naked put. The put has a finite risk, whereas the call's risk is simply unknown, but certainly greater. Because delta is one way to predict an option's likely price movement relative to the underlying, ATM option movement is worth observing. The responsiveness of the ATM call or put in comparison with out-of-the-money price action demonstrates why proximity is so critical.

Out-of-the-money (OTM) options include underlying trading below the strike of a call, or above the strike of a put. OTM options have zero intrinsic value, so it is easier to observe how time and extrinsic value behave. Time value is going to decline in a predictable curve, so extrinsic value accounts for all the variables in OTM premium. The closer to the strike the underlying stock's price moves, the more responsive the premium will be, as though anticipating how the whole premium picture will change if and when the option moves ITM. A deep OTM option will see little or no change in premium other than decline in time value, often accelerated by the same direction of change in extrinsic value. The deeper OTM the option is and the closer its expiration, the less action in the premium. Even a sharp favorable change in the price of the underlying stock will have little or no effect on the deep OTM option. Its delta is at or close to 0.00, and as long as the likelihood of gaining any intrinsic value is remote, the status remains the same.

Expiration and Option Valuation

Time and price are intricately related in all option premium. Time value is predictable in a very specific manner. The decay in time value is predictable but is often cloaked by the volatility of the underlying stock and the resulting adjustments in extrinsic value. A common but inaccurate explanation of option premium value includes only intrinsic and time value. Predictability of time value decay is not easily recognized when it is broken down in this way.

Although time to expiration is a major factor in premium levels, it is best observed in conjunction with the evolving proximity between underlying price and strike. The relationship between time and proximity is exponentially related. This is seen in the emerging trends of extrinsic value. So just as intrinsic value might be offset by contrary adjustments in extrinsic value, the time value premium might be similarly distorted or altered. Time value premium in isolation will decline predictably, but when the combination of proximity (underlying to strike) and time to expiration are considered as a single feature of premium value, it will be seen that (even in OTM options) time value and extrinsic value often counter-balance one another. With a deep OTM option quite unresponsive to movement in the underlying stock (especially as expiration approaches), the expected rapid acceleration in time value decay might appear even greater than normal. This occurs when extrinsic value has been inflated in the past and, after movement of the underlying far from the strike, that extrinsic value declines rapidly. This may look like an increase beyond a normal curve in time value decay. As extrinsic value falls away, it appears that time value is moving more quickly than normal.

With the proximity being a factor in this alteration of otherwise predictable forces, the entire matter of premium tracking becomes quite complex. It is helpful to remember a few key features of how premium values work, as follows:

1. Intrinsic value is specific and predictable and is always equal to the number of points the option is ITM (underlying above a call's strike or below a put's strike).

2. Time value premium is also predictable, regardless of proximity factors. The closer the time to expiration, the greater the time decay. Time value reaches zero on the day of expiration, without exception.

3. Extrinsic value, a measure of volatility, is where all the variation is going to occur. This includes a measurement of implied volatility expressed in the changing option delta and historical volatility of the underlying stock. It is further influenced by the proximity between strike price and underlying stock's current market value; by the time to expiration; and by whether the option is in, at, or out of the money.

Most traders are keenly aware of expiration and the decay of time value, even when the other mitigating factors (specifically related to implied volatility) are not as evident. However, traders (both long and short) might also benefit by observing how implied volatility changes based on proximity. It would be reasonable to attempt to assign a "proximity value" to option premium, and to a degree, this is what delta achieves. A deep OTM option, for example, displays a delta of 0.00, and when ATM, calls tend to be slightly above 0.50 and puts slightly below. If a trader considers delta a predictor of whether the option is likely to end in or out of the money, it becomes easier to predict likely success of particular strategies.

This proximity value is used to greatest advantage by long traders. A long position trader has to overcome time and extrinsic value changes *and* experience an option ending up far enough ITM to create a profit on the day of expiration. However, long position traders might also profit by closing positions early when implied volatility inflates premium value. This may be predictable to a degree when the timing of entry into long positions allows for swings in the prices of the underlying stock. There are no guaranteed methods, but attempting to time entry into long option positions with such swings improves the outcomes. When prices fall considerably in a very rapid move, long call entry is signaled and may easily produce immediate profits when implied volatility is high. This is made more so when the option is close to ATM or even ITM. For example, on a weaker-than-expected earnings report, a stock's value might fall as much as 10 or 15 percent in a single trading session. This over-reaction invariably corrects over the following two to three sessions.

The same swing trading approach can take advantage of implied volatility using puts. For example, when a stock's price spikes upward in a single session on momentary news or even a rumor, it is likely to correct within two to three sessions following, especially once other traders recognize the over-extension of the price. Buying puts at this price spike creates a situation where correction is likely. ATM or ITM puts will benefit the most from this tendency.

Short sellers may use the same swings even more advantageously. Time value decay creates profits for short sellers in both ITM and ATM situations. Even OTM options may be sold short with some confidence. Remembering that 75 percent of all options expire worthless unless closed early, short selling presents a considerable advantage, and the trader will be able to wait out the last phases of time decay and extrinsic narrowing. An ATM option is somewhat higher-risk for the short seller because exercise is always a possibility. However, if movement is away from ITM, the higher delta will produce short profits rapidly.

Even ITM short sellers can be profitable when close to strike because any decline in intrinsic value is likely to be close to a one-to-one point change as expiration nears, especially within one strike increment of ATM. In fact, short traders have considerable advantage over long traders because (a) they receive payment rather than making it, broadening their breakeven point spread; (b) time decay always favors the short positions; (c) short options can be rolled forward to further exploit time value; and (d) the strategy can be quite conservative when covered (coverage includes short calls with long stock, as well as short options with longer-expiring long options).

Interest and Dividends

The best-known factors affecting and influencing option value are proximity of underlying stock and the option's strike price; time to expiration; historical volatility of the stock and implied volatility of the option; and two additional features that, while not directly involved with the setting of premium value, are certainly a part of the equation. These are interest rate and dividend yield.

Interest rate applies regarding a trader's account. Interest is paid on credit balances and charged on debit balances (also known as the cost of carry of open positions on margin). If a trader is highly leveraged and using maximum margin, the interest will be relatively high. Another trader, limiting positions only to cash available, will have no debit on which interest is charged and may earn interest income on a credit balance. The open options and stock positions in a portfolio are influenced by interest rate, most notably when the margin balance is high and interest is being paid. This cost increases when time to expiration is extended (that is, through rolling forward to new positions). If this extension requires additional margin, interest will also be part of the net outcome.

Dividend yield has a direct affect as well and in several respects. For example, when a company increases its dividend, it usually causes lower call premium levels and higher put premium levels. Knowing this may represent valuable information, especially for short sellers. A higher dividend often makes a particular company more valuable as a long-term investment, but at the same time richer put premium levels might make short put writing more profitable and even less risky. But the same argument also applies in reverse. When a company decreases or suspends its dividend, call premium levels tend to rise, and puts tend to fall.

Dividends play an additional role as elements of value. Clearly, the value of an outcome in any position relies on the net profit or loss. This is especially true in analyzing comparable returns for positions such as covered calls. The net income from a covered call on two different underlying stocks is going to vary based on different dividend yields. Even if the annualized return from dividends is identical and even if potential capital gains are also identical, dividends represent a significant portion of overall return. If one company pays a 4 percent dividend and another pays nothing, it makes no sense to ignore the dividend.

This observation is more important than its relevance to an accurate net profit calculation. It also affects which companies are to be selected for writing options. Because accurate comparisons rely on annualized returns, the difference between dividend yields cannot be ignored in this comparative analysis. For conservative investors interested in long-term price appreciation, covered calls are excellent vehicles for enhancing current profits; but so are dividends. The basic selection of stocks for option writing should include dividend yield and, for some investors, might even exclude companies whose annual yield is low or which do not pay any dividend.

Stock Selection as Part of the Option Value Equation

It is often true that options traders ignore or minimize stock risks. For speculators who may never take a long position in stock, the distinction between growth and value (or between volatile or safe stocks) might be less important than the implied volatility of options and relative differences in the *volatility skew* (relative value of options on one stock that vary based on differences in strikes and their distance from current market value). For those who combine long-term investing with options trading, the question of stock selection is clearly an important consideration in selecting both stocks and options strategies.

The selection of companies in which to invest has two aspects for options traders. First is consideration of the basic investment value of that stock, and second is the analysis of option premium value and implied volatility. Ideally, options traders seek a degree of historical volatility adequate to enrich option premium (on the short side) and implied volatility to provide momentary bargain pricing (on the option side). However, if the option side of the matter is allowed to overrule basic stock selection, it is likely that traders will choose the wrong stocks, especially if they will be taking up positions in those companies.

For example, covered call writing should be led by the stock and not by the option. It is a common practice to review option opportunities and compute various outcomes and the yields they represent and then buy shares of that stock specifically to write covered calls. This is a popular method for picking covered calls, but it ignores the requirements of sound stock selection as a first step.

Basic Investment Value of Stock

Every investor and trader has to determine what levels of risk are appropriate and what positions belong in the portfolio. This is not a simple matter, nor are the standards identical for everyone. Some investors are interested in short-term profits (and consequently, also need to accept short-term risk). Others want to fill their portfolio with value investments, high-yielding dividend stocks, or stocks of companies that dominate their industry or offer exceptional and rapid competitive growth. All of these criteria may be in the mix for stock selection.

The criteria for stock selection (see Chapter 5, "Options and Stock Selection") used by options traders is likely to cover a range of fundamental and technical tests, preferably a combination of both. However, in picking companies in which to trade options, several questions should be addressed, as follows:

1. Will you take long positions in the stock or simply trade options? If you are only going to trade options, analysis of a stock can be limited to short-term technical features such as price volatility, strength or weakness of movement, recent breakout patterns or trading gaps, and the beta tendency of the stock (a measurement of price volatility relative to the overall market).

    However, if a trader plans to take positions in the short such as covered calls, the technical analysis should be augmented with a careful fundamental review as well. The fundamental tests should be designed to test capital strength, profitability, price/earnings trend, and dividend yield. More detailed tests beyond these basics is often unnecessary. Applying tests is a reasonable method for eliminating unsuitable companies for stock purchase and options trading.

2. Are you willing to accept the market risk of owning this stock? Even with a sound or conservative option policy, accepting the risk of long positions in stock might be considerable. In recent years investors in financial companies, for example, discovered that the once solid and safe industry went through serious credit crises, and many of the larger financial institutions lost 50 percent or more of their value. For example, Citicorp (C) was once considered an exceptionally safe blue chip investment with an attractive dividend yield and strong capitalization. In 2007 and 2008, the company lost more than half of its market value. Even a rich program of options trading would be unlikely to offset such losses entirely. Positions can be protected with short calls to a degree or with long puts for a period of time. But why would an investor take long positions unless they can live with the risks as well? Buying shares in "safe" companies like Citicorp is far from a sure thing, and options can protect long stock positions only to a degree.

3. What is your long-term goal involving stock and options trading? Too often, investors buy shares of stock with the initial intention of holding those shares for long-term appreciation, only to change the goal later. This might be unintentional. Writing covered calls may expose traders to exercise, and even though profitable, the unintended consequence is that desirable investments are moved out of the portfolio. These must be replaced with other, equally desirable shares of companies; however, if traders misuse their portfolios by trading options in ways that are contrary to their long-term goals, the purpose of investing capital is contradicted.

Traders will improve their overall portfolio performance by defining their goals in advance. For example, it could make sense to distinguish long positions in two categories. First are those stocks intended as long-term hold investments, on which no options trading should occur that could threaten this long position. (However, as prices rise or fall, traders may swing trade in long options to take advantage of short-term volatility or to protect paper profits.) A second group might include those stocks whose primary purpose in the portfolio is to provide coverage for unusually rich premiums in a covered call strategy.

Selection of Appropriate Option Positions

When investors begin mixing their stock and options trades, it is easy to lose track of the initial goal and risk tolerance levels. For this reason, definition of appropriate strategies not only helps to keep goals on line; it also helps traders to identify value within both stock and option positions.

Value itself is a variable. For example, for some investors, using short puts makes sense as a form of contingent purchase that also generates short-term income. As long as a trader is willing to acquire shares at the strike price and would be happy to have that company's stock in the portfolio, naked puts present a reasonable strategy. For other investors, this approach would be inappropriate and a violation of risk tolerance standards. The value of long or short strategies further depends on the portfolio goals, as well as the individual's experience and knowledge, income, available capital, and size of the portfolio.

As an individual's portfolio grows, options strategies are likely to evolve as well. A base of covered calls on exceptionally high-quality shares is sensible in most portfolios because it represents a conservative and high-yield strategy. But as the dollar value of the portfolio grows, additional strategies might acquire value as well. These may include strategies of greater risk or strategies of more conservative requirements.

Higher-risk strategies include straddles, strangles, and spreads, as well as ratio writes and even the use of multiple-option combinations. As traders acquire experience in trading options, risk tolerance levels evolve too, and this might lead to more exotic levels of trading and acceptance of greater risks. For others, more conservative hedging strategies will become desirable. For example, the use of long puts to protect paper profits might become highly desirable for many investors, notably those tending to be more conservative than average or beginning to think about retirement and preservation of capital as a primary goal.

In many stock-focused portfolios, options strategies may also be considered as a means of recovering paper losses when market values fall within stock positions. The rescue strategies available with options can make up losses far more rapidly than simply waiting out the market. If a company has been selected for its high quality, a temporary decline in market value is simply one possible outcome in a stock position; however, the recovery of a loss position can be accelerated in three specific ways, as follows:

1. *Covered call writing.* This provides downside protection from the premium received. In addition, a moderate loss in stock may be recovered with subsequent covered call writes; however, traders have to take care to avoid programming capital losses by picking the wrong strike prices for covered calls. The covered call is one of the more conservative strategies, but strike selection is essential in controlling and managing profits and losses. If the strike is lower than the net basis in stock, it makes no sense to write the covered call.

   Covered call writing is a conservative strategy, with one qualification: The strike must be greater than the net basis in stock (original cost minus premium of the covered call). Judgment should prevail as well. If the margin is minimal between net basis and strike, is it sensible to write the covered call? It could make more sense to wait out the price trend and (a) write a higher-strike call later, (b) simply wait for the price level to return, or (c) employ one of the other recovery strategies.

2. *Short straddles against long stock positions.* Although many consider this a high-risk strategy, the short straddle is actually not that risky; it is a combination of a covered call and a naked put. Remember that either or both sides of a short straddle can be closed when time value declines. In addition, both positions are initially OTM in the properly structured short straddle, and exercise of either side is often more of an advantage than a disadvantage. The receipt of a two-part credit may be substantial and may even make up all or most of a paper loss. If the short call is exercised, the stock is called away at the strike, and as long as the net basis of stock (original cost minus straddle premium income) is lower than the strike, exercise will be profitable. If the short put is exercised, the trader acquires an additional 100 shares. This presents the opportunity for subsequent covered calls on more shares or multiple-contract short straddles.

3. *Naked put writing.* When a trader would be happy to acquire additional shares of stock at the put's strike, the naked put is an advantageous strategy. It produces income, so even the strike is discounted if and when the put is exercised. If it is not exercised, the premium income is entirely profit. Upon expiration or close, the strategy can be repeated indefinitely. If exercised, the opportunity to repeat any of the three rescue strategies is not only present, but expanded. Exercise also represents acquisition of more shares, which averages the cost of stock and also helps to reduce the paper loss.

The reasons for acquiring stock often mandate how options trading occurs. The kinds of options trading undertaken may also dictate which companies end up in your portfolio. As long as the risks are understood and accepted by an options trader, those consequences may be quite acceptable. The goal, however, should be to avoid unwanted surprises. Some options strategies are assumed to offer one level of outcome, where actual outcome is quite different. Many covered call writers are surprised when their stock is called away, and naked put writers may be equally surprised when they are required to accept stock at inflated value based on current market value. Neither outcome should come as a surprise.

The next chapter involves calculation of returns from options trading. This might seem to be a rather straightforward process, but in practice, it is quite complex. The goal should be to achieve consistency and accuracy for comparative analysis and to ensure that risks of specific positions are acceptable given the potential returns.

chapter 4

Return Calculations

Figuring out how profitable a particular strategy will be is not as simple as it sounds at first glance. The variations of both outcome and calculation are complex, and this makes valid comparisons difficult.

Return calculations are valuable primarily as a means for monitoring the results of strategic decisions and for tracking portfolio performance over a period of time. This continual monitoring helps all traders to fine-tune their strategies, abandoning strategies that did not work out or that were too risky and focusing on higher-yield or lower-risk approaches to options.

These calculations are also used to anticipate likely outcomes given a set of facts. So calculations like "expected return" are designed to apply probability to options trading outcomes. For most traders, this is not a useful calculation because it includes estimates and is quite complex. Most people want to restrict their calculations to an analysis of risk and reward for a series of possible strategies.

Expected Return and Pricing Models

Expected return is simply the return you *should* earn if trades were made many times in identical situations. In other words, it is a statistical average. However, as most options traders quickly discover, the averages only apply historically. In the real world of trading, numerous new variables make the past useful only in comparison between different options, but not as actual estimates of return.

The likely return from a trade is also likely to be influenced by the current price. If an option's premium is exceptionally high based on a model of what it should be, the advantage goes to the short seller; if the price is exceptionally low, option long positions have a momentary advantage based on these models. However, models are just that: They predict and estimate, but they do not provide any guarantee of outcome. The best-known option pricing model is the Black-Scholes Model (see Chapter 12 "Option Glossary," for a complete description and the formula for this model). First introduced in 1973, this has become the industry standard for estimating what an option's price should be. However, there are several problems with this model. It is accurate for European-style options (which may be exercised only at or near the time of expiration). Thus, the formula applies to most index and sector options but not to listed options and LEAPS premium values, which can be exercised at any time (American-style). In addition, the formula is accurate for options on stocks that do not pay dividends, but less so for dividend-yielding stocks and their options.

Because dividend yield is excluded from the calculation of Black-Scholes, it is a difficult formula to use comparatively. Dividends reduce call premium as they are increased, so the importance of dividends in price modeling cannot be ignored. The originators of the model recommended that by discounting the current stock price to adjust for dividend payments until option maturity, this flaw could be offset. The formula can also be adjusted by weighting call premium when dividends are applicable. The formula also is based in part on historical volatility; however, stock volatility changes with the passage of time, so the formula is lacking in cases where the most recently displayed volatility is dissimilar to the period used in the calculation.

The importance of Black-Scholes was that it demonstrated how option pricing could be calculated to identify an *ideal* risk-free hedge. This works as a theory, but the model also serves as a means for making pricing calculations universal within the industry. The inaccuracies of Black-Scholes can be adjusted for by discounting the present value of dividends, which is the current stock price minus that discounted dollar value of dividends to be paid until option expiration. Models allowing for this include adjustments for option yield, discount of the dividend, and historical volatility. Additional methods for calculating premium include R.C. Merton's jump-diffusion model, put-call parity modeling, and many other complex calculations.

Pricing is valuable to the extent that it sets a standard, which also leads to observations and calculations of return from specific strategies. Options traders select specific options for their trades based on preferences of risk level, particular stocks and the implied volatility of their options, and favored strategic approaches to trading. However, the selection of a specific option within a stock's choices (based on proximity between strike and stock value, time to expiration, and the richness of each option's price) will produce a wide range of possible profit and risk exposure. If you study a range of option premium levels at any particular time, you will easily spot inconsistencies, however. In other words, even given the same expiration time and proximity between strike and underlying value, strike patterns alone do not predict a uniform change in option values.

The volume of trading in each option creates disparities in premium value, and these are best quantified by applying models such as Black-Scholes. However, because of that model's inconsistency, it is only fully accurate when applied to the options that (a) are available on a single stock, (b) that pay no dividend, and (c) if a dividend is paid, on options that expire at the same time. By limiting the application of any pricing model, these restrictions are acceptable because they are equally applied to all the options being studied. Once the analysis moves between stocks, it loses accuracy. After it is applied to varying expirations, the existence of a dividend further distorts the pricing model.

The anticipated or expected return based on pricing models is an interesting exercise and at times is useful for comparing options to one another. However, the majority of traders are going to be more interested in selecting strategies with profitable outcomes or with limited and well-understood risks. The following sections provide guidelines for this level of option return analysis.

Annualized Return

The starting point for return calculations is ensuring that comparisons between dissimilar holding periods are expressed on a valid basis. If you have one position open for three months and another for 18 months, their identical stated yield is not really identical. Because the holding periods are not the same, the returns have to be annualized.

A word of caution: Annualizing return should not be performed to estimate consistent outcome from a particular strategy. In short-term trades, it is quite easy to produce double-digit annualized returns and, in some instances, triple-digit returns. But any claims that this is a likely consistent type of yield are going to be inaccurate. Annualizing is useful in comparing and selecting options based on their holding period.

The first application of annualized return applies in the selection of particular options. For example, in a covered call strategy, which option is going to produce the best yield? If you seek only the highest dollar amount from a covered call strategy, it will make sense to always sell the one that has the longest possible expiration, especially with a strike close to current value. However, this is not always going to produce the most desirable yield. The selection of a particular strike is going to affect the likelihood of exercise, a factor that cannot be ignored in picking an option. The higher the strike, the lower the option yield, but the higher the capital gain on the underlying stock if and when the call is exercised. In the basic comparison between calls, begin by the relatively simple comparison of possible covered call candidates of the same strike but with different expirations.

In the case of JCN, for example, assume you bought 100 shares at $100 per share on February 1, 2007. Current value as of December 31 is $108.10. You consider writing covered calls at 110, based on the observation that exercise will produce not only income from the short call, but 10 points of capital gain in the stock position as well. The following calls were available at the 110 strike as of December 31, 2007:

Expiration	Time (Months)	Last Trade
January 08	0.70 *	2.15
February 08	1.70	3.63
April 08	4.70	6.00
July 08	7.70	8.30
January 09	12.70	11.70
January 10	24.70	16.64

* Based on average expiration of 21 out of 30 days in each month.

Based on JCN'S current price of $108.10 at the time of these premium levels, it is clear that—as is always the case—the longer the time to expiration, the higher the dollar value of the call. Many inexperienced covered call writers are immediately attracted to the higher dollar values, failing to realize the two flaws in this approach. First, the longer the time to expiration, the more time for the stock's price to develop and move; this means the longer the term, the higher the odds of exercise. Second, picking the highest dollar amounts ignores the probability that shorter-term options yield a higher annualized return; writing several shorter-term options is going to be more profitable than writing one very long-term option.

To annualize return, first calculate the unadjusted yield based on current option price and current stock value. The January 2008 call is worth 2.15, and the stock value is 108.10:

$$2.15 \div 108.10 = 1.99\%$$

Next, divide the unadjusted yield by the number of months in the holding period (in this case, 0.70); then multiply by 12 (months) to calculate the annualized return, which is the return that would be earned on this option if it were open exactly one full year:

$$(1.99 \div 0.70) \times 12 = 34.1\%$$

Remember that annualizing is intended to serve as a comparative tool to determine which options are most feasible for a particular strategy. It would be reckless to perform this calculation and conclude that a covered call strategy will consistently yield 34.1 percent per year. The strategy might yield that well, but annualizing should not be applied to draw that conclusion.

The complete formula for the annualized return is:

$$\left((d \div s) \div h \right) \times 12 = a$$

when:

d = Dollar amount of return

s = Current price of underlying stock

h = Holding period (in months)

a = Annualized yield

The annualized return for all the positions in the example is as follows:

January 08 $\left((2.15 \div 108.10) \div 0.70 \right) \times 12 = 34.1\%$

February 08 $\left((3.63 \div 108.10) \div 1.70 \right) \times 12 = 23.7$

April 08 $\left((6.00 \div 108.10) \div 4.70 \right) \times 12 = 14.2$

July 08 $\left((8.30 \div 108.10) \div 7.70 \right) \times 12 = 12.0$

January 09 $\left((11.70 \div 108.10) \div 12.70 \right) \times 12 = 10.2$

January 10 $\left((16.64 \div 108.10) \div 24.70 \right) \times 12 = 7.5$

Many first-time traders are surprised to realize that annualized return declines with time. The higher time value premium looks rewarding, but actual yield is invariably better with short-term covered calls, as this example demonstrates.

Annualized return is useful in the initial analysis of positions for short writing. The opposite is true for long call positions. You might also consider annualized return as annualized cost when trying to decide which long call to buy. The longer-out expirations cost more money, but the cost as a percentage of stock value is less. This provides greater time exposure for the long position. Accordingly, there is greater potential for a profitable outcome in distant expirations, if the trader believes that stock value will rise high enough to surpass the time value premium.

For example, a trader would like to buy 100 shares of JCN and pay no more than $110 per share. Buying a January 110 call provides a very low premium but only a remote chance of profit. However, a January 2010 call with a strike of 110 can be bought for 16.64, providing more than two years for the stock value to grow. The price of stock would have to reach a level of 126.64 per share by expiration in January 2010 in order for this trade to be profitable. However, for $1,664 in option premium, the trader controls 100 shares at 110. Buying those shares today would cost $10,810. For an annualized cost of 7.5 percent, the trader controls JCN shares and fixes the future exercise price.

Annualized return is valuable in comparing calls for any strategy. On the short side, annualized return enables traders to study comparable yields for a range of expiration times. On the long side, the cost of a position can be compared on the same annualized basis among a series of possible option positions.

Strike Selection for Covered Calls

Picking an expiration date is one-half of the covered call equation. Determining how long you are willing to remain at risk versus the dollar amount and yield of the premium for each option is the exercise that covered call writers go through. The other half of this equation is selection of the most appropriate strike.

The first guideline in this regard is based on the assumption that exercise is always a possibility for any short call at any strike. Exercise is most likely to occur on the last trading day, but it can occur at any time. Covered call writers must be willing to accept this risk and to structure call selection with the possibility in mind that exercise can occur. So the strike must conform to an important limitation: If the call is exercised, the strike price must be greater than the net basis in the underlying stock. "Net" basis is the original net cost minus premium received for writing the call, as follows:

Basis in stock − Call premium = Net basis

If strike price is lower than this net basis, exercise will create a net loss. For example, if original basis was $54 per share and premium from writing a covered call is 6, net basis is $48 per share ($54 − 6). Acceptable strikes include 50 or above, but anything below the net of $48 per share will not be appropriate.

The selection of the right strike should be undertaken in the same way as selection of the expiration date. Premium levels are going to produce varying returns, and the balance between one strike and another has to consider a number of factors, including time to expiration, net basis in the underlying stock, and annualized return. The higher the strike, the lower the premium income will be, and the more remote the chances of exercise. At the same time, the higher the strike, the greater the capital gain on the underlying stock will be if exercised. Most covered call writers will select a call that is OTM by one increment or less (for example, a 45 call when the underlying is currently worth between 40 and 44, or a 60 call when the underlying is between 55 and 59). This tends to produce maximum return premium. Once this limitation is set, selection can be coordinated between strike and expiration, all on an annualized basis to make comparisons accurate.

It is not accurate to include capital gain in the underlying stock in the comparison between premiums. However, this is a very real consideration. Strictly for the purposes of comparison, this does have to be included in the decision-making process. A two-part analysis is recommended. First, check various annualized returns on options with acceptable strikes and expirations. Second, evaluate and select a covered call with one eye to the contingency of exercise. When two different options are close in terms of annualized return, the differences in strike and consequential capital gain may become a determining factor.

Returning to a previous example, that of JCN as of December 31, 2007, the underlying stock closed at 108.10. Various expirations for the 100 call were compared on an annualized basis. However, this analysis might be expanded to also consider other strikes within the possible ranges for covered calls. The analysis is limited to strikes of 110 or above (even though, in the example, the original basis in stock was $100 per share). This limitation is appropriate given that the current value is at $108.10; most covered call writers prefer writing OTM calls based on current value. The distinction of net basis becomes most critical when original net basis is higher than current value of the stock. In that situation, writing a covered call that will exercise below net basis is self-defeating. Writers may need to wait until prices evolve or accept lower margins of profit in that situation. However, original cost will be brought into the equation to make the final determination of which option to write.

Return if Exercised or Unchanged

Expanding the JCN example to additional calls, the following are included in the range of possibilities, all calculated on the basis of annualized returns:

Month, Year	Strike	Option Premium	Stock Value	Holding Period	Full Year	Annualized Return
January 08	110	$((2.15 \div 108.10\,)$		$\div\ 0.70) \times$	$12 =$	34.1%
February 08	110	$((3.63 \div 108.10\,)$		$\div\ 1.70) \times$	$12 =$	23.7

Month, Year	Strike	Option Premium	Stock Value	Holding Period	Full Year	Annualized Return
February 08	115	$\big((1.71 \div 108.10\,) \div$		$1.70\big) \times$	$12 =$	11.2
April 08	110	$\big((6.00 \div 108.10\,) \div$		$4.70\big) \times$	$12 =$	14.2
April 08	115	$\big((3.90 \div 108.10\,) \div$		$4.70\big) \times$	$12 =$	9.2
July 08	110	$\big((8.30 \div 108.10\,) \div$		$7.70\big) \times$	$12 =$	12.0
July 08	115	$\big((6.10 \div 108.10\,) \div$		$7.70\big) \times$	$12 =$	8.8
July 08	120	$\big((4.30 \div 108.10\,) \div$		$7.70\big) \times$	$12 =$	6.2
January 09	110	$\big((11.70 \div 108.10) \div$		$12.70\big) \times$	$12 =$	10.2
January 09	115	$\big((9.40 \div 108.10) \div$		$12.70\big) \times$	$12 =$	8.2
January 09	120	$\big((7.30 \div 108.10) \div$		$12.70\big) \times$	$12 =$	6.4
January 10	110	$\big((16.64 \div 108.10) \div$		$24.70\big) \times$	$12 =$	7.5
January 10	120	$\big((12.30 \div 108.10) \div$		$24.70\big) \times$	$12 =$	5.5
January 10	125	$\big((11.30 \div 108.10\,) \div$		$24.70\big) \times$	$12 =$	5.1
January 10	130	$\big((9.30 \div 108.10\,) \div$		$24.70\big) \times$	$12 =$	4.2

If the writer wants double-digit returns, that is one way to narrow down this list. Of the 15 options listed, only six calculate out at double digits on an annualized basis. These are the following:

January 08	110	34.1%
February 08	110	23.7
February 08	115	11.2
April 08	110	14.2
July 08	110	12.0
January 09	110	10.2

The original January and February 110 calls remain the most promising. However, both of these are only 1.90 points from strike price. It might be possible to reduce chances of exercise by selecting the February 115. Although this yields only 11.2 percent on the option, it may be favored for two reasons. First, it remains a fairly short-term option with much more remote chances of exercise than the February 110. Second, if exercise does occur, the capital gain on the underlying stock will be much greater. In the example, you had bought 100 shares of JCN the previous February 1, making these options even more desirable; exercise will produce long-term capital gains, which are taxed at a lower rate. Here is a comparison between the two February calls, including option premium and capital gain:

Month	Strike	Option Yield	Gain	Stock Capital Gain Adjust to Annualized	Total Yield
February 08	110	23.7%	$\left((1{,}000 \div 10{,}000) \div 12.7\right) \times 12 = 9.4\%$		33.1%
February 08	115	11.2	$\left((1{,}500 \div 10{,}000) \div 12.7\right) \times 12 = 14.2$		25.4

In this example, the 110 call is more profitable in either case. Considering the option alone, income is 23.7 percent versus 11.2 percent. The only important benefit of the 115 call is that exercise is much more remote due to the distance to the strike. A trader might prefer this smaller net return in exchange for the greater likelihood that the option will expire worthless. The gap in net profit is narrowed somewhat by inclusion of the capital gain. The after-tax benefit relies on the overall tax rate for the trader and, of course, the larger question of whether exercise would occur.

In developing a truly comparable calculation of return if exercised, it is important to also include dividend income in the equation. Covered call writers continue to earn dividends on the underlying stock until exercise occurs. In comparing possible selection of calls on the same stock, as in the preceding example, this is not critical. However, in comparing overall return if exercised among different stock possibilities, dividend yield can make a significant difference.

For example, JCN yielded between 1.5 and 2.0 percent dividend during 2008. This might be in line for numerous other stocks on which options will be written as part of a covered call strategy. However, many other stocks yield no dividend or a far higher dividend. For example, Altria Corporation (MO) and Consolidated Edison (ED) each paid out approximately 6.0 percent during 2008. Comparable covered call returns if exercised may be quite close, but when dividend income is added, higher-yielding stocks may be far more attractive.

Dividend yield represents a significant portion of any option strategy involving holding long positions in the stock, most notably for covered call writing. In the preceding example, if different companies were involved in the comparison between calls, dividend yield could influence a decision to pick one call over the other. Given the lower likelihood of exercise with an incrementally higher strike on a short-term expiration (as with JCN's 110 and 115 February calls), if the 115 belonged to an issue paying three times more dividend yield, the selection might have been quite different.

As a consequence, any comparisons between two or more different companies have to include the dividend yield as part of the picture. This raises yet another question: Should you base dividend yield on (a) original price paid, (b) current value of the stock, or (c) the yield at the strike? Arguments may be made for any of these three selections. However, the strongest and most compelling decision is to base the yield on the yield at the time the stock was purchased. Because the amount of investment at that time and at that price determines the actual yield that will be received, it is justified to keep dividend yield at this original level. However, if one of the two alternatives is picked, it should be used consistently among those different stocks being compared.

A second calculation involves a covered call that expires. The premium from this call is entirely profit. However, the yield should be based on the original price of the stock, given that this is what provides cover for the short position.

Annualized return is calculated in this instance based on the day of expiration. The reference to "unchanged" means that OTM stock remains OTM (or ATM at worst), and so the option expires worthless. This is a less complex calculation because no stock sale is involved, and dividend income is unaffected by the net outcome. In other words, the trader owned the stock before and continues to own the stock after the option expires. The previously demonstrated method of calculating return and then adjusting it for annualized return applies in this case as well. An alternate method of calculation involves basing the return on the strike rather than current value or original basis of stock. However, because the covered call was entered at the time the current value prevailed, it is that value that most affects the value of the option premium. To remain consistent in a comparative analysis, return if unchanged should be calculated based on the market value of the underlying stock at the time the position was opened and annualized based on the period between opening date and expiration.

Also note an inconsistency in the consideration of underlying stock capital gains when brought into the overall calculation. Option return is calculated as a percentage of the current value of the underlying at the time the position is opened; but the capital gain is based on original cost of the stock. Remember, though, that the inclusion of the stock profit is used only to make valid value judgments concerning the selection of one strike price and expiration over another. The disparity in methods is justified because the exercise is not a "total return" calculation, but rather a comparative analysis. Because option premium varies based on proximity between underlying stock current value and the strike price, it is only accurate to base return from the option on the value of the stock. However, because the capital gain is only accurate when original cost is compared to sales cost, the exercise price (and variation of the strike between calls) affects overall yield and has to be calculated on that basis, even though it is dissimilar from the method used in calculating the option return.

Return if Closed

For any option position, long or short, a final method of return calculation occurs when that position is closed before expiration. For covered positions, calculation of return is normally related to the underlying stock position, as explained in the previous section. When you are dealing only in option positions, return calculations are going to be based on net cash invested (in the case of long positions) or the return based on changes in premium value (for short positions).

For example, if you enter a long position for $300 net and close that position at $600, the return is 100 percent (before annualizing). If you close it at $150, it represents a 50 percent loss (before annualizing). Remember, the process of annualizing returns, whether for profits or for losses, is only meaningful for purposes of comparison between positions and not to calculate what you should expect to experience throughout an entire year of options trades.

With short positions, the calculation is performed in reverse, just like the trade. If you enter a short position and received $400 and close that position at $200, your profit is 50 percent (before annualizing). If you close at a loss, the process is also reversed. For example, a $400 short closed for a net of $500 represents a 25 percent loss. Because short positions are transacted in reverse order from long positions, it is not entirely accurate to treat these calculation as "return on investment" because of this reversal in sequence. In fact, return if closed is an oddity for either long or short trades because the basis is not the same as that for covered calls.

In the covered call, option profit or loss is a percentage of the long stock position and, very much like dividend yield, that profit is a percentage of the long investment. For short positions, the return if closed calculation is an approximation only. With this in mind, the calculation itself is only useful when applied to compare a series of option-only trades. It is not the same as a covered position, but it does provide a means for tracking performance. It enables you to judge your timing and option selection, based on the artificial but comparative "yield" percentages.

A more accurate method for calculating a return on investment would be to identify a fixed dollar amount you have put aside strictly for options trades and to track profits and losses as trades are entered and then closed. The net profit (or loss) as a percentage of that fixed amount would be a more accurate measure of return on investment. For a majority of traders, this is not a practical approach, even though it makes sense mathematically. Most traders do not isolate a fixed dollar amount for options trades, but move in and out of positions as part of the overall portfolio. The decision to increase or to decrease trades relies on market prices, perceptions, and volatility levels. Traders tend to leave idle cash in a money market account as part of a portfolio and use a more generalized portfolio fund to execute trades or even combined with the use of margin. So identifying a fixed fund is a great concept, but one that is going to be difficult to apply for most traders.

The purpose of attempting to identify return on any type of option strategy, or on a range of different strategies, is not so much to specifically define return itself, but to (a) measure timing and success, (b) compare different outcomes by strategy and risk level, and (c) simply measure performance in options trading over time. Ultimately, the real measure of return is going to be based on annual net profit or loss in the entire portfolio, including capital gains or losses on stocks, dividend and interest income, and profits on options trades.

To calculate annual return at the end of each year, begin with the basic dollar value of profits and losses. Next, calculate the percentage this represents of the portfolio's value. If your portfolio has not been increased during the year with additional investment dollars or decreased by withdrawals, this is simple. The dollar value of profit or loss is divided by the initial portfolio dollar value to arrive at the annual return.

Most investors experience a change in their portfolio throughout the year, consisting of additional investment deposits and withdrawals at various times. In this case, the annual return has to be calculated using a weighted average. This requires adding together portfolio value at various times during the year and finding the average value (excluding the addition of profits).

For example, your portfolio began the year with a value of $26,000. Your overall profits during the year were $3,714. You added $3,000 each on March 1, June 1, and September 1. On December 1, you withdrew $2,000. Your pre-profit/loss portfolio value during the year was as follows:

January–February	$26,000 (2 months)
March–May	29,000 (3 months)
June–August	32,000 (3 months)
September–November	35,000 (3 months)
December	33,000 (1 month)

Weighted average is so-called because longer periods are given more weight than shorter periods. The calculation isolates each period; in this example, there were five separate periods, each with different dollar values. To calculate:

$$\big((26{,}000 \times 2) + (29{,}000 \times 3) + (32{,}000 \times 3) + (35{,}000 \times 3) + (33{,}000 \times 1) \big) \div 12$$

Reducing the formula:

$$52{,}000 + 87{,}000 + 96{,}000 + 105{,}000 + 33{,}000 \div 12 = \$31{,}083$$

In this example, the weighted average value of the portfolio for the year was $31,083. This can also be calculated with partial months when changes occur midway or even with the exact number of days. As long as the total of the months adds up to 12, or the total of the exact days adds up to 365, the formula works. Your profits for the year were $3,714, so the overall yield on this portfolio for the full year was the following:

$$\$3{,}714 \div \$31{,}083 = 11.95\%$$

Any discussion of return on investment has to include the success of stock selection as well as of options trading. A basic premise of any portfolio program, even one heavily focused on options, is that isolating trades to high-quality and well-selected stocks is a sensible and wise concept. This increases net return not only short-term but long-term as well. The selection of the best and safest stocks depends on both fundamental and technical tests and comparisons. The next chapter examines stock selection for options trading.

chapter 5

Options and Stock Selection

The selection of options based on appropriate risk levels and stocks makes more sense than the selection of stocks to maximize option returns. In other words, any position combining option and stock positions should be based on appropriate stocks held in a trader's portfolio as long-term investments. The alternative, for those intent solely on speculating in options, is to (a) accept higher-risk positions from speculation trading, (b) hedge high-risk positions with option-based coverage, or (c) be aware that long positions in stock are taken up not as investments, but as hedges for option positions.

If you buy stock strictly to provide cover for short call positions, it may be a poor strategy. This is especially true for those traders seeking the richest possible option premium. That invariably leads to focus on high-volatility stocks. This means the portfolio ends up with many risky stocks, which is often contrary to long-term goals. An assumption that most options traders want safety in their stock positions is granted for the following discussion; the assumption is that the majority of traders begin with the premise that the core portfolio should consist of long-term hold stocks (value investments) and that option activity is undertaken to increase current income, hedge long positions, or accept exercise if and when it occurs.

The following sections provide very basic criteria for stock selections, whether for trading options or simply for narrowing down a list of potential investment candidates. In picking options, remember these key points:

1. Higher historical volatility usually is accompanied by higher implied volatility in option premium *and* by higher market risks in both stock and option positions.

2. Stock selection should rule the decision about which stocks to buy and which ones to avoid, based on the risk profile for most traders. If this guideline is not followed, traders should acknowledge that they are accepting higher risks or select alternative methods for covering short option positions (for example, through buying longer-term expiring options as offset to shorter-term ones).

3. In narrowing down a list of potential stocks, remember that dividend yield represents a significant portion of overall return on investment. So dividends should always be part of a comparative analysis between stocks being considered. The relationship between dividend yield and call value might not be completely offsetting, so comparisons may have to include valuation of implied volatility as well as dividend yield.

4. Both technical and fundamental tests may be used to narrow the list of candidates for investment. However, the long-term value and safety of stocks should be a primary selection standard, with potential options trading a secondary consideration.

Diversification by Risk Profile

The methods used to diversify an individual portfolio might be quite varied. A preliminary opinion about diversification simply observes that investors should not place all their capital into a single stock. However, additional, perhaps more subtle, expansions of this concept are important. These include the following:

- Diversification among stocks of different sectors.

- Selecting sectors not subject to the same economic cycles or forces.

- Utilizing mutual funds as an alternative to direct ownership of stocks.

- Allocation among non-stock investments (real estate, long-term debt, money market, futures).

- Using options to hedge market risks or increase income.

- Diversification by risk profile within the stock market.

The last method in this list is quite similar to the preceding one: the use of options to hedge risk or even to eliminate it altogether. Risk profile varies by individual, of course, but for many, it is not a question of managing risk to ensure that *all* investments reside at the same risk level. Rather, portfolio management may also involve dividing up segments of total capital into different risk profiles. For example, a core of 75 percent may be invested in value companies with long-term appreciation in mind, and the remaining 25 percent used to speculate, swing trade, or pursue positions with exceptionally high current income. This diversification by risk profile is the most appealing for many investors, who recognize that they do not want to be restricted to a single risk level.

Options play an important role in this level of diversification. Not only are options valuable for hedging risk (that is, buying puts to insure existing paper profits in long positions) and for increasing current income (via covered call writing and limited risk positions like butterflies or strangles), but also for seeking varying levels of historical volatility.

The moderate to conservative trader is likely to stay away from highly volatile stocks simply because the market risks are not acceptable—at least not over the entire portfolio. However, such risks, because they may also produce exceptionally high returns, might be appealing for a segment of capital. In this situation, diversification by risk profile can improve the overall return potential for a portfolio without also increasing the overall risk beyond acceptable levels.

Most investors will be drawn to covered calls with risk diversification in mind. This is an appropriate method for portfolio management and return enhancement, as long as the primary objectives are allowed to remain intact. A great risk in using options is a volatility trap. This comes up when stocks are selected because they have high premium value in their options, rather than on other, sound technical and fundamental criteria. Any trader who gives in to the temptation to pick stocks based on option income potential is likely to increase market risks beyond levels they would otherwise consider acceptable.

With this trap in mind, a few guidelines for selecting stocks help avoid this trap, as follows:

1. Always select stocks based on stock-specific analysis and never due to the current implied volatility in option premium.

2. Be aware of volatility levels on a technical basis when including companies on a short list, making certain that the selection criteria are valid and not based on opportunities for option profits as an overruling factor.

3. Track stocks in the portfolio to identify changes in volatility levels, remembering that even when you use an appropriate set of criteria for picking stocks, it may change over time.

Fundamental Selection Indicators

There are numerous possible fundamental criteria used for picking stocks. The individual risk profile will lead each investor to a range of attractive analytical tools. The following five general categories provide a general overview of the analytical tools that are most useful for most investors:

1. *Revenue and earnings.* The most obvious of all fundamental indicators is tracking revenue and earnings. Both the current year's status and longer-term trend are crucial indicators of a company's ability to continue growth and to expand in a competitive environment. Tracking both top-line and bottom-line results over a 10-year period is quite revealing because this reveals the overall direction in which the company is moving. If revenue and earnings are declining over many years, it is unusual for the company to recover or to reverse the trend. A flat movement is an indicator that the markets for a company are not expanding. A growing level of both revenue and earnings is a strong sign of improving markets and profitability. Earnings are most often tracked through EPS, or earnings per share, which is a valuable indicator to track but not to compare. EPS varies between companies based not only on dollar amount of earnings but also on the number of outstanding shares. So this is useful only for tracking within one company over a period of years.

   A sensible fundamental rule: *Limit your list of investment candidates to companies whose revenue and earnings are improving over the long term.*

2. *Core earnings and fundamental volatility.* Standard & Poor's Corporation devised a common-sense method for reviewing a company's earnings. The *core earnings* are a restated version of net earnings excluding nonrecurring items and adding in core items that have been excluded. Because the accounting rules are flawed, companies are allowed to publish earnings with some very inaccurate interpretations, and the S&P core earnings fixes this. Core earnings are published and compared to reported earnings on the S&P *Stock Reports* service. Analysis of core earnings further reveals that companies with relatively small core earnings adjustments also tend to report steady outcomes for revenue and earnings. This correlation, which may be called "fundamental volatility," is a valuable test of a company's long-term trading risk. When a company's revenue and earnings are erratic and inconsistent from year to year, it is very difficult to predict long-term

growth. Such companies with frequent correlation in higher than average core earnings adjustments, are fundamentally higher-risk than the opposite: companies with low fundamental volatility.

A sensible fundamental rule: *Limit investment candidates to those with long-term steady trends in revenue and earnings (low fundamental volatility) and that are subject to only small core earnings adjustments.*

3. *Working capital tests.* There are two very critical tests of working capital. These are the current ratio and the debt ratio. The current ratio compares current assets to current liabilities. A current ratio consists of cash and assets that are convertible to cash within 12 months (accounts receivable, inventory, and marketable securities). Current liabilities are payable within 12 months (accounts payable, taxes payable, and the current portion of long-term notes or other obligations). When the current assets are divided by the current liabilities, the result (expressed as a single digit) is the current ratio. As a general guideline, a current asset of 2 or higher is considered the norm of acceptable working capital control.

The debt ratio is a test of capitalization. This refers to the sources of capital for a company, which consist of equity (stock) and debt (long-term bonds and notes). The higher the debt, the worse the news. To calculate the debt ratio, add together all capitalization (shareholders' equity and long-term debt) and then divide long-term debt by the total. The resulting percentage is the debt ratio. If a long-term trend shows this level steady or declining, it is a positive sign. A debt ratio between zero and 25 percent is very healthy. However, if the debt ratio is rising, that is a red flag; if it is exceptionally high (above 65 percent, for example), it is going to be very difficult for the company to expand in the future. The larger the debt, the more profits have to go to paying interest and repaying the debt itself; and the less remains for paying dividends or for financing market expansion.

A sensible fundamental rule: *Seek consistency or improvement in both current ratio and debt ratio; avoid investing in companies with high debt ratio or a rising debt ratio.*

4. *Dividend yield and history.* The dividend yield is going to represent a significant portion of overall portfolio income. Yet it is most often overlooked, both by stock investors and by options traders. The yield you will earn is the yield paid based on the price you pay for shares of stock. This remains true no matter how much the per-price value changes. The yield after purchase date changes only if the company changes its declared dividend per share. Higher than average yield is valuable because it

represents a very real return to investors; the value is accelerated when dividends are reinvested to buy additional shares. The long-term history of dividend yield is a valuable tracking tool. Reduce your list of candidates by looking for those companies that have increased their dividend every year for at least the last 10 years. This test is valuable because a company must have funds available (profits) to be able to afford dividends. Thus, a consistent record of growth in dividend payments indicates high quality in the investment itself.

A sensible fundamental rule: *Invest in stock of companies that pay better than average dividend yield and that have increased their dividend per share every year for at least the last 10 years.*

5. *P/E ratio.* P/E (price divided by earnings) is actually a hybrid indicator. The price is a technical indicator, and the earnings a fundamental. This ratio is calculated on a per-share basis, with the ratio expressed as a single number, also called the multiple. The P/E is the number of years' earnings equal to the current share price. When P/E is exceptionally high, shares are expensive and, if also volatile, it is also likely that option premium will have higher than average implied volatility. However, high-P/E stocks are also risky. A reasonable P/E level is generally between 10 and 20, although this really depends on the trend for the company and for its industry. In narrowing down your list of potential stocks, seek companies with moderate to low P/E levels and trends.

A sensible fundamental rule: *Limit investment candidates to those companies whose P/E has been consistent through the past decade and whose P/E is not excessively high (above the 20–25 range).*

Technical Selection Indicators

Fundamental indicators are focused on profit and loss and valuation of the company. In other words, it is backward-looking and tests market success and financial strength. On comparison, technical analysis is a study of current price trends and related issues, such as volatility in price itself and the volume of trading activity. Many technicians are also chartists, those who study price charts to seek trading patterns and to anticipate the most likely price direction to evolve in the near future.

Technical indicators, like the fundamentals, come in many different varieties, from very simple to quite complex. However, the essential technical analysis science can be broken down into four major divisions, as follows:

1. *Basic price volatility.* The calculation of price volatility normally is performed over a 52-week period and is quantified and compared in terms of how far price has varied off its 52-week low. This is inaccurate in many ways. It would be more accurate to compare the oldest 52-week price and study the range of deviation either above or below that price to get a realistic view of price volatility. Otherwise, the outcomes are vastly different for a stock near its 52-week high and another near its 52-week low.

   Another problem is that the normal method does not allow for spikes. Statistically, an accurate range allows for exclusion of unusually high or low spikes in relation to a "normal" distribution. A price spike should be excluded when (a) it happens as an isolated price movement, (b) trading range returns fairly quickly to the previously established trading range, and (c) the aberration does not recur during the 52-week period.

   A sensible technical rule: *In placing a value on volatility, exclude price spikes and also be aware of the trend itself, remembering that price direction affects the importance of 52-week volatility.*

2. *Breadth of the current trading range and its general trend.* A trading range may move only within two to three points in a typical 5- to 10-day trading period, or it may cover many more points. The breadth of the trading range is important not only as it relates to the price per share, but also in how quickly it moves within the range. In addition, a trading range might be defined as a specific number of high-to-low points, but it may also demonstrate an overall trend. Interpreting the technical aspects of price should also take into account whether the price trend is moving upward, downward, or sideways and whether the breadth of the trading range is widening or narrowing.

   A sensible technical rule: *Analyze trading range of a stock over recent periods, remembering that farther-away ranges are less important to the current price direction. Be aware of price breadth itself, as well as whether the overall price direction is upward, downward, or sideways and whether it is narrowing or widening.*

3. *The trading range today compared to the past.* It is a mistake to view a narrow or brief series of trading days and try to draw conclusions from it. The trading range a stock experiences today is built on past price direction and the interaction among buyers and sellers. The supply and demand affects the trading range just as the range affects buying and selling behavior. Although technicians focus on price patterns and trends, the impact of economic and earnings news on a company and its sector (not to mention the overall market) is likely to further impact trading range. From the technical point of view, one difficulty is in determining whether a recent change is a temporary one or the beginning of an important change in the trading range.

   A sensible technical rule: *Remember that short-term analysis is difficult because reading the latest trend is not reliable. Evaluate today's trading range in light of its past volatility, price direction, breadth trends, and trading volume.*

4. *Occurrence and frequency of support and resistance tests or breakouts.* Technicians are always looking for strong price indicators that change the existing breadth of a stock's trading range. Resistance (the highest price in the trading range) and support (the lowest price level) establish order and predictability but only for as long as the current trading range remains in effect. Eventually, trading ranges evolve and change, sometimes gradually and at other times quite dramatically. Certain price patterns predict breakouts above resistance or below support. These include head and shoulders patterns, double and triple tops (or bottoms), and changes in volume relative to price. When a breakout occurs—meaning price moves beyond the established trading range—it may continue to move in the breakout direction, or it may retreat back to the trading range. This trend is often interpreted by the occurrence of various kinds of gaps (space between one period's close and the next period's open) and by the speed of price movement, changes in volume, and entry of buyers or sellers into the action.

   A sensible technical rule: *Look for strong signals of important changes in price movement and trading range. Especially important are tests of resistance or support and breakouts, followed by price retreat or by continued movement.*

Options traders will benefit by spending time analyzing stocks, notably for any strategies involving the combined positions of options with stock holdings. Another topic every options trader needs to remember is option taxation. The federal law includes many quirks and special rules affecting options trades, timing and recognition of tax losses, and even the possibility that long-term capital gains on stocks could be lost by entering an ill-advised options trade. These topics are covered in the next chapter.

chapter 6

Option Taxation

Taxes are complex no matter what kinds of investments are involved. However, if you trade options, the complexity of taxation is exponentially greater. Many rules apply only to options trading, and poor planning or unawareness of the rules may lead to expensive mistakes. These mistakes might even include the loss of favorable long-term capital gains rates on stock profits, even when positions were open for more than the required 12 months.

This chapter provides a brief overview of the rules related to option taxation, limitations, and special rules that apply to wash sales, constructive sales, and short call positions.

Capital Gains and Losses

The general rule for capital gains is that long-term gains are taxed at lower rates than ordinary income. Short-term gains, those on investments held for less than one year (under rules in forces in 2008), are taxed at the higher ordinary income rates. Qualified dividends are also taxed at the same rate as that for net capital gains.

The rules prevailing as of the end of 2008 are those carried over or changed under the Jobs and Growth Tax Relief Reconciliation Act of 2003. Short-term capital gains apply on investments held for less than one full year and are taxed at the federal level at rates up to 35 percent. Long-term gains are taxed based on a calculated "net" capital gains (long-term net gains minus any short-term losses), with a maximum rate of 15 percent. These rates are increased under calculations of the alternative minimum tax when it applies. Gains and losses on investments are required to be recognized and reported in the year that positions are closed (thus, a short position is not taxed until it is closed, exercised, or expired). Gains and losses may not be deferred. However, the maximum annual net capital loss is limited to $3,000. Any excess must be carried forward and applied to capital gains or losses in future periods, perpetually limited to the $3,000 ceiling. These net losses do not expire but are carried forward indefinitely.

Long calls are taxed under the holding period rules if they expire or are closed with a closing sale order. They may be short-term (held less than one year) or long-term (held over one year, as in the case of long LEAPS positions). If a long call is exercised, a different calculation is involved. The premium paid for the call, net of brokerage commission, is added to the price of the stock acquired at the strike. The holding period for stock acquired under exercise of the call begins on the day following exercise and may not include the holding period of the call.

Long puts, like calls, may be long-term or short-term, depending on the holding period of the option. If a long put is exercised, resulting in the sale of the underlying stock, the cost of the put, net of brokerage commissions paid, is deducted from the amount realized upon sale of the stock.

Short calls result in receipt of premium upon opening the short position. However, this receipt is not taxed until the position has been closed by way of expiration with a closing purchase order. If a short call is held until expiration, it is always treated as a short-term capital gain regardless of the holding period.

If the call is closed with a closing purchase order, the net gain is also treated as a short-term capital gain in all cases. If the short call is assigned, the stock price consists of the strike price plus net premium received. A covered call that is assigned creates a profit in the underlying stock equal to the difference between original net basis (purchase) and strike, plus short premium received net of brokerage costs (sale). This overall transaction is treated as either long-term or short-term depending on the holding period of the stock. There is an exception, however: If the covered call is unqualified, the stock profit might be treated as short-term gain regardless of its holding period (see the next section).

Short puts result in the receipt of premium, but this is not taxed until the position has been closed. If the short put is closed prior to expiration with a closing purchase order, it is always treated as a short-term capital gain regardless of the holding period. The same rule applies if the short put is held until expiration. If a short put is assigned, the basis of the acquired stock is reduced by the net premium received in writing the put. The stock's holding period begins the day after the stock is acquired in this manner, regardless of the holding period of the short put.

Qualified and Unqualified Covered Calls

An exception to the general rule of capital gains applies to some covered calls. In order for the rules in the previous section to apply, the covered call must be "qualified." This generally means that the call has to have at least 30 days to go before expiration, and the strike may not be less than the first strike price level below the closing price of the stock on the day prior to writing the call. This definition varies based on the time to expiration and the strike price range.

For example, if you write a covered call that expires in two months, it is qualified as long as the strike rule applies. If the previous day's closing price was $32 and the call's strike is 30, it is a qualified covered call. However, if the strike is 27.50, or 25.00, it is unqualified. This affects the calculation of capital gains on the stock, even if the call is never exercised. Another restriction: If the stock's market value at the opening of the day is higher than 110 percent of the prior day's close, that opening price is used to determine qualification rather than the previous day's close.

The distinction between qualified and unqualified covered calls varies with the stock price and with time to expiration. These distinctions are summarized in Table 6.1.

Table 6.1   Rules for Qualified Covered Calls

Prior Day's Stock Closing Price	Time Until Expiration	Strike Price Limits
$25 or below	Over 30 days	One strike under close of the prior trading day (however, no call can be qualified if the strike is lower than 85% of stock price).
$25.01–$60	Over 30 days	One strike under close of the prior trading day.
$60.01–$150	31–90 days	One strike under close of the prior trading day.
$60.01–$150	Over 90 days	Two strikes under close of the prior trading day (but no more than 10 points ITM).
Above $150	31–90 days	One strike under close of the prior trading day.
Above $150	Over 90 days	Two strikes under close of the prior trading day.

Investors and traders are not barred from writing unqualified covered calls. However, there will be consequences in the way their capital gains will be calculated and taxed. In addition, if a covered call is ATM or OTM, based on the preceding definitions, the call cannot expire within the next 30 days to be considered qualified.

Unqualified covered calls result in capital gains adjustments under the anti-straddle rule. This is a tax rule designed to limit or prevent mismatching of gains and losses in related transactions (for example, long stock and short calls). There are five possible consequences to writing unqualified covered calls, as follows:

1. *ATM and OTM covered calls.* There is no change in the treatment of capital gains on stock as long as those short calls do not expire within 30 days. The status of these calls is based on a comparison between the short call strike and closing price in the stock on the prior day (or opening price on the current day if it exceeds the prior close by 110 percent or more).

2. *There is no affect on capital gains as long as ITM calls meet the qualification rules.* Traders are able to write ITM short calls, but qualification is restricted to those close strike prices. As long as these limitations are observed, long-term gain rates remain in effect for the underlying stock.

3. *The holding period to calculate capital gains on the underlying stock is suspended when an unqualified covered call is written.* For example, if you owned stock for five months and wrote an unqualified covered call, the count is suspended until the short position is closed, expired, or exercised.

So if the short position were open for six months, it would require a total holding period in the stock of 18 months before long-term capital gains rates applied (12 months plus the holding period of the unqualified covered call).

4. *Covered call losses are treated as long-term losses.* Regardless of the holding period, any losses on covered calls, qualified or unqualified, are treated as long-term capital losses, even when underlying stock profits are treated as long-term capital gains.

5. *The stock holding period is affected when short call positions have been closed.* When qualified short calls are sold at a loss, the underlying stock must be held for at least 30 days in order for the call to be treated as qualified.

Some long-term options (exceeding 33 months) are subject to special rules. However, for the majority of options traders, these options (exceeding the maximum life span of a LEAPS) will not normally be traded.

Rules for Offsetting Positions

Under the wash sale rule, traders are not allowed to sell and then repurchase the same positions within 30 days. For example, you may sell shares of stock on December 15 and claim a loss in the current year, with plans to repurchase the stock on January 5. This strategy would not work; the loss would not be deductible because the position is a wash sale (repurchase occurred in under 30 days).

The definition of a wash sale is applied not only to identical positions, but also to "substantially identical" ones. This is where options enter the picture. For example, if you sell stock and within 30 days you sell an ITM put anticipating exercise, that is a substantially identical security. So the intent would be to claim a loss on the stock but also to replace the stock at a selected strike through the short put. This transaction would result in disallowing the deduction of the stock sold.

These offsetting positions are carefully defined under federal rules to prevent a mismatching of profits and losses between tax years. Any time offsetting positions involve "substantial diminution of risk or loss," additional restrictions apply. Any time a strategy includes one position designed to reduce or eliminate the loss in another on the same security, four more rules also apply, as follows:

1. The holding period for purposes of capital gains is suspended during the period that offsetting positions are open.

2. Wash sale limitations are applied in many straddles, requiring that losses are deferred on one side until the second position has also been closed.

3. No tax deductions are allowed as long as "successor positions" are open. A successor position is on the same side as the original position (long or short), but replaces that original position and is entered within 30 days before or after the loss occurred. (Essentially, this boils down to a rule stating that losses are not deductible in the year incurred if other portions of the offset remain open into the following year; those losses are deferred so that all profit or loss is reported in the same year.)

4. All costs of carry, including brokerage fees and margin interest, are added to the basis of the long position and may not be deducted during the period the offsetting position remains open.

Exceptions to the "offsetting position" rules generally applied to straddles include two specific strategies: qualified covered calls and married puts. A *married put* is the same-day acquisition of shares of stock and a put on that stock. If the put expires in this situation, its cost is added to the price of the stock rather than being separately deductible, but the offsetting positions disallowance of losses does not apply.

Strategic Considerations

Some traders want to force exercise of covered calls and have an incentive to write deep ITM calls. However, because this strategy may affect the taxation of gain on the underlying stock, it is important to ensure that the call in question meets the definition of qualified covered call. If the 12-month qualifying period has already been met, there is no tolling of the time period to count up to that requirement. However, it is important to know how the rules affect this when additional offsetting positions are involved.

If you are trading options within a qualified retirement plan, the restrictions associated with qualified and unqualified covered calls are not an issue. Many self-directed plans allow covered call writing. However, because net gains are all deferred in these accounts, there is no long-term capital gain at risk. In this situation, the rules of qualification do not matter.

However, there may be conditions in which it is desirable to write unqualified covered calls. Specifically, if you are carrying over an exceptionally large capital loss each year, you cannot deduct more than $3,000 per tax period. However, writing unqualified covered calls produces good premiums with one of two outcomes. First, if stock value falls, the deep ITM calls can be closed at a profit. Second, if exercised, these covered calls result in capital gains. Even if long-term rates are not allowed due to the rules governing option taxation, current-year gains can be used in this situation to reduce the net carry-forward to capital losses. This provision actually shelters the unqualified gain and the fully-taxed short-term capital gains on stock.

It is possible for traders to create unqualified covered calls unintentionally. For example, a trader originally acquired 100 shares of stock 11½ months ago at $35 per share. Today, market value is $62 per share. The trader sells a covered call with a strike of 60. However, the call expires in three weeks, which makes it unqualified. In this situation, because shares were owned for less than 12 months at the time the short call was opened, the count to the 12-month long-term holding period is suspended. If the call is exercised, it will result in a short-term capital gain.

Another situation arises when a covered call writer rolls forward to exercise. For example, a 60-strike call on stock valued at $60 per share is qualified as long as the call does not expire within 30 days. Later, though, if the stock market price rose to $67 per share, the covered call writer may want to roll forward to avoid exercise. Replacing a soon-to-expire 60 call with a 60 call expiring in 45 days makes sense to avoid exercise, but it closes out the original qualified call and replaces it with a new, unqualified call. If stock was owned for under 12 months, this suspends the period counting up to the required long-term gain holding period. If that later call is exercised, it results in short-term capital gain treatment for the underlying stock.

The tax rules for options are complex and often illogical. The purpose in many of the rules was to prevent options traders from using combination and hedging positions to defer tax liabilities or to create tax losses in ways that got around the 30-day wash sale rule or the constructive sale rules. However, anyone trading options based on hedging positions or employing multiple-option positions, such as butterflies, straddles, or strangles, needs to consult with a tax professional to ensure that the tax consequences are as well understood as the potential tax benefits.

chapter 7

Option Strategies A–C

The strategies in this and the two following chapters are arranged alphabetically. Option and stock values have been used based on a close of business value on the same trading session, December 31. Three companies have been used, and these are called JCN, NDE, and YPN. Because values change significantly over time, fictitious names have been provided with these quotes. A complete summary of the option listings for these three companies are included in the appendix at the back of this book.

Although current option and stock values will be different for all of these sample listings, the relative values should be approximately the same at any time, given current price relative to strike, and time to expiration. Option premium values are expressed in the per-share price values. Thus, a cited price of 2.40 is per share of the underlying, and the option contract related to 100 shares is translated as $240.00.

Examples exclude trading costs; given the widespread use of online discount brokerage services in which fees are quite low, this is a minor exclusion. However, costs of entering and exiting positions should be taken into account in calculating potential profit. Examples generally are limited to single options. In practice, the use of multiple option contracts further reduces the transaction cost, which is another point to be factored into the calculation of net outcome.

The tables provided to accompany many of the examples of spreads, straddles, and combinations are provided on the comparable basis assuming that the full position is left open until the day of expiration for each option contract. In practice, stock movement may provide opportunities to close out part of a position at a profit. The short side of a multiple-option strategy can be closed when time value evaporates, leaving only the long side (or a separate short contract for a call versus a put, or a put versus a call). However, if a long side is closed due to substantial change in the price of the underlying, that may leave short positions open in uncovered status, greatly increasing risk. In evaluating each strategy, the comparison of outcomes, if held open to expiration, helps to define risk and identify profit potential. This does not mean a multiple-option position will always remain open that long.

The majority of examples employ the least number of contracts possible. However, the use of multiple contracts may enhance profits, as well as add greater profit potential. For example, in rolling forward to avoid exercise, replacing a single short option with two, three, or more later-expiring short contracts may produce a net credit while improving future profit potential. This is a practical idea for short calls if and when enough underlying stock is owned to provide coverage for a flexible rolling strategy. This point should be kept in mind for all strategies. The number of open contracts as well as ratio levels in combinations can be varied based on risk levels, the amount of underlying stock held, and available margin credit.

Alligator spread—Any spread involving complex combinations of offsetting options, to the extent that the trading costs will in all likelihood "eat up" any profits. It is possible to design a strategy to provide virtually no loss exposure with limited profit potential, as in the well-known *butterfly* spread. However, if the number of offsetting positions is too great, the potential profits will not materialize on a net basis. Trading costs and broker commissions make the position not worthwhile. Options traders also have to consider the possibility that in overly complex option spreads and combinations, they might face (a) brokerage security deposits, which may tie up capital, and (b) unexpected tax consequences, as seen with the *anti-straddle rules* that penalize traders entering two-sided transactions and realizing losses and profits in different years.

Bear call spread—A variation of the bear spread employing only calls, as in the preceding example. The profit is maximized when the market value of the underlying stocks declines; however, risk is limited to the difference between long and short positions. The spread creates a limited profit potential or offers a limited loss.

The breakeven on this position resides in between the two strike prices. Profit is equal to the point spread above the short position (the bear call spread always creates a credit because current value of the lower short call will always exceed the value of the higher long call). Referring again to the previous example, a trader receives a net of $450 in this bear call spread. If the underlying were to close at $89.50 on expiration day, the short position breaks even (strike of 85 plus 4.5 points for the net credit). The trader could satisfy the call with the long call or accept exercise.

A loss occurs when the stock's price rises above both call strikes and is limited to the point spread, minus the original credit received when the position was opened.

Bear put ladder—A strategy employing a long put spread and, in addition, a short put at a strike below the spread strikes. For example, a trader could create a bear put ladder by buying a January JCN (value $108.10) put at 110 and selling a February put at 105 (the typical put spread)—and also selling an April put at 100. Maximum profit will be earned when the stock closes between the two short strikes by expiration. Profit would be the net of (a) the credit gained when the position was opened or, if a net debit, a negative; and (b) the point spread between the higher long and short positions. In this example, that would be five points, or $500 (110 minus 100). If the stock were to decline below the lower put's strike, exposure nets out to one uncovered put, minus the point spread described previously.

Bear Put Ladder on JCN

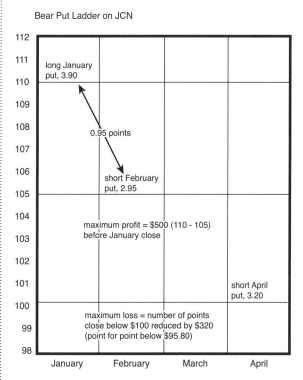

Figure 7.1 Bear put ladder on JCN

Bear put spread—A spread designed to produce maximum profit if and when the underlying stock's market value declines. It involves selling a put and buying another at a higher strike price.

Profit potential on this spread is identical to that of the bear call spread. Both potential profit and loss are limited. As the stock declines (moves in the desired direction), intrinsic value of the higher long put grows. If and when the stock's price falls below the lower short put strike, the profit is equal to the difference between the strike prices (so a five-point difference would represent a gross profit of $500). However, this is reduced by the debit required to open the position, which reduces maximum profit.

Minimum risk level is equal to the cost of opening the position. Maximum profit is equal to the difference between the two put strikes, minus the initial cost. And the breakeven point is equal to the difference between the higher put's strike price and the debit incurred to open the position (assuming the higher put closes ITM).

The bear put spread can be established with a significant advantage over the bear call spread. Because it can be set up with neither option in the money, there is a lower risk of early exercise in comparison with the same strategy involving calls. For example, a bear put spread on NDE ($58.91 market value) may involve selling a February 60 put (at 2.20) and buying a February 62.50 put (at 3.40). The net cost is 1.20 ($120); the maximum loss if the stock moves upward is $120, and maximum profit is $130.

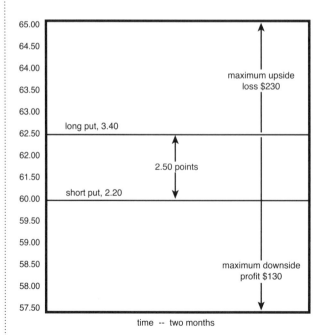

Bear Put Spread on NDE

Figure 7.2   Bear put spread on NDE

Bear spread—A spread strategy in which the position will be profitable if the underlying stock's market value falls. The bear spread can be designed using either puts or calls.

Here is an example of a bear spread using puts: A bear spread is created by selling a put with a lower strike and buying a put with a higher strike. This limits both profits and losses; however, profit occurs if and when the underlying stock's value falls. The previous example of a bear put spread illustrates this.

In a bear spread using calls, a higher short position is offset by a lower long position. For example, a bear spread is created on JCN ($108.10) by buying a July 120 call (at 4.30) and selling a July 115 call (at 6.10) for a net credit of 1.80. As long as the underlying stock remains below the short position's strike price of 115, the short call will lose value; if the stock's price rises above the short call's value, losses will be limited by the higher 120 call, and dollar amount of the maximum loss will be $320 (five points difference in the strikes minus 1.80 credit in the position).The greatest advantage is gained when the stock remains below $115 per share in this example. If that occurs, maximum profit is equal to the net 1.80 points in the position.

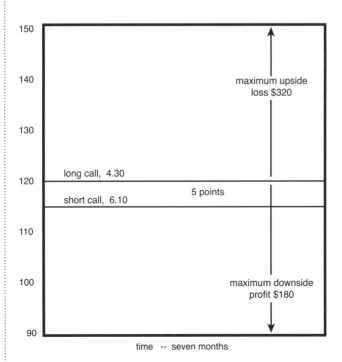

Bear Spread On JCN

Figure 7.3   Bear spread on JCN

Box spread (debit)—A four-part spread position used as a form of arbitrage (buying and selling of related positions at varying price levels). This is used to create a limited but risk-free level of profit.

Example: NDE's price is $58.91 at the close on December 31. A box spread is created by combining a call bull spread with a put bear spread, all based on March options. The first half consists of buying a March 55 call at 5.70 and selling a March 60 call at 2.40. The second half consists of buying a March 60 put at 2.85 and selling a March 55 put at 1.10:

Buy March 55 call	- 5.70
Sell March 60 call	2.40
Net debit	- 3.30
Buy March 60 put	- 2.85
Sell March 55 put	1.10
Net debit	- 1.70
Box spread debit	- 5.00

This position locks in a profit of 5.00 ($500) while costing exactly the same. Accordingly, risk has been eliminated in the position. This riskless feature can be tested at any price level:

If the stock closes above 60, the puts would both be worthless, and the calls would net out at a value of 5 points, the difference between the spreads. If the stock were to close between 55 and 60, the OTM options (March 60 short call and March 55 short put) would be worthless, and the ITM options (March 55 long call and March 60 long put) would net out with an intrinsic value of 5. (No matter where expiration existed, the difference between strike prices and expiration price will always be 5. For example, if the stock closed at 57.50, both options would be worth 2.50.). If the stock closes below 55, the calls would expire worthless, and the net value of the puts would be 5, the spread between the two strikes.

Although this example ensures a breakeven at any price, the position can be used to create additional profits by exiting short positions upon decline in time value and holding open call and put positions, converting to a simple long spread. The risk at that point consists of the original cost (5) minus profits from selling the short options. For example, if the short call and put were both closed for a net of 2, the remaining debit is 3. The position needs movement of 3 points or more, either above the long call strike of 55 or below the long put strike of 60. This narrow range requirement makes an additional small profit quite possible.

Box spread (credit)—Similar to the debit spread described previously, but working with a net credit instead of a debit. In this case, the trader sells the spread and creates a credit. The position can be closed (bought out) at any time at a fixed price.

Example: YPN closed on December 31 at $93.69. A credit box spread is created by buying an April 95 call at 4.90 and selling an April 90 call at 7.94; and buying an April 90 put at 3.40 and selling an April 95 put at 5.50:

Buy April 95 call	- 4.90
Sell April 90 call	7.94
Net credit	3.04
Buy April 90 put	- 3.40
Sell April 95 put	5.50
Net credit	2.10
Box spread credit	5.14

This box spread can be closed at any time and at any price for 5, although the net credit was at 5.14. This creates a riskless profit of 0.14 and potentially higher profits from early close of short positions due to declined time value. If the stock were to close above 95, the puts would expire worthless, and the calls retain their spread of 5 points. If the stock were to close between 90 and 95, the long OTM options would both expire worthless, and the net cost to close the remaining short options would remain at 5 points. If the stock closed below 90, both calls would expire worthless, and the net difference between long and short put would remain at 5 points.

Bull call ladder—The combination of a long call spread plus an additional *short* call at a higher strike price. The concept holds that in the event the stock price rises, the lowest (long) strike price call will increase in value enough to offset the mid-level (short) call and to satisfy exercise; and the highest strike price (short) call is far enough out of the money so that possible exercise is remote.

Example: JCN closed at 108.10 on December 31. You buy a July 110 call at 8.30 and sell a 115 call at 6.10. This is the typical spread pattern using calls. However, you also sell a 120 call for 4.30 at the same time, creating the ladder (the term "ladder" is normally used in the U.K., whereas the same strategy is often called a "Christmas tree" in the U.S.). The net position is as follows:

July 110 long call   - 8.30
July 115 short call   6.10
July 120 short call   4.30
    Net credit   2.10

If none of these positions are closed by expiration, the following profit or loss occurs.

Stock price 127 approximates a breakeven price. This consists of intrinsic value in the long call of 17 (127 – 110); less intrinsic value in the 115 short call of 12 and in the 120 short of 7; plus the original net credit of 2.10:

Long call profit   17.00
Short 115 call loss   - 12.00
Short 120 call loss   - 7.00
Original position credit   2.10
    Net   0.10

Above 127, the net loss grows by two points for every point increase (due to the combination of two short positions and one long position, adjusted by a fixed 2.10 initial credit).

If the stock closes between the two short positions, profit consists of the 5-point spread between the lower short and the long; plus the initial credit of 2.10. The higher short of 120 expires worthless. For example if the stock closes at 117:

Long call profit   7.00
Short 115 call loss   - 2.00
Short 120 call expiration   0
Original position credit   2.10
    Net   7.10

If the stock closes between 120 and 127, the profit declines by one dollar per point in the stock increase. For example, at 122, the 7.10 profit above falls to 5.10; at 126, it falls to 1.10.

If the stock closes between the long and the lower short, profit consisted on long call intrinsic value plus the initial credit of 2.10. For example, if the stock closes at 112, profit would be 4.10:

Long call profit   2.00
Short 115 call expiration   0
Short 120 call expiration   0
Original position credit   2.10
    Net   4.10

If the stock closes below the long position, all options expire worthless and the initial credit of 2.10 is a fixed profit.

Bull Call Ladder on JCN

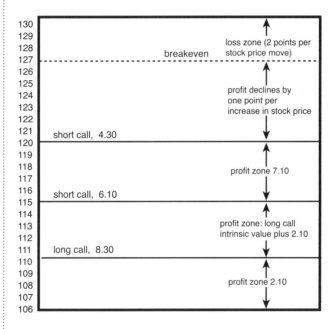

time -- seven months

Figure 7.4   Bull call ladder on JCN

Bull call spread—A popular variation of the spread, designed to produce maximum profits when the underlying stock rises. This position involves a long call at one strike with a short call at a higher strike. As long as expiration is identical, it is a vertical spread. If expiration is different, then it becomes a diagonal spread.

The bull call spread offers a combined limited profit and limited risk. Risk never exceeds the net cost to open the position, and the strategy is favored by many investors over a simple long call purchase because the cost is smaller. Even so, the position always creates a net debit when both sides are opened at the same time because the lower strike call always trades at a higher price than those calls with higher strikes. An exception: If each side of the spread is opened at different times and based on stock price movement, an original long or short position is converted to a spread. In this case, it is possible to create a bull call spread with a net credit.

Net breakeven on this strategy resides between the two strike prices. A limited profit zone exists above the higher strike; this is always a fixed profit equal to the point difference between strikes minus the cost to create the position. Maximum loss is realized if the underlying stock's price ends up at expiration below the lower strike. The maximum loss in the position is equal to the net debit involved in opening the position.

Example: You create a bull call spread in YPN. The stock is at $93.69 per share. You buy a February 90 at 4.70 and sell a February 95 at 1.45.

Table 7.1

YPN Price at Expiration	Feb 90	Profit or Loss Feb 95	Total
105	+10.30	−8.55	+ 1.75
100	+ 5.30	−3.55	+ 1.75
95+	0.30	+ 1.45	+ 1.75
94	−0.70	+ 1.45	+ 0.75
93	−1.70	+ 1.45	−0.25
92	−2.70	+ 1.45	−1.25
91	−3.70	+ 1.45	−2.25
90	−4.70	+ 1.45	−3.25
89	−4.70	+ 1.45	−3.25
88	−4.70	+ 1.45	−3.25

Bull Call Spread on YPN

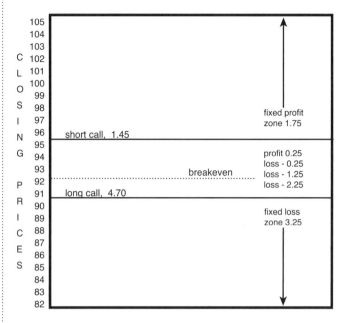

Figure 7.5 Bull call spread on YPN

Bull put ladder—Also called the short put ladder, this strategy combines unlimited profit potential with a limited risk. It is an effective strategy when volatility is expected to be high.

The bull put ladder consists of selling one in the money put, and buying a put at or close to the money, and buying another put out of the money. Profit will be limited if and when the stock price rises above the upper breakeven point; larger, potentially unlimited profits will occur if the stock price falls below the lower breakeven point. Losses will occur if the stock price closes between the strikes of the two long puts. The position has two breakeven points: one above the short put strike and the other below the two long put strikes.

Example: NDE closed at $58.91 on December 31. You sell a February 62.50 put for 3.40; buy a February 57.50 put for 1.30; and buy a February 52.50 put for 0.33. The net credit you receive for this position is 1.77. The two breakeven points occur on the upside between 60 and 61 with a fixed net profit from that point upward; and on the downside between 49 and 50 per share with profit increasing dollar for dollar with decline in the stock from that point downward.

Table 7.2

NDE Price at Expiration	Feb 62.50	Profit or Loss Feb 57.50	Feb 52.50	Total
65	+ 3.40	- 1.30	- 0.33	+ 1.77
64	+ 3.40	- 1.30	- 0.33	+ 1.77
63	+ 3.40	- 1.30	- 0.33	+ 1.77
62	+ 2.90	- 1.30	- 0.33	+ 1.27
61	+ 1.90	- 1.30	- 0.33	+ 0.27
60	+ 0.90	- 1.30	- 0.33	- 0.73
59	- 0.10	- 1.30	- 0.33	- 1.73
58	- 1.10	- 1.30	- 0.33	- 2.73
57	- 2.10	- .80	- 0.33	- 3.23
56	- 3.10	+ .20	- 0.33	- 3.23
55	- 4.10	+ 1.20	- 0.33	- 3.23
54	- 5.10	+ 2.20	- 0.33	- 3.23
53	- 6.10	+ 3.20	- 0.33	- 3.23
52	- 7.10	+ 4.20	+ 0.17	- 2.73
51	- 8.10	+ 5.20	+ 1.17	- 1.73
50	- 9.10	+ 6.20	+ 2.17	- 0.73
49	- 10.10	+ 7.20	+ 3.17	+ 0.27
48	- 11.10	+ 8.20	+ 4.17	+ 1.27
47	- 12.10	+ 9.20	+ 5.17	+ 2.27

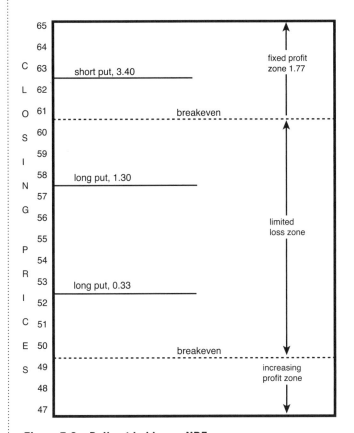

Bull Put Ladder on NDE

Figure 7.6   **Bull put ladder on NDE**

Bull put spread—A variation of spread using puts. This strategy combines a long put at one strike with a short put at a higher strike. The greatest potential profit is achieved when the stock price rises.

For example, JCN closed on December 31 at 108.10. A bull put spread—to be used if you believe the stock price is going to rise—is constructed by buying a buying a February 105 put for 2.95 and selling a 110 put for 5.00. The net credit in this example is 2.05. The spreads between the two strikes is five points. If the stock price rises above the higher (short) strike, the maximum profit of 2.05 ($205) will be earned since both puts will expire worthless. Risk is limited as well. If the stock closes between the two put strikes, profit or loss depends on the net credit received. If the stock price closes below the lower strike, the maximum loss of 2.95 will be realized, which is the difference between the five-point spread and the net cost of the position (5.00 – 2.05).

Table 7.3

JCN Price at Expiration	Profit or Loss		Total
	Feb 105	Feb 110	
112	- 2.95	+ 5.00	+ 2.05
111	- 2.95	+ 5.00	+ 2.05
110	- 2.95	+ 5.00	+ 2.05
109	- 2.95	+ 4.00	+ 1.05
108	- 2.95	+ 3.00	+ 0.05
107	- 2.95	+ 2.00	- 0.95
106	- 2.95	+ 1.00	- 1.95
105	- 2.95	0	- 2.95
104	- 1.95	- 1.00	- 2.95
103	- 0.95	- 2.00	- 2.95
102	+ 0.05	- 3.00	- 2.95
101	+ 1.05	- 4.00	- 2.95
100	+ 2.05	- 5.00	- 2.95

Bull Put Spread on JCN

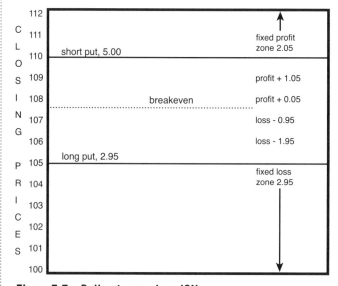

Figure 7.7   Bull put spread on JCN

Bull spread—Any spread that will produce profits when the underlying stock's market price rises. The strategy may involve either calls or puts. The trader accepts the potential of a limited profit in exchange for the limited risk.

A bull spread employing calls combines a long strike below a short strike. Because the long strike will have more ITM value if and when the underlying stock moves higher than the short call, profit is limited to the point spread between the strikes minus the cost of creating the position.

A bull spread with puts is designed in a similar manner, and a limited profit will exist upon a rise in the underlying stock because the short put loses its premium value when out of the money. Risk is also limited because a higher long position put will offset the short put risk, plus the point spread.

Butterfly spread—A complex spread involving the simultaneous use of offsetting calls or puts. On one side, a range of strike prices are employed and offset by a range of either higher or lower strike price ranges at the same time. Traders may employ either calls or puts in the butterfly spread.

An example involving calls: YPN closed at $93.69 on December 31, 2007. You construct a spread involving calls ranging between 85 and 95 strikes, as follows:

February 85 call	9.90
February 90 call	5.90
February 95 call	2.85

A butterfly spread combines two separate spreads in a single position: one a bull spread and the other a bear spread. For a relatively small cost, risk is limited. So if you believe the stock will not experience much volatility between now and expiration, you might earn a limited profit from this position. However, two attributes have to be considered, given the severely limited profit potential of the butterfly. First is trading costs, which may absorb much of the maximum profit. Second is margin requirement, which expands with the number of outstanding option contracts. If the margin requirement stretches your portfolio resources, it may not be worth the exchange of limited risk and limited profit.

In the example using the YPN calls, a butterfly is created by buying the high and low call strikes and selling two of the middle strikes:

Buy 1 February 85 call	- 9.90
Sell 2 February 90 calls	+11.80
Buy 1 February 95 call	- 2.85
Net debit	- 0.95

For less than $100 (before calculating brokerage fees), this butterfly is set up with limited risk on both the upside and the downside. The greatest risk in this position, in fact, is 0.95 ($95) plus trading expenses.

Table 7.4

YPN Price at Expiration	1 Feb 95	Profit or Loss 2 Feb 90	1 Feb 85	Total
100	+ 2.15	- 8.20	+ 5.10	- 0.95
99	+ 1.15	- 6.20	+ 4.10	- 0.95
98	+ 0.15	- 4.20	+ 3.10	- 0.95
97	- 0.85	- 2.20	+ 2.10	- 0.95
96	- 1.85	- 0.20	+ 1.10	- 0.95
95	- 2.85	+ 1.80	+ 0.10	- 0.95
94	- 2.85	+ 3.80	- 0.90	+ 0.05
93	- 2.85	+ 5.80	- 1.90	+ 1.05
92	- 2.85	+ 7.80	- 2.90	+ 2.05
91	- 2.85	+ 9.80	- 3.90	+ 3.05
90	- 2.85	+11.80	- 4.90	+ 4.05
89	- 2.85	+11.80	- 5.90	+ 3.05
88	- 2.85	+11.80	- 6.90	+ 2.05
87	- 2.85	+11.80	- 7.90	+ 1.05
86	- 2.85	+11.80	- 8.90	+ 0.05
85	- 2.85	+11.80	- 9.90	- 0.95
84	- 2.85	+11.80	- 9.90	- 0.95
83	- 2.85	+11.80	- 9.90	- 0.95
82	- 2.85	+11.80	- 9.90	- 0.95
81	- 2.85	+11.80	- 9.90	- 0.95
80	- 2.85	+11.80	- 9.90	- 0.95

In this example, for a fixed price and limited loss of $95 above or below the mid-range price level, you gain the potential of profit up to $405. The butterfly combines a spread between the 95 and 90 strike, with another at the 90 and 85 strike.

Butterfly Spread on YPN

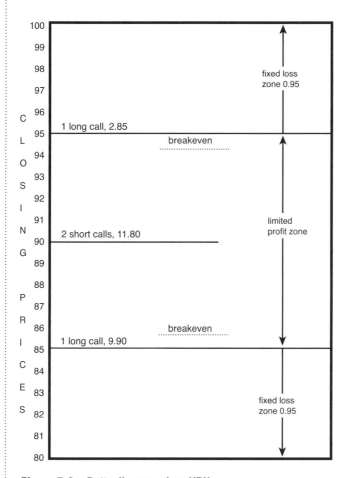

Figure 7.8 Butterfly spread on YPN

A similar strategy can be constructed employing puts, in which short puts are opened on the middle range with long puts above and below. In all butterfly spreads, the number of long and short positions are identical. (If and when a dissimilar number of options are employed, it becomes a variation of a *ratio* on either long or short side, such as the ladder or the ratio *calendar combination spread*).

Butterfly spreads can be reversed as well. Using calls, a high and low short position can be opened and offset with the purchase of two mid-range long calls. Using puts, a high and low short position would be opened and offset with mid-range long puts. However, in both of these instances, the likelihood of exercise would be greatly increased. The concept of the butterfly spread makes sense for most traders when short positions reside in between higher- and lower-strike price long positions.

The theory of the butterfly spread may be mathematically interesting, but in practice it is less practical. The creation of a strategy with initial breakeven or credit benefit limits potential profits, but trading costs in opening and closing positions are likely to eliminate or even exceed the limited profit levels, a situation known as an *alligator spread*—one in which any limited profits are "eaten up" by the trading costs.

Buy-write—Alternative name for the covered call, the two sides representing a buy (of stock) and a short sale of a call.

Calendar spread—A spread with both sides having the same strike price but with varying expiration dates. The short-term option is sold, and the longer-term option is bought to cover the short position. The greater time value in the later position creates a net debit; the strategy assumes the short call can be closed profitably or allowed to expire, and the longer-term long position may benefit from a rising stock price and increased intrinsic value. Also called a *horizontal spread*.

Example: You are able to sell an NDE February 60 call for 1.65. With the stock price at 58.91, this call is 1.09 OTM. At the same time, you buy a June 60 call for 4.00. Your net cost for this position is 2.35. Consider the three possible outcomes, as follows:

1. The short position is exercised. In this case, you cover the position with the long call with the same strike, and your net loss is 2.35.

2. The short position expires worthless. You continue to hold the long June call, which you acquired for a net cost of 2.35, hoping for a profit. A variation of this theme is that the short position is closed at a small profit. For example, its value falls to 0.35, and you buy to close. Your basis in the June call is then adjusted to 2.70 (2.35 + 0.35).

3. The short position expires worthless, and you close the June call at a loss. In this case, the loss on the June call is reduced by the profit on the February call, creating either a smaller loss or a net profit.

Collar—A protective strategy combining a short covered call and a long put. This position is commonly opened on an existing stock position to protect paper profits and may involve identical or different strikes and expirations.

For example, assume you had purchased shares of JCN at $95 per share, and it is currently valued at $108.10. A collar may be used to protect some of the paper profits by buying a July 105 put for 6.40 and selling a July 110 covered call for 8.30. The net credit on this collar is 1.90. If the stock's price rises and the covered call is exercised, profit will consist of the net credit of 1.90 ($190), plus the appreciated stock (strike of 110 minus original basis of 95, or 15 points ($1,500). If the stock's price remains below the 110 strike until expiration, the call position is entirely profit; if the stock's price falls below the put strike of 105, the put offsets the loss below that level point for point.

This collar protects almost the entire amount of paper profit in the stock. With the current value of stock at $108.10, the credit on the collar of 1.90 reduces current basis value to 106.20 (looking at this another way, you could view the original basis in stock to be reduced from 95 per share down to 93.10 (95 less 1.90). If the stock price rises, the short call will be exercised, and stock called away at the 110 strike; if the stock price falls between 105 and 110, the net 1.90 is all profit; and if the stock price falls below 105, the long put insures profits and picks up one dollar in intrinsic value for every dollar lost in market value of the stock.

Combination—Any position involving two or more option strategies that are open at the same time, but which are not straddles. A long combination exists when a call and a put are both included; a short combination is defined as simultaneous opening of a call and a put. For example, whereas a straddle will contain identical strike price and expiration, a combination will vary. For example, you create a combination when you buy two options both expiring in the same month, with call and put having different strike prices.

Example: NDE closed at 58.91 per share. You create a long combination when you buy a March 60 call for 2.40 and a March 55 put for 1.10. Your total cost is 3.50. To profit from this position, you will require movement in the stock's price more than two breakeven prices: 3.5 points above 60 or 3.5 points below 55 (strike prices of top and bottom option minus the net cost of the position).

A short combination requires selling of two positions rather than buying. For example, if instead of buying options on NDE, you sold them, it would create a credit combination. This would be achieved by selling a March 60 call for 2.40 and selling a March 55 put for 1.10. The net credit is 3.50. Now a profit is possible as long as the stock price remains between the two strikes, below the call strike of 60 and above the put strike of 55. Breakeven now exists 3.5 points above the call strike and 3.5 points below the put. Because these are five points apart, that creates a no-loss zone of 12 points (a five-point spread between the strikes plus 3.5 points on either side).

The short combination is easier to manage and create profits because it is a credit position. Additionally, profits can be managed and created in one of two ways. First, as time value declines in either option or in both, one or both sides can be closed at a profit. Second, as either side goes ITM, exercise can be avoided by closing the short position or by rolling forward to a later expiration. In the roll, either option can be kept at the same strike but a later expiration, the call can be rolled forward and up, or the put can be rolled forward and down. By changing the strike, the chances of exercise are eliminated for the moment, and in the event of later exercise, this creates additional exercise profit.

Condor spread—Also called a flat-top butterfly, the condor combines a bull and a bear spread in a single, four-part position. The typical butterfly involves three different strikes. For example, you would hold two long calls, each with different strike prices, and sell two calls at the same strike in between the other two. A condor involves four separate strikes, and the position sequence is long, short, short, long.

Example: YPN closed at $93.69 on December 31. You construct a condor position using four calls with different strikes:

Buy 1 July 90 call   - 10.10

Sell 1 July 95 call   + 7.30

Sell 1 July 100 call   + 5.00

Buy 1 July 105 call   - 3.20

    Net debit   - 1.00

Table 7.5

YPN Price at Expiration	July 90	Profit or Loss July 95	July 100	July 105	Total
110	+ 9.90	- 7.70	- 5.00	+ 1.80	- 1.00
109	+ 8.90	- 6.70	- 4.00	+ 0.80	- 1.00
108	+ 7.90	- 5.70	- 3.00	- 0.20	- 1.00
107	+ 6.90	- 4.70	- 2.00	- 1.20	- 1.00
106	+ 5.90	- 3.70	- 1.00	- 2.20	- 1.00
105	+ 4.90	- 2.70	0	- 3.20	- 1.00
104	+ 3.90	- 1.70	+ 1.00	- 3.20	0
103	+ 2.90	- 0.70	+ 2.00	- 3.20	+1.00
102	+ 1.90	+ 0.30	+ 3.00	- 3.20	+2.00
101	+ 0.90	+ 1.30	+ 4.00	- 3.20	+3.00
100	- 0.10	+ 2.30	+ 5.00	- 3.20	+4.00
99	- 1.10	+ 3.30	+ 5.00	- 3.20	+4.00
98	- 2.10	+ 4.30	+ 5.00	- 3.20	+4.00
97	- 3.10	+ 5.30	+ 5.00	- 3.20	+4.00
96	- 4.10	+ 6.30	+ 5.00	- 3.20	+4.00
95	- 5.10	+ 7.30	+ 5.00	- 3.20	+4.00
94	- 6.10	+ 7.30	+ 5.00	- 3.20	+3.00
93	- 7.10	+ 7.30	+ 5.00	- 3.20	+2.00
92	- 8.10	+ 7.30	+ 5.00	- 3.20	+1.00
91	- 9.10	+ 7.30	+ 5.00	- 3.20	0
90	-10.10	+ 7.30	+ 5.00	- 3.20	- 1.00
89	-10.10	+ 7.30	+ 5.00	- 3.20	- 1.00
88	-10.10	+ 7.30	+ 5.00	- 3.20	- 1.00
87	-10.10	+ 7.30	+ 5.00	- 3.20	- 1.00
86	-10.10	+ 7.30	+ 5.00	- 3.20	- 1.00
85	-10.10	+ 7.30	+ 5.00	- 3.20	- 1.00

The condor expands the profitable middle range over a comparable three-strike butterfly.

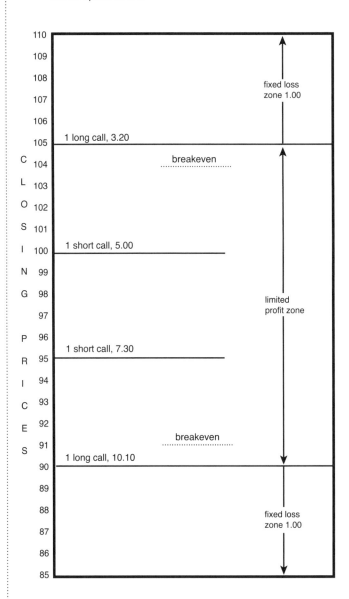

Condor Spread on YPN

Figure 7.9   Condor spread on YPN

Conversion—A strategy combining three parts together: a long put, a short call, and 100 shares of long stock. Both options share expiration and strike, and this position creates locked-in profits, as long as the position cost is lower than the option strike levels.

Example: NDE stock closed December 31 at 58.91. You buy 100 shares at that closing price. You also buy a March 55 put for 1.10 and sell a March 55 call for 5.70. Your credit for the option positions is 4.60. This reduces your net cost to 54.31 (58.91 − 4.60). If the stock remains above the 55 strike, the call is exercised, and stock is called away at 55, for a profit of 0.69. If the stock price falls below 55, the entire call premium is profit, and the put value offsets decline in the stock price point for point. The net position profit of 0.69 is the profit this position can earn in either event. This may be varied if the short position can be closed profitably prior to expiration, in which case the outstanding put provides continuing downside protection for the long stock.

A reversal is similar to a conversion with the long and short positions opposite: short stock, short put, and long call.

Covered call—A strategy requiring ownership of 100 shares of the underlying stock. One call is sold short against 100 shares, thus covering the risk. If you do not own 100 shares, the call is not covered, but is *naked*, and risks are much greater.

For example, you own 100 shares of JCN that you purchased for $103 per share. In selecting an appropriate call for this strategy, you need to plan for the contingency of exercise. So if you were to sell a 100 call, the calculation of net return would have to allow for the loss of three points (basis of 103 less strike of 100). It makes sense to always write covered calls so that in the event of exercise, the combined stock and option outcome will create an overall net profit.

Downside protection: Covered calls essentially discount the basis in stock, providing downside protection. In the preceding example, the basis is $103 per share; if you sell a call and receive 4.00 in premium, this reduces your net basis in the stock to $99 per share. The option premium you receive when you sell a covered call is credited to your account and is yours to keep, pending one of several possible outcomes. In the example of acquiring JCN at $103 per share, you see that current value as of December 31 is $108.10. You may select a number of different calls based on strike price and time to expiration. These include, among others, the following:

January 105	4.90 (Immediate income of $490 plus $200 in profit from stock if the short call is exercised. The call expires in three weeks.)
January 110	2.15 (Immediate income of $215 plus $700 in profit from stock if the short call is exercised. The call expires in three weeks.)
February 105	6.30 ($630 + $200) with nearly two months until exercise.
February 110	3.63 ($363 + $700) with nearly two months until exercise.

The preceding examples are all short-term covered calls. The two 105 calls are more than three points ITM, meaning chances for exercise are strong; however, the richer premium might justify this strategy if you are willing to sell the stock. The 110's are OTM and offer less option premium but potentially higher capital gains if the short call is exercised.

Return calculations: In calculating the return from a covered call strategy, consider all possible outcomes:

(a) Stock value falls, time value declines, and the call can be bought to close at a profit, freeing you to repeat the strategy with a different call.

(b) Stock remains at or below the option's strike and expires worthless; all the option premium is profit, and you are free to repeat the strategy.

(c) Stock price rises and you accept exercise.

(d) Stock price rises to or above strike, and you roll forward (or forward and up) to avoid exercise.

To accurately compare outcomes from various covered call selections, remember that dividends continue to be earned even when the short call is opened and remain earned until the call is exercised or stock is sold. Comparisons should be annualized as well so that they are accurate. To annualize, divide the projected return by the number of weeks until expiration and multiply the result by 52 (weeks) to approximate the return you would earn over an entire year. Return calculations may include option premium only or by compared with dividend and capital gain for total return if and when exercised.

Appropriate use: Covered calls are appropriate to use when exercise is among the acceptable outcomes and when you want to discount your basis to either force an exercise sale or later avoid exercise and repeat the covered call strategy several times. It is one of many ways to take paper profits without selling stock or to use as part of a combined strategy involving long calls or either long or short puts.

Conservative strategy: The covered calls define the extent of a conservative option strategy because all outcomes are going to be profitable if the strategy is properly timed, no matter what the outcome. The only negative to the covered call occurs when a stock's market price rises dramatically and stock is called away when the short call is exercised. In that outcome, you lose the appreciated value because the short call fixes your income at the strike price. For most covered call enthusiasts, this is a risk worth adopting, considering the consistency or returns and safety in the strategy.

Tax considerations: Tax law affects capital gains based on the type of covered call selected. A *qualified* covered call enables you to claim long-term gains on stock profits after exercise, but an *unqualified* covered call may toll the 12-month count or start it over. This type of call is deemed too far ITM at the time the covered call is opened. Thus, traders selecting deep in-the-money calls should be aware of the potential for loss of favorable capital gains treatment due to this important tax rule.

Covered combination—A strategy with three parts: ownership of 100 shares of stock, a short call, and a short put. The options have the same expiration but different strike prices. The call is covered, and the put is uncovered. In the event the put is exercised, the trader acquires an additional 100 shares at the strike. In the event the call is exercised, the 100 shares of stock are called away, and only the short put remains.

Example: You own 100 shares of NDE, which you acquired at $55 per share. As of December 31, the price is $58.91. You open a covered combination by selling a February 55 call for 4.90 and selling a February 60 put for 2.20. Your total credit for this combination is 7.10 ($710). Although both options are ITM, the 7.10-point range extends the breakeven point between 48 and 67 (seven points below the call strike and seven points above the put price). If either option is exercised within this zone, the position is profitable. For example, if the stock falls to $52 per share, the put is exercised, and you purchase an additional 100 shares at $60 (a loss of eight points). However, with an additional 100 shares, subsequent option positions can be opened to offset the loss of 0.90 ($90). This loss is the difference between the eight points and the 7.10 premium received. If the stock rises and is called away at $55, you keep the $710 received for the position, and you break even on the stock (basis was $55 per share, and strike of the call is 55).

The most likely outcome of a short-term covered combination is rapid decline in time value, resulting in one of the two positions expiring worthless and the other being closed at a profit or rolled forward to avoid exercise. In the preceding example, although both options are ITM, time value is considerable. The call contains 0.99 of time value (premium 4.90 less intrinsic value of 3.91), and the put contains 1.11 in time value (premium 2.20 less intrinsic value of 1.09). With less than two months to expiration, time value will decline quickly, so the strategy's most likely outcome will be to close one or both positions when this occurs or to roll forward to take advantage of additional time value with later expiration dates.

Covered put—A strategy opposite a covered call. With the call, owning 100 shares of stock covers the short position, but a put cannot be covered in the same way. To "cover" the position, one of two situations is required. First, the trader maintains adequate cash in an account or combined with margin to pay for exercise at a put's strike. Second, the put covers a short position in stock. For example, a trader is short 100 shares in the belief that the price will decline. However, concerned with the risk that the price will rise, the trader sells one put per 100 short shares.

Covered short straddle—A strategy combining a short call and a short put, also known as a covered combination. It is not accurate to describe the position as covered because exercise of the short put requires purchase of additional shares.

Credit spread—Any spread in which the net receipt from short positions exceeds the net cost of long positions, with the net deposited in the trader's account. The credit is used as part of the calculated breakeven, profit, or loss pricing. The larger the credit, the more likely a profit in any spread.

chapter 8

Option Strategies D–P

The strategies in this chapter, as well as Chapters 7 and 9, are arranged alphabetically. Option and stock values have been used based on a close of business value on the same trading session, December 31. Three companies have been used, and these are called JCN, NDE, and YPN. Because values change significantly over time, fictitious names have been provided with these quotes. A complete summary of the option listings for these three companies are included in the appendix at the back of this book.

Debit spread—A spread in which the net cost of long positions is higher than the net receipt from short positions, with that net to be paid by the trader. The debit is used to adjust calculated breakeven, profit, and loss pricing. The larger the debit, the less likely a profit in any spread.

Delta hedge—A strategy based on option price change (measured by delta) compared with price change in the underlying. When the option's price movement is dissimilar to the point movement in the underlying, the delta quantifies this difference. Delta for options always ranges between 0.00 and 1.00 (for calls) and between 0.00 and -1.00 (for puts). For example, if the stock rises one point, but the option rises only one-half point, its delta is 0.50. When the underlying and option premium move exactly the same number of points, the delta is 1.00.

The delta hedge takes advantage of the adjustments in price movement. For example, out-of-the-money calls tend to have very low delta factors. A delta hedge strategy can be devised assuming that with less responsive price movement, some positions (especially short positions) are likely to be more profitable than in the money (ITM) options, whose delta is closer to 1.00. Options with higher ratios may be better trades for long positions because of the delta, meaning that less time value erosion and closer intrinsic value tracking can be anticipated.

Delta spread—A ratio designed to maximize returns from two separate delta values of options on the same underlying stock. The delta of a long and short option are opened at the same time, with likelihood that the short side will erode more quickly and the long side will hold value or increase in value to a greater extent. The delta spread (also called a ratio spread because the value is determined by dividing one delta by the other) is designed to anticipate how changes in each side's delta will change and how option premium levels will react.

Diagonal spread—Any spread involving options with different strike prices and expiration dates. In comparison, a horizontal spread has different expirations and the same strikes; a vertical spread has the same expirations but different strikes.

Types of Spreads

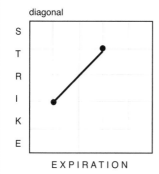

diagonal

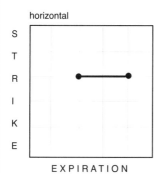

horizontal

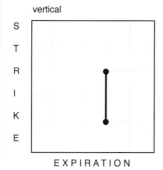

vertical

Figure 8.1   Types of spreads

Hedge—A strategy set up to offset one position with another, usually resulting in combining limited profits with limited risk, often set up to limit losses in one position. For example, the owner of stock may buy a put to protect paper profits. In the event the stocks' price fell below the put strike, the decline will be matched point-for-point in intrinsic value of the put. In this instance, the put hedges the risk of loss in the stock.

Hedge ratio—The delta of a ratio, a comparison between the delta of two offsetting options. The purpose of the ratio is to identify the point where a neutral hedge exists so that offsetting positions approximate zero risk.

Horizontal spread—A spread consisting of options with the same strikes but different expirations (see Figure 8.1 for diagonal hedge).

Iron butterfly (long)—A combined straddle and combination (compared with the simple butterfly, which is two spreads), providing limited profit potential with limited risk. A long iron butterfly consists of four options (compared with three in the standard butterfly). Profit occurs when the stock's price ends up below the lowest strike or above the highest strike in the position (in a short iron butterfly, profit occurs between the strike ranges).

Example: YPN closed on December 31 at 93.69. The long iron butterfly is constructed with options with 90, 95, and 100. The following positions are opened, with all options expiring in February:

Long	Short
	90 put, 1.85
95 put, 2.50	
95 call, 1.45	
	100 call, 1.05

The net cost of this position is 1.05 (2.50 + 1.45 – 1.85 – 1.05). The breakeven range occurs in a mid-range, and profit occurs if the stock closes above or below that range.

Table 8.1

YPN Price at Expiration	90 Put	Profit or Loss 95 Put	95 Call	100 Call	Total
105	+ 1.85	- 2.50	+ 8.55	- 3.95	+ 3.95
104	+ 1.85	- 2.50	+ 7.55	- 2.95	+ 3.95
103	+ 1.85	- 2.50	+ 6.55	- 1.95	+ 3.95
102	+ 1.85	- 2.50	+ 5.55	- 0.95	+ 3.95
101	+ 1.85	- 2.50	+ 4.55	+ 0.05	+ 3.95
100	+ 1.85	- 2.50	+ 3.55	+ 1.05	+ 3.95
99	+ 1.85	- 2.50	+ 2.55	+ 1.05	+ 2.95
98	+ 1.85	- 2.50	+ 1.55	+ 1.05	+ 1.95
97	+ 1.85	- 2.50	+ 0.55	+ 1.05	+ 0.95
96	+ 1.85	- 2.50	- 0.45	+ 1.05	- 0.05
95	+ 1.85	- 2.50	- 1.45	+ 1.05	- 1.05
94	+ 1.85	- 1.50	- 1.45	+ 1.05	- 0.05
93	+ 1.85	- 0.50	- 1.45	+ 1.05	+ 0.95
92	+ 1.85	+ 0.50	- 1.45	+ 1.05	+ 1.95
91	+ 1.85	+ 1.50	- 1.45	+ 1.05	+ 2.95
90	+ 1.85	+ 2.50	- 1.45	+ 1.05	+ 3.95
89	+ 0.85	+ 3.50	- 1.45	+ 1.05	+ 3.95
88	- 0.15	+ 4.50	- 1.45	+ 1.05	+ 3.95
87	- 1.15	+ 5.50	- 1.45	+ 1.05	+ 3.95
86	- 2.15	+ 6.50	- 1.45	+ 1.05	+ 3.95
85	- 3.15	+ 7.50	- 1.45	+ 1.05	+ 3.95

This example involves only three prices at which losses will result. The higher or lower the price away from this very small zone, the more profitable the iron butterfly.

Iron Butterfly (Long) on YPN

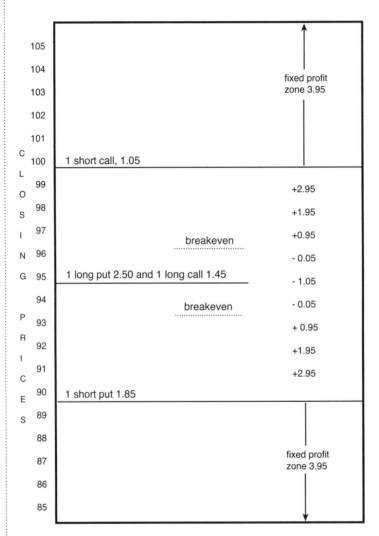

Figure 8.2   Iron butterfly (long) on YPN

Iron butterfly (short)—A combined straddle and combination (compared with the simple butterfly, which is two spreads), providing limited profit potential with limited risk. A short iron butterfly consists of four options (compared with three in the standard butterfly). Profit occurs when the stock's price ends up between the strike ranges (in a long iron butterfly, profit occurs below the lowest strike or above the highest strike).

Example: YPN closed on December 31 at 93.69. The short iron butterfly is constructed with options with 90, 95, and 100 just like the long iron butterfly, but in reverse (long positions become short and vice versa). The following positions are opened, with all options expiring in February:

Long	Short
90 put, 1.85	
	95 put, 2.50
	95 call, 1.45
100 call, 1.05	

The net credit of this position is 1.05 (2.50 + 1.45 − 1.85 − 1.05). Whereas the long iron butterfly based on the same options created a debit, if you assume you can reverse the long and short for the same prices, the short credit is the same value as the long debit.

This example offers only three prices with potential profits, with the remaining outcomes all losses, and with losses increasing to the fixed maximum as the price moves higher or lower away from the mid-range. It is likely that this position's components would be closed early to avoid the restricted likelihood of a profitable result.

Table 8.2

YPN Price at Expiration	90 Put	Profit or Loss 95 Put	95 Call	100 Call	Total
105	- 1.85	+ 2.50	- 8.55	+3.95	- 3.95
104	- 1.85	+ 2.50	- 7.55	+2.95	- 3.95
103	- 1.85	+ 2.50	- 6.55	+1.95	- 3.95
102	- 1.85	+ 2.50	- 5.55	+0.95	- 3.95
101	- 1.85	+ 2.50	- 4.55	- 0.05	- 3.95
100	- 1.85	+ 2.50	- 3.55	- 1.05	- 3.95
99	- 1.85	+ 2.50	- 2.55	- 1.05	- 2.95
98	- 1.85	+ 2.50	- 1.55	- 1.05	- 1.95
97	- 1.85	+ 2.50	- 0.55	- 1.05	- 0.95
96	- 1.85	+ 2.50	+ 0.45	- 1.05	+ 0.05
95	- 1.85	+ 2.50	+ 1.45	- 1.05	+ 1.05
94	- 1.85	+ 1.50	+ 1.45	- 1.05	+ 0.05
93	- 1.85	+ 0.50	+ 1.45	- 1.05	- 0.95
92	- 1.85	- 0.50	+ 1.45	- 1.05	- 1.95
91	- 1.85	- 1.50	+ 1.45	- 1.05	- 2.95
90	- 1.85	- 2.50	+ 1.45	- 1.05	- 3.95
89	- 0.85	- 3.50	+ 1.45	- 1.05	- 3.95
88	+ 0.15	- 4.50	+ 1.45	- 1.05	- 3.95
87	+ 1.15	- 5.50	+ 1.45	- 1.05	- 3.95
86	+ 2.15	- 6.50	+ 1.45	- 1.05	- 3.95
85	+ 3.15	- 7.50	+ 1.45	- 1.05	- 3.95

Iron Butterfly (Short) on YPN

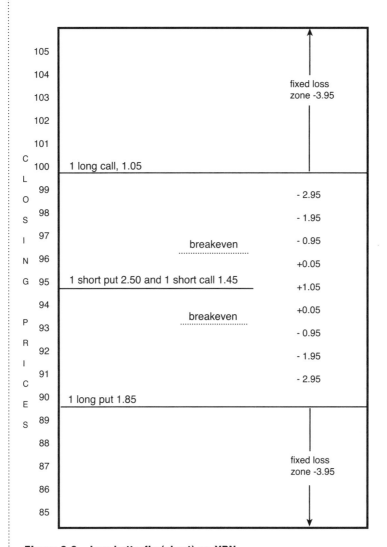

Figure 8.3   Iron butterfly (short) on YPN

Leg in / leg out—A leg consists of the parts in a combination option strategy. Simple straddles and spreads have two legs, consisting of long and short options or of option type (calls or puts). A combination is created when one side exists and the trader enters a subsequent transaction that creates a straddle or spread (leg in). Similarly, when a combination already exists, a trader may close one side to take partial profits, converting a combination to a single long or short position (leg out).

Long call—An open option contract including the contractual right to buy 100 shares of the underlying stock at the fixed strike price and on or before the expiration date. In comparison, a long put gives its owner the right to sell 100 shares of the underlying; a short call is an open contract in which the call rights are granted to someone else in exchange for receipt of the option premium.

Long calls are employed by traders in numerous ways, as follows:

1. *Swing trading.* If you own shares of stock as a long-term investment, you will not want to sell when prices rise or fall. However, when prices dip, buying calls is one way to swing trade on the temporary price movement.

2. *Simple speculation.* The most popular form of long call trading is to earn short-term profits. Even though 75 percent of all long options expire worthless or lose money, this remains a popular activity.

3. *To tie in a future price.* If you plan to buy shares in the future, buying a call today provides leverage and locks in the price for future purchase.

4. *To cover a short position.* The long call is used by short sellers of stock to insure against the contingency of loss in the event the stock's price rises. The open long call offsets each point lost with an increase of one point in intrinsic value.

5. *As part of a straddle or spread.* The combination strategies involving two or more sides require the use of offsetting positions. Long calls offset short calls or long puts.

Long call butterfly—A butterfly position combining a bull spread and a bear spread together and using calls. It is designed to produce profits when the underlying stock price remains within the boundaries of high and low strikes. This position includes four trades and three strikes with the same expiration. One call is purchased at the high and at the low strikes, and two calls are sold at a strike in between. This strategy limits both profit and risk.

Example: NDE closed December 31 at $58.91. You construct a long call butterfly with calls and at June strikes of 55, 60, and 65. You buy one 55 at 7.60 and one 65 call at 1.90, and sell two 60 calls at 4.00 each. Your net debit is 1.50.

Table 8.3

NDE Price at Expiration	1 Jun 65	Profit or Loss 2 Jun 60	1 Jun 55	Total
70	+ 3.10	- 12.00	+ 7.40	- 1.50
69	+ 2.10	- 10.00	+ 6.40	- 1.50
68	+ 1.10	- 8.00	+ 5.40	- 1.50
67	+ 0.10	- 6.00	+ 4.40	- 1.50
66	- 0.90	- 4.00	+ 3.40	- 1.50
65	- 1.90	- 2.00	+ 2.40	- 1.50
64	- 1.90	0	+ 1.40	- 0.50
63	- 1.90	+ 2.00	+ 0.40	+ 0.50
62	- 1.90	+ 4.00	- 0.60	+ 1.50
61	- 1.90	+ 6.00	- 1.60	+ 2.50
60	- 1.90	+ 8.00	- 2.60	+ 3.50
59	- 1.90	+ 8.00	- 3.60	+ 2.50
58	- 1.90	+ 8.00	- 4.60	+ 1.50
57	- 1.90	+ 8.00	- 5.60	+ 0.50
56	- 1.90	+ 8.00	- 6.60	- 0.50
55	- 1.90	+ 8.00	- 7.60	- 1.50
54	- 1.90	+ 8.00	- 7.60	- 1.50
53	- 1.90	+ 8.00	- 7.60	- 1.50
52	- 1.90	+ 8.00	- 7.60	- 1.50
51	- 1.90	+ 8.00	- 7.60	- 1.50
50	- 1.90	+ 8.00	- 7.60	- 1.50

Long Call Butterfly on NDE

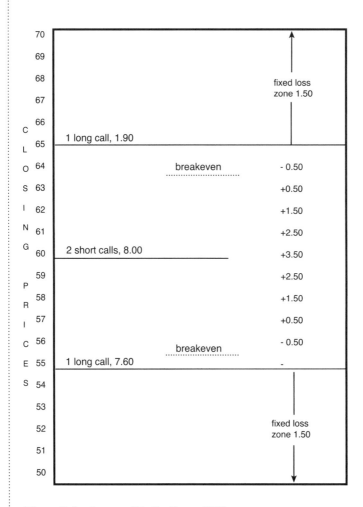

Figure 8.4   Long call butterfly on NDE

Long call condor—A strategy similar to the butterfly and using long and short calls, with the distinction that the two middle calls are opened with different strikes. Thus, four different strikes are used instead of three (the butterfly involves doubling up the middle-strike with twice as many options, but the condor employs the same number of calls at all strike prices with the two middle positions offsetting the higher and lower). This expands the potential profit price range beyond that of the butterfly.

Example: You open a condor on JCN by selling two middle-strike calls and protecting that position with one higher-strike and one lower-strike long call.

The short positions are July 105 (11.00) and 110 (8.30), and the long positions are July 100 (15.80) and 115 (6.10). Your net debit is 2.60.

Table 8.4

JCN Price at Expiration	Jul 100	Profit or Loss Jul 105	Jul 110	Jul 115	Total
123	+ 7.20	- 7.00	- 4.70	+ 1.90	- 2.60
122	+ 6.20	- 6.00	- 3.70	+ 0.90	- 2.60
121	+ 5.20	- 5.00	- 2.70	- 0.10	- 2.60
120	+ 4.20	- 4.00	- 1.70	- 1.10	- 2.60
119	+ 3.20	- 3.00	- 0.70	- 2.10	- 2.60
118	+ 2.20	- 2.00	+ 0.30	- 3.10	- 2.60
117	+ 1.20	- 1.00	+ 1.30	- 4.10	- 2.60
116	+ 0.20	0	+ 2.30	- 5.10	- 2.60
115	- 0.80	+ 1.00	+ 3.30	- 6.10	- 2.60
114	- 1.80	+ 2.00	+ 4.30	- 6.10	- 1.60
113	- 2.80	+ 3.00	+ 5.30	- 6.10	- 0.60
112	- 3.80	+ 4.00	+ 6.30	- 6.10	+ 0.40
111	- 4.80	+ 5.00	+ 7.30	- 6.10	+ 1.40
110	- 5.80	+ 6.00	+ 8.30	- 6.10	+ 2.40
109	- 6.80	+ 7.00	+ 8.30	- 6.10	+ 2.40
109	- 7.80	+ 8.00	+ 8.30	- 6.10	+ 2.40
107	- 8.80	+ 9.00	+ 8.30	- 6.10	+ 2.40
106	- 9.80	+ 10.00	+ 8.30	- 6.10	+ 2.40
105	-10.80	+ 11.00	+ 8.30	- 6.10	+ 2.40
104	-11.80	+ 11.00	+ 8.30	- 6.10	+ 1.40
103	-12.80	+ 11.00	+ 8.30	- 6.10	+ 0.40
102	-13.80	+ 11.00	+ 8.30	- 6.10	- 0.60
101	-14.80	+ 11.00	+ 8.30	- 6.10	- 1.60
100	-15.80	+ 11.00	+ 8.30	- 6.10	- 2.60
99	-15.80	+ 11.00	+ 8.30	- 6.10	- 2.60
98	-15.80	+ 11.00	+ 8.30	- 6.10	- 2.60

Long Call Condor on JCN

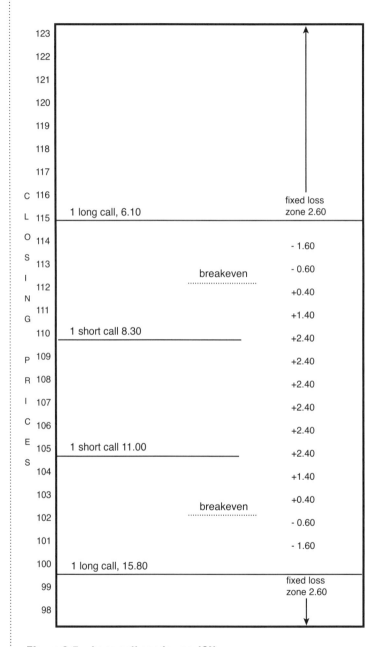

Figure 8.5   Long call condor on JCN

Long combination—A strategy involving long options, including the following:

1. Synthetic long stock, involving a long call and a short put at the same strike.

2. Any grouping that is designed to minimize risk, often in exchange for a limited potential profit.

3. Straddles or spreads using long positions rather than short positions.

Long iron butterfly—A butterfly employing both calls and puts. The middle strike consists of one short call and one short put with the same strike; the higher and lower strikes are long: a call at the higher strike and a put at the lower strike. All options have the same expiration unless it is constructed as a diagonal position; in that case, the short options are usually shorter-term. In the traditional butterfly strategy, either calls or puts are used exclusively; the long iron butterfly used both types of options. Losses are limited at both top and bottom; maximum profit is equal to the credit on the position.

Example: You construct a long iron butterfly on YPN. Using February options, the short positions include a 95 call (2.85) and a 95 put (4.00). The long positions are a 100 call (1.05) and a 90 put (1.85). The net credit on this position is 3.95. That represents maximum profit. Maximum loss occurs both above the highest strike and below the lowest strike, and the loss level is fixed at 1.05 (five-point spread between strikes minus net credit of 3.95).

Table 8.5

YPN Price at Expiration	Long 90 Put	Short 95 Put	Profit or Loss Short 95 Call	Long 100 Call	Total
105	- 1.85	+ 4.00	- 7.15	+ 3.95	- 1.05
104	- 1.85	+ 4.00	- 6.15	+ 2.95	- 1.05
103	- 1.85	+ 4.00	- 5.15	+ 1.95	- 1.05
102	- 1.85	+ 4.00	- 4.15	+ 0.95	- 1.05
101	- 1.85	+ 4.00	- 3.15	- 0.05	- 1.05
100	- 1.85	+ 4.00	- 2.15	- 1.05	- 1.05
99	- 1.85	+ 4.00	- 1.15	- 1.05	- 0.05
98	- 1.85	+ 4.00	- 0.15	- 1.05	+ 0.95
97	- 1.85	+ 4.00	+ 0.85	- 1.05	+ 1.95
96	- 1.85	+ 4.00	+ 1.85	- 1.05	+ 2.95
95	- 1.85	+ 4.00	+ 2.85	- 1.05	+ 3.95
94	- 1.85	+ 3.00	+ 2.85	- 1.05	+ 2.95
93	- 1.85	+ 2.00	+ 2.85	- 1.05	+ 1.95
92	- 1.85	+ 1.00	+ 2.85	- 1.05	+ 0.95
91	- 1.85	0	+ 2.85	- 1.05	- 0.05
90	- 1.85	- 1.00	+ 2.85	- 1.05	- 1.05
89	- 0.85	- 2.00	+ 2.85	- 1.05	- 1.05
88	+ 0.15	- 3.00	+ 2.85	- 1.05	- 1.05
87	+ 1.15	- 4.00	+ 2.85	- 1.05	- 1.05
86	+ 2.15	- 5.00	+ 2.85	- 1.05	- 1.05
85	+ 3.15	- 6.00	+ 2.85	- 1.05	- 1.05

Long Iron Butterfly on YPN

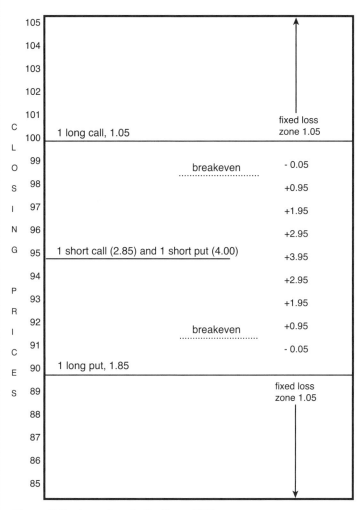

Figure 8.6 Long iron butterfly on YPN

Long put—An open option contract including the contractual right to sell 100 shares of the underlying stock at the fixed strike price and on or before the expiration date. In comparison, a long call gives its owner the right to buy 100 shares of the underlying; a short put is an open contract in which the put rights are granted to someone else in exchange for receipt of the option premium.

Long puts are employed by traders in numerous ways, as follows:

1. *Swing trading.* If you own shares of stock as a long-term investment, you will not want to sell when prices rise or fall. However, when prices rise, buying puts is one way to swing trade on the temporary price movement.

2. *Simple speculation.* The most popular form of long put trading is to earn short-term profits. Even though 75 percent of all long options expire worthless or lose money, this remains a popular activity.

3. *To tie in a future sale price.* If you plan to sell shares in the future, buying a put today provides leverage and locks in the price for future sale. Thus, if the stock price declines, the put offsets that decline point for point with increased intrinsic value once the put is in the money.

4. *To cover or insure a long stock position.* The long put is used by stock owners to insure against the contingency of loss in the event the stock's price declines. The open long put offsets each point lost with an increase of one point in intrinsic value.

5. *As part of a straddle or spread.* The combination strategies involving two or more sides require the use of offsetting positions. Long puts offset short puts or long calls.

Long put butterfly—A butterfly position combining a bull spread and a bear spread together and using puts. It is designed to produce profits when the underlying stock price remains within the boundaries of high and low strikes. This position includes four trades and three strikes with the same expiration. The highest and lowest strikes are long puts, and two short puts are sold at the middle strike. This strategy limits both profit and risk.

Example: You construct a long put butterfly on NDE based on June puts. This consists of a long 65 put at 6.60, two short puts at 60 for 3.70 each (7.40 total), and one long 55 put at 2.10. Net debit is 1.30, which is also the maximum loss on this strategy.

Table 8.6

NDE Price at Expiration	1 Jun 65	Profit or Loss 2 Jun 60	1 Jun 55	Total
70	- 6.60	+ 7.40	- 2.10	- 1.30
69	- 6.60	+ 7.40	- 2.10	- 1.30
68	- 6.60	+ 7.40	- 2.10	- 1.30
67	- 6.60	+ 7.40	- 2.10	- 1.30
66	- 6.60	+ 7.40	- 2.10	- 1.30
65	- 6.60	+ 7.40	- 2.10	- 1.30
64	- 5.60	+ 7.40	- 2.10	- 0.30
63	- 4.60	+ 7.40	- 2.10	+ 0.70
62	- 3.60	+ 7.40	- 2.10	+ 1.70
61	- 2.60	+ 7.40	- 2.10	+ 2.70
60	- 1.60	+ 7.40	- 2.10	+ 3.70
59	- 0.60	+ 5.40	- 2.10	+ 2.70
58	+ 0.40	+ 3.40	- 2.10	+ 1.70
57	+ 1.40	+ 1.40	- 2.10	+ 0.70
56	+ 2.40	- 0.60	- 2.10	- 0.30
55	+ 3.40	- 2.60	- 2.10	- 1.30
54	+ 4.40	- 4.60	- 1.10	- 1.30
53	+ 5.40	- 6.60	- 0.10	- 1.30
52	+ 6.40	- 8.60	+ 0.90	- 1.30
51	+ 7.40	- 10.60	+ 1.90	- 1.30
50	+ 8.40	- 12.60	+ 2.90	- 1.30

Long Put Butterfly on NDE

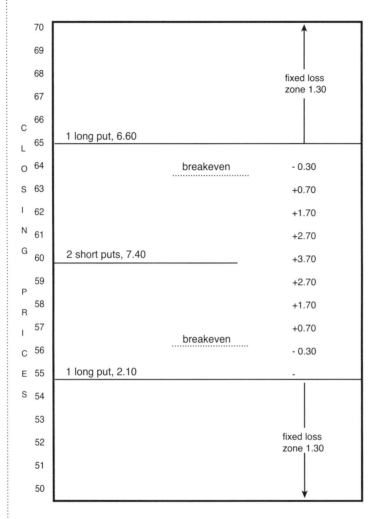

Figure 8.7   Long put butterfly on NDE

Long put condor—An expansion on the long put butterfly, consisting of spreading the two middle puts between two different strikes. This expands the total range into four different strikes, with the two long positions at highest and lowest, and the two short puts in the two middle-range strikes.

Example: Referring to the NDE example of a long put butterfly, you modify it by expanding to include four strikes, all with June expirations. This consists of a long 65 put 6.60, a short 62.50 put at 4.90, a short 60 put at 3.70, and a long 55 put at 2.10. Net debit is 0.10. In this strategy, maximum loss on the upside is limited to the net cost of 0.10. On the downside, that loss is expanded to 2.60 maximum (cost of 0.10, plus additional 2.5 points for the expanded short positions in the middle (62.50 – 60.00)).

Table 8.7

NDE Price at Expiration	1 Jun 65	1 Jun 62.50	1 Jun 60	1 Jun 55	Total
70	- 6.60	+ 4.90	+ 3.70	- 2.10	- 0.10
69	- 6.60	+ 4.90	+ 3.70	- 2.10	- 0.10
68	- 6.60	+ 4.90	+ 3.70	- 2.10	- 0.10
67	- 6.60	+ 4.90	+ 3.70	- 2.10	- 0.10
66	- 6.60	+ 4.90	+ 3.70	- 2.10	- 0.10
65	- 6.60	+ 4.90	+ 3.70	- 2.10	- 0.10
64	- 5.60	+ 4.90	+ 3.70	- 2.10	+ 0.90
63	- 4.60	+ 4.90	+ 3.70	- 2.10	+ 1.90
62	- 3.60	+ 4.40	+ 3.70	- 2.10	+ 2.40
61	- 2.60	+ 3.40	+ 3.70	- 2.10	+ 2.40
60	- 1.60	+ 2.40	+ 3.70	- 2.10	+ 2.40
59	- 0.60	+ 1.40	+ 2.70	- 2.10	+ 1.40
58	+ 0.40	+ 0.40	+ 1.70	- 2.10	+ 0.40
57	+ 1.40	- 0.60	+ 0.70	- 2.10	- 0.60
56	+ 2.40	- 1.60	- 0.30	- 2.10	- 1.60
55	+ 3.40	- 2.60	- 1.30	- 2.10	- 2.60
54	+ 4.40	- 3.60	- 2.30	- 1.10	- 2.60
53	+ 5.40	- 4.60	- 3.30	- 0.10	- 2.60
52	+ 6.40	- 5.60	- 4.30	+ 0.90	- 2.60
51	+ 7.40	- 6.60	- 5.30	+ 1.90	- 2.60
50	+ 8.40	- 7.60	- 6.30	+ 2.90	- 2.60

Long Put Condor on NDE

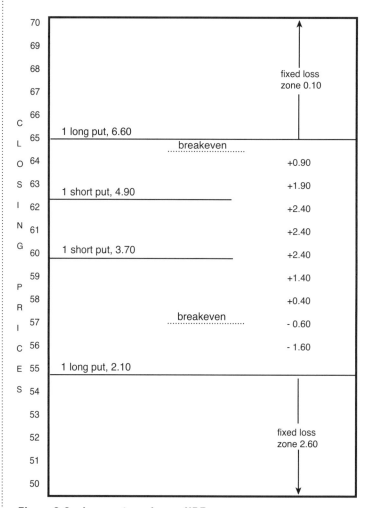

Figure 8.8   Long put condor on NDE

Long stock (synthetic)—An option position that approximates the performance of stock, whether rising or falling in price. The synthetic position enables you to take a position in the stock for less money than it would require to purchase shares. This is accomplished by entering into a long call and a short put with identical strike and expiration. If the stock's price rises, the short put becomes worthless, and the long call gains value. If the stock remains at or slightly above the strike, the position expires without creating either profit or loss. If the stock price falls, the call becomes worthless and the put is exercised, resulting in acquisition of 100 shares at the strike.

Example: You create a long stock synthetic position by purchasing a YPN July 95 call for 7.30 and selling a July 95 put for 7.00. Your net cost is 0.30 ($30). Because the cost of this position is quite small and there are nearly seven months until expiration, the leverage advantage is considerable. Buying 100 shares cost $9,369 on December 31, and for $30, you achieve the same market advantage with a long synthetic position. The primary risk—having 100 shares put to you after a decline—is the same risk as purchasing 100 shares at about the strike of the put and then facing a declining market. However, investing over $9,000 less presents a considerable opportunity because those funds can be invested elsewhere or if the portfolio holds adequate assets, the synthetic approach can be expanded beyond this single position. The position at various stock prices show a one-point value movement mirroring how the stock would perform if you were to simply buy 100 shares.

Table 8.8

YPN

Price at Expiration	Jul 95 Call	July 95 Put	Net
103	+ 0.70	+ 7.00	+7.70
102	- 0.30	+ 7.00	+6.70
101	- 1.30	+ 7.00	+5.70
100	- 2.30	+ 7.00	+4.70
99	- 3.30	+ 7.00	+3.70
98	- 4.30	+ 7.00	+2.70
97	- 5.30	+ 7.00	+1.70
96	- 6.30	+ 7.00	+0.70
95	- 7.30	+ 7.00	- 0.30
94	- 7.30	+ 6.00	- 1.30
93	- 7.30	+ 5.00	- 2.30
92	- 7.30	+ 4.00	- 3.30
91	- 7.30	+ 3.00	- 4.30
90	- 7.30	+ 2.00	- 5.30
89	- 7.30	+ 1.00	- 6.30
88	- 7.30	0	- 7.30
87	- 7.30	- 1.00	- 8.30

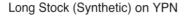

Long Stock (Synthetic) on YPN

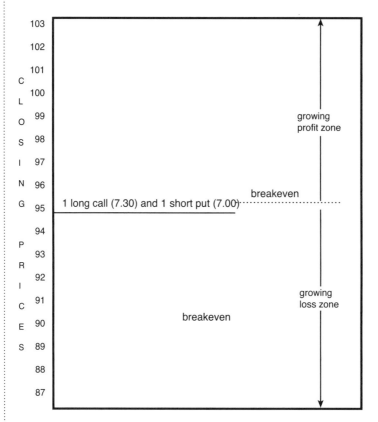

Figure 8.9   Long stock (synthetic) on YPN

Long straddle—The simultaneous purchase of a call and a put on the same underlying, with the same strike, and with the same expiration. This strategy becomes profitable only if the stock's price exceeds the total cost of the position on either the upside or the downside.

For example, the long stock (synthetic) position involves a long call and a short put. Using the same contracts to create a long straddle, you would the call for 7.30 and buy the put for 7.00. Your debit is 14.30, so you need a price movement of more than 14 points to break even on the long straddle. Using YPN and the July 95 call and put, the range required to create a profit is quite wide. This strategy would be worthwhile only if you anticipate exceptional volatility in either direction from the strikes.

Table 8.9

YPN Price at Expiration	Jul 95 Call	July 95 Put	Net
112	+ 9.70	- 7.00	+ 2.70
111	+ 8.70	- 7.00	+ 1.70
110	+ 7.70	- 7.00	+ 0.70
109	+ 6.70	- 7.00	- 0.30
108	+ 5.70	- 7.00	- 1.30
107	+ 4.70	- 7.00	- 2.30
106	+ 3.70	- 7.00	- 3.30
105	+ 2.70	- 7.00	- 4.30
104	+ 1.70	- 7.00	- 5.30
103	+ 0.70	- 7.00	- 6.30
102	- 0.30	- 7.00	- 7.30
101	- 1.30	- 7.00	- 8.30
100	- 2.30	- 7.00	- 9.30
99	- 3.30	- 7.00	- 10.30
98	- 4.30	- 7.00	- 11.30
97	- 5.30	- 7.00	- 12.30
96	- 6.30	- 7.00	- 13.30
95	- 7.30	- 7.00	- 14.30
94	- 7.30	- 6.00	- 13.30
93	- 7.30	- 5.00	- 12.30
92	- 7.30	- 4.00	- 11.30
91	- 7.30	- 3.00	- 10.30
90	- 7.30	- 2.00	- 9.30
89	- 7.30	- 1.00	- 8.30
88	- 7.30	0	- 7.30
87	- 7.30	+ 1.00	- 6.30
86	- 7.30	+ 2.00	- 5.30
85	- 7.30	+ 3.00	- 4.30

Table 8.9   continued

YPN Price at Expiration	Jul 95 Call	July 95 Put	Net
84	- 7.30	+ 4.00	- 3.30
83	- 7.30	+ 5.00	- 2.30
82	- 7.30	+ 6.00	- 1.30
81	- 7.30	+ 7.00	- 0.30
80	- 7.30	+ 8.00	+ 0.70
79	- 7.30	+ 9.00	+ 1.70

Long Straddle on YPN

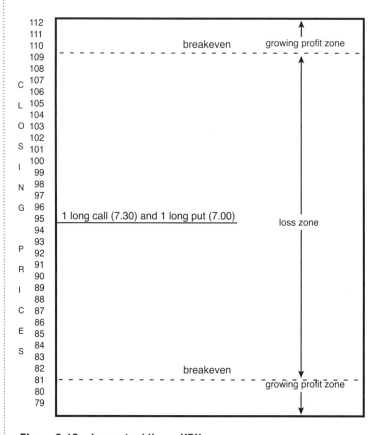

Figure 8.10   Long straddle on YPN

Married put—The purchase of 100 shares and a put at the same time. Also known as a synthetic long call, maximum profit is unlimited in the event of the stock's price rise (equal to the number of points above stock basis, minus the cost of the put). Risk is limited because decline in the stock's price is offset by increase in the put's intrinsic value. Risk is equal to the premium paid for the put, plus any distance between the basis in stock and the put's strike.

For example, you buy 100 shares of JCN on December 31, paying $108.10 per share. You purchase an April 105 put for 4.55. Stock risk is 3.10 points (108.10 – 105.00), and the put risk is the premium of 4.55. The breakeven on the position is 112.65 on the upside (basis of 108.10 + put premium of 4.55). On the downside, fixed loss risk maximum is 7.65 (gap between stock basis and put strike, plus put premium, or 108.10 – 105.00 + 4.55). So in exchange for unlimited profit potential above breakeven, you would be willing to fix the maximum potential loss.

Table 8.10

YPN Price at Expiration	Stock	July 105 Put	Net
115	+ 6.90	- 4.55	+ 2.35
114	+ 5.90	- 4.55	+ 1.35
113	+ 4.90	- 4.55	+ 0.35
112	+ 3.90	- 4.55	- 0.65
111	+ 2.90	- 4.55	- 1.65
110	+ 1.90	- 4.55	- 2.65
109	+ 0.90	- 4.55	- 3.65
108	- 0.10	- 4.55	- 4.65
107	- 1.10	- 4.55	- 5.65
106	- 2.10	- 4.55	- 6.65
105	- 3.10	- 4.55	- 7.65
104	- 4.10	- 3.55	- 7.65
103	- 5.10	- 2.55	- 7.65
102	- 6.10	- 1.55	- 7.65

Married Put on JCN

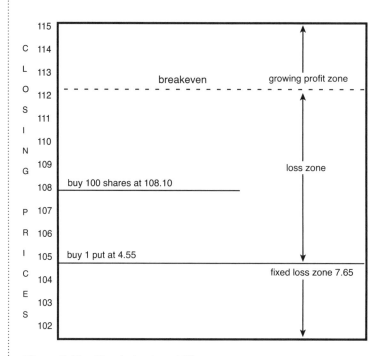

Figure 8.11   Married put on JCN

Money spread—*See* vertical spread.

Naked option—A short position not hedged or covered by an offsetting long position. A call is naked (uncovered) when it is written without (a) owning 100 shares of the underlying, (b) owning a call that provides complete or partial hedging in a straddle or spread position, or (c) also holding an uncovered put, in which case the combined premium from selling both naked options provides a point spread of profit or reduced gain.

A put is uncovered whenever the position is sold without being offset by (a) a short stock position (thus, if the stock price rises, the loss in intrinsic value of the put offsets all or some of the loss on the short stock), (b) owning a put that offsets the short position in a straddle or spread position, or (c) holding a short call that provides a degree of protection against loss due to the combined short premium income of both options.

A naked call has unlimited risk, in theory, because a stock's price may rise indefinitely. On a practical level, the real market risk is limited to the *likely* maximum price increase, minus premium received from selling the call. A naked put does not have unlimited risk because a stock's price can fall only so far. This analysis usually refers to a zero value as the maximum risk, but in realistic terms, the risk faced when holding a naked put is the difference between strike price and the stock's tangible book value, minus the premium received from selling the put.

Naked calls and puts will not be exercised as long as they remain at the money or out of the money. Exercise can be avoided by closing the position with a buy to close order. It can also be avoided by rolling forward to a later-expiring option. A call may also be rolled forward and up to extend the strike to an additional point level; a put may be rolled forward and down to achieve the same benefit. Rolling may be accomplished for a small debit or, if time value has evaporated from the option, for a credit.

Neutral hedge ratio—Reference to the price movement of an option in relation to the price movement of the underlying stock, or the delta of the option.

Neutral position—A spread or straddle that is neither bullish nor bearish. With the delta calculated, a trader will adjust each side of a two-part strategy to approximate neutrality. For example, if one option has a delta of .25 and another is .50, a neutral ratio will be 2:1 (.50 ÷ .25). In adjusting a position to neutral, you will open twice as many of the lower-delta options (two short .25 positions against one long of the .50 delta, or two long .25 positions against one short of the .50 delta).

Put diagonal spread (bear)—A spread using puts and entered when you believe the price of the underlying will decline in the near future. It involves buying a higher-strike, in-the-money put and selling an out-of-the-money, lower-strike put that expires sooner.

Example: You create a put diagonal spread (bear) on NDE. The stock closed December 31 at 58.91. You buy a June 60 put for 3.70 and sell a March 55 put for 1.10. Your net debit is 2.60. If the underlying price remains at or above 55 until the March expiration, the short put expires worthless; if the stock subsequently remains below the 60 strike, you can close the long put for intrinsic value before expiration. The timing is crucial for this position. Movement above or below each strike determines whether the position will be profitable or not. For a net debit of 2.60, you gain control over the longer-term put, assuming that the shorter-term put either expires worthless or loses time value by expiration. (It was out of the money at sale, so the entire premium represented time value.) The stock would need to fall to 53.90 to create breakeven on the short position (55 strike less premium of 1.10). Given the current price of 58.91, that is a five-point drop. If that were to occur, the long 60 strike put would contain 6.10 in intrinsic value (whereas the short put's offsetting intrinsic status would be 1.10, or a net advantage of five points).

Put diagonal spread (bull)—A diagonal spread using puts, entered when you believe the price of the underlying will rise in the near future. It involves selling a higher-strike out-of-the-money put and buying a lower-strike, in-the-money put that expires later.

Example: Reversing the situation in the bear put spread example, you open a put diagonal spread (bull) on NDE. The stock closed December 31 at 58.91. You sell a March 60 put for 2.85 and buy a June 55 put for 2.10. Your net credit is 0.75. If the stock price declines below the lower strike, your maximum loss is fixed at 4.25 (the five-point difference in strikes, minus the premium you received). If the stock price remains in between the two strikes, your maximum loss will be the difference between 60 and the actual price, minus the premium. So if the stock closes at 57, your loss is 2.25 (60.00 − 57.00 − 0.75). If the underlying price rises above the higher 60 strike, both puts expire worthless, and the profit is fixed at 0.75. However, the shorter-term expiration for the short put occurs first. The best possible outcome involves the underlying rising above the 60 strike; in this case, the short put expires worthless, for a profit of 2.85, followed by a decline in the stock's price before the June expiration, so that the long position can be closed at a profit.

Put ratio backspread—Also called a reverse put ratio spread, a position when one or more puts are sold and a higher number of puts are bought with the same expiration but at a lower strike. This strategy features limited risk with potentially unlimited profits (limited only to the difference between long put strikes and zero). The strategy is worthwhile when you believe the underlying stock's price will decline before long put expiration.

Example: JCN closed on December 31 at 108.10. You believe that by mid-year, this price will fall, so you open a 2:1 put ratio backspread. You sell one July 110 put for 7.70 and buy two July 105 puts for 6.40 each, for a total of 12.80. Your net debit is 5.10. The advantage in this position is that for a relatively small cost, you create significant profit potential in the event of a price decline. Because the ratio is 2 to 1, an in-the-money price decline will result in profits of two points in the long put for each point lost in the short put. The major drawback is that it might require a considerable point drop in the underlying to create a profitable outcome.

Table 8.11

JCN Price at Expiration	1 July 110	2 July 105	Net
113	+ 7.70	- 12.80	- 5.10
112	+ 7.70	- 12.80	- 5.10
111	+ 7.70	- 12.80	- 5.10
110	+ 7.70	- 12.80	- 5.10
109	+ 6.70	- 12.80	- 6.10
108	+ 5.70	- 12.80	- 7.10
107	+ 4.70	- 12.80	- 8.10
106	+ 3.70	- 12.80	- 9.10
105	+ 2.70	- 12.80	- 10.10
104	+ 1.70	- 10.80	- 9.10
103	+ 0.70	- 8.80	- 8.10
102	- 0.30	- 6.80	- 7.10
101	- 1.30	- 4.80	- 6.10
100	- 2.30	- 2.80	- 5.10
99	- 3.30	- 0.80	- 4.10
98	- 4.30	+ 1.20	- 3.10
97	- 5.30	+ 3.20	- 2.10
96	- 6.30	+ 5.20	- 1.10
95	- 7.30	+ 7.20	- 0.10
94	- 8.30	+ 9.20	+ 0.90
93	- 9.30	+ 11.20	+ 1.90
92	- 10.30	+ 13.20	+ 2.90

Put Ratio Backspread on JCN

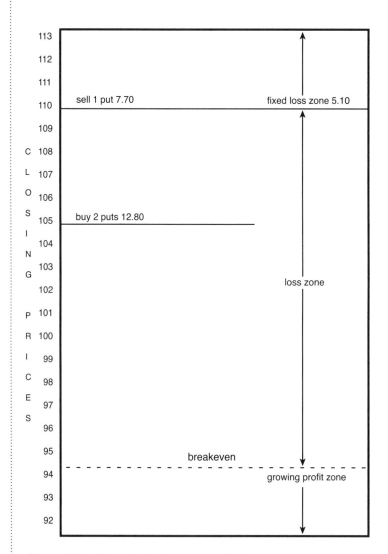

Figure 8.12   Put ratio backspread on JCN

chapter 9

Option Strategies R–Z

The strategies in this chapter, as well as in Chapters 7 and 8, are arranged alphabetically. Option and stock values have been used based on a close of business value on the same trading session, December 31. Three companies—JCN, NDE, and YPN—have been used. Because values change significantly over time, fictitious names have been provided with these quotes. A complete summary of the option listings for these three companies are included in the appendix.

Ratio backspread (call)—Also called a reverse call ratio spread, a strategy in which more calls are bought than sold. The long positions are bought at a higher strike but with the same expiration and are greater in number to the extent of the ratio (in a 2:1 ratio, there will be two long calls and one short call, for example).

Example: You open a 2:1 ratio backspread (call) on YPN. The stock closed on December 31 at 93.69. You buy two July 95 calls for 7.30 each, for a total of 14.60, and sell one July 90 call for 10.10. Your net debit is 4.50. If the stock price rises, the two long positions offset the one short position by two points to one at each rise in the underlying stock. If the stock price ends up at expiration between the two strikes, the maximum loss equals the debit plus the intrinsic value of the short position. If the stock's price falls below both strikes, the maximum loss is fixed at the debit of 4.50.

Table 9.1

YPN Price at Expiration	1 July 90	2 July 95	Net
109	- 8.90	+ 13.40	+ 4.50
108	- 7.90	+ 11.40	+ 3.50
107	- 6.90	+ 9.40	+ 2.50
106	- 5.90	+ 7.40	+ 1.50
105	- 4.90	+ 5.40	+ 0.50
104	- 3.90	+ 3.40	- 0.50
103	- 2.90	+ 1.40	- 1.50
102	- 1.90	- 0.60	- 2.50
101	- 0.90	- 2.60	- 3.50
100	+ 0.10	- 4.60	- 4.50
99	+ 1.10	- 6.60	- 5.50
98	+ 2.10	- 8.60	- 6.50
97	+ 3.10	- 10.60	- 7.50
96	+ 4.10	- 12.60	- 8.50
95	+ 5.10	- 14.60	- 9.50
94	+ 6.10	- 14.60	- 8.50
93	+ 7.10	- 14.60	- 7.50
92	+ 8.10	- 14.60	- 6.50
91	+ 9.10	- 14.60	- 5.50
90	+ 10.10	- 14.60	- 4.50
89	+ 10.10	- 14.60	- 4.50
88	+ 10.10	- 14.60	- 4.50
87	+ 10.10	- 14.60	- 4.50

Ratio Backspread (Call) on YPN

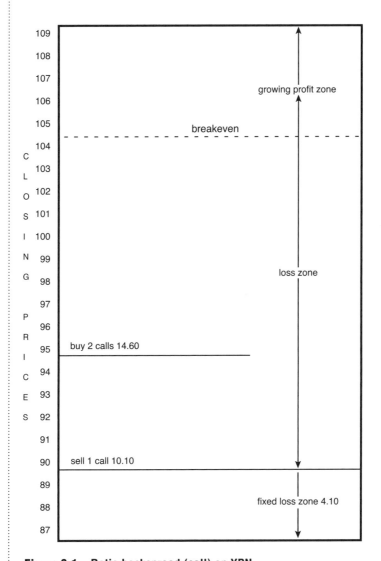

Figure 9.1   Ratio backspread (call) on YPN

Ratio backspread (put)—Also known as the reverse put ratio spread, a strategy combining short puts with a larger number of long puts. All share the same expiration date; however, the long puts are at a lower strike. This position creates limited risk on the upside with theoretically unlimited profits if the underlying declines. The ratio is defined by the number of short and long positions; if there are two long and one short puts, it is a 2:1 ratio backspread.

Example: You open a 2:1 ratio backspread (put) on NDE, which closed at 58.91 on December 31. This involves one short June 60 put at 3.70 and two long July 55 puts at 2.10, for a total of 4.20. Your net debit is 0.50. The advantage in this position is that as the underlying price falls below 50, you gain one point for each point of decline in the stock; if the price rises above 60, the loss is fixed at 0.50. The major disadvantage is the extended middle loss range.

Table 9.2

NDE Price at Expiration	1 June 60	2 June 55	Net
63	+ 3.70	- 4.20	- 0.50
62	+ 3.70	- 4.20	- 0.50
61	+ 3.70	- 4.20	- 0.50
60	+ 3.70	- 4.20	- 0.50
59	+ 2.70	- 4.20	- 1.50
58	+ 1.70	- 4.20	- 2.50
57	+ 0.70	- 4.20	- 3.50
56	- 0.30	- 4.20	- 4.50
55	- 1.30	- 4.20	- 5.50
54	- 2.30	- 2.20	- 4.50
53	- 3.30	- 0.20	- 3.50
52	- 4.30	+ 1.80	- 2.50
51	- 5.30	+ 3.80	- 1.50
50	- 6.30	+ 5.80	- 0.50
49	- 7.30	+ 7.80	+0.50
48	- 8.30	+ 9.80	+ 1.50
47	- 9.30	+ 11.80	+ 2.50

Ratio Backspread (Put) on NDE

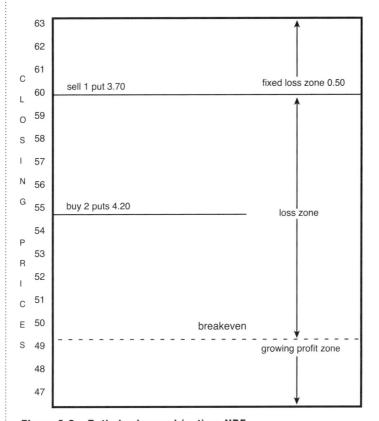

Figure 9.2   Ratio backspread (put) on NDE

Ratio calendar combination spread—A position coupling two ratio calendar spreads, one using calls and the other using puts. The call strike prices are higher than the put strike prices. This strategy is complex and profits limited, but if a high amount of time value is involved in the short positions, it can also be a profitable strategy with limited risk.

Example: JCN closed at 108.10 on December 31. You initiate a ratio calendar combination spread with the following positions:

Sell January 105 put	1.70
Sell January 110 call	2.15
Credit	3.85
Buy February 105 put	2.95
Buy February 110 call	3.63
Debit	6.58
Net debit	2.73

The advantage to this combination is maximized when the underlying stock price remains in the middle range until the earlier short options expirations and then moves above or below that middle range. In this way, the short positions expire worthless or at a profit, leaving the potential for profits from the longer-term long positions.

Table 9.3

JCN Price at Expiration	Profit or Loss January Combination			Profit or Loss February Combination		
	Jan 105 Put	Jan 110 Call	Total	Feb 105 Put	Feb 110 Call	Total
120	+ 1.70	- 7.85	**- 6.15**	- 2.95	+ 6.37	**+ 3.42**
119	+ 1.70	- 6.85	**- 5.15**	- 2.95	+ 5.37	**+ 2.42**
118	+ 1.70	- 5.85	**- 4.15**	- 2.95	+ 4.37	**+ 1.42**
117	+ 1.70	- 4.85	**- 3.15**	- 2.95	+ 3.37	**+ 0.42**
116	+ 1.70	- 3.85	**- 2.15**	- 2.95	+ 2.37	**- 0.58**
115	+ 1.70	- 2.85	**- 1.15**	- 2.95	+ 1.37	**- 1.58**
114	+ 1.70	- 1.85	**- 0.15**	- 2.95	+ 0.37	**- 2.58**
113	+ 1.70	- 0.85	**+ 0.85**	- 2.95	- 0.63	**- 3.58**
112	+ 1.70	+ 0.15	**+ 1.85**	- 2.95	- 1.63	**- 4.58**
111	+ 1.70	+ 1.15	**+ 2.85**	- 2.95	- 2.63	**- 5.58**
110	+ 1.70	+ 2.15	**+ 3.85**	- 2.95	- 3.63	**- 6.58**
109	+ 1.70	+ 2.15	**+ 3.85**	- 2.95	- 3.63	**- 6.58**
108	+ 1.70	+ 2.15	**+ 3.85**	- 2.95	- 3.63	**- 6.58**
107	+ 1.70	+ 2.15	**+ 3.85**	- 2.95	- 3.63	**- 6.58**
106	+ 1.70	+ 2.15	**+ 3.85**	- 2.95	- 3.63	**- 6.58**
105	+ 1.70	+ 2.15	**+ 3.85**	- 2.95	- 3.63	**- 6.58**
104	+ 0.70	+ 2.15	**+ 2.85**	- 1.95	- 3.63	**- 5.58**
103	- 0.30	+ 2.15	**+ 1.85**	- 0.95	- 3.63	**- 4.58**
102	- 1.30	+ 2.15	**+ 0.85**	+ 0.05	- 3.63	**- 3.58**
101	- 2.30	+ 2.15	**- 0.15**	+ 1.05	- 3.63	**- 2.58**
100	- 3.30	+ 2.15	**- 1.15**	+ 2.05	- 3.63	**- 1.58**
98	- 4.30	+ 2.15	**- 2.15**	+ 3.05	- 3.63	**- 0.58**
97	- 5.30	+ 2.15	**- 3.15**	+ 4.05	- 3.63	**+ 0.42**
96	- 6.30	+ 2.15	**- 4.15**	+ 5.05	- 3.63	**+ 1.42**
95	- 7.30	+ 2.15	**- 5.15**	+ 6.05	- 3.63	**+ 2.42**

Ratio Calendar Combination on JCN

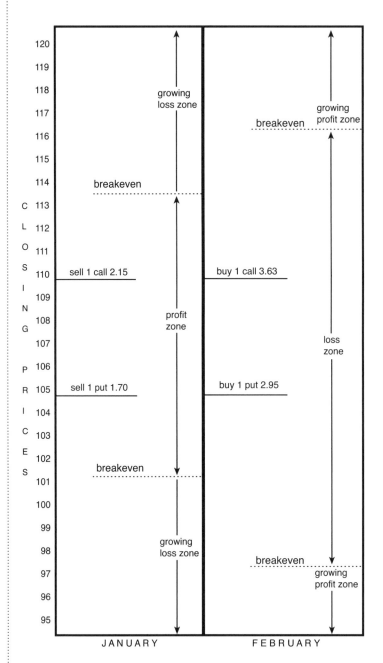

Figure 9.3   Ratio calendar combination on JCN

Ratio calendar spread (call)—A form of calendar spread in which more calls are sold than bought. For example, a 2:1 ratio would consist of selling two calls and buying one call. The short calls expire earlier than the long call. The narrower the ratio, the less risk; for example, a 3:2 is less risky than a 2:1 because the uncovered portion of the strategy is reduced.

Example: You set up a 3:2 ratio calendar spread (call) on YPN, which closed at 93.69 on December 31. You sell three July 90 calls for 10.10 each (30.30 total), and you buy two January 90 calls for 13.40 each (total 26.80). Your net credit is 3.50. In this case, you have a five-month span between the short and long positions, creating significant profit potential if the shorter-term, short calls expire worthless or can be closed at a profit. Because expiration is different for the short and long positions, the usual comparison is not entirely applicable. However, if the shorts can be closed profitably, the long positions will appreciate if the underlying later rises.

Table 9.4

YPN Price at Expiration	3 Jul 90	2 Jan 90	Net
106	- 17.70	+ 5.20	-12.50
105	- 14.70	+ 3.20	-11.50
104	- 11.70	+ 1.20	-10.50
103	- 8.70	- 0.80	- 9.50
102	- 5.70	- 2.80	- 8.50
101	- 2.70	- 4.80	- 7.50
100	+ 0.30	- 6.80	- 6.50
99	+ 3.30	- 8.80	- 5.50
98	+ 6.30	- 10.80	- 4.50
97	+ 9.30	- 12.80	- 3.50
96	+ 12.30	- 14.80	- 2.50
95	+ 15.30	- 16.80	- 1.50
94	+ 18.30	- 18.80	- 0.50
93	+ 21.30	- 20.80	+ 0.50
92	+ 24.30	- 22.80	+ 1.50
91	+ 27.30	- 24.80	+ 2.50
90	+ 30.30	- 26.80	+ 3.50
89	+ 30.30	- 26.80	+ 3.50
88	+ 30.30	- 26.80	+ 3.50
87	+ 30.30	- 26.80	+ 3.50
86	+ 30.30	- 26.80	+ 3.50
85	+ 30.30	- 26.80	+ 3.50

Ratio Calendar Spread (Call) on YPN

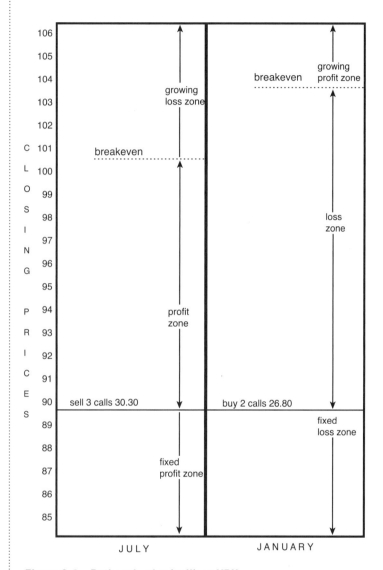

Figure 9.4   Ratio calendar (call) on YPN

Ratio calendar spread (put)—A strategy with both short puts and long puts. The short puts expire before the long puts, and all positions are opened with the same strike price. More short positions are opened, and the relationship between short-term short puts and longer-term long puts is expressed as a ratio. Selling two puts for every one bought creates a 2:1 ratio. Because short positions are partially uncovered, the closer the ratio and the less risk. For example, a 3:2 ratio calendar spread contains less risk than a 2:1 with the same contracts.

Example: You create a 3:2 ratio calendar spread (put) on NDE. The stock closed at $58.91 on December 31. You sell three March 60 puts at 2.85 each for a total credit of 8.55. You buy two June 60 puts at 3.70 each, for a total debit of 7.40. Your net credit is 1.15. Because expiration months are not the same, a side-by-side comparison is not complete. The best possible outcome is for the underlying to remain above the 60 strike until the March expiration and to then fall below the 60 strike by the June expirations.

Table 9.5

NDE Price at Expiration	3 Mar 60	2 Jun 90	Net
65	+ 8.55	- 7.40	+ 1.15
64	+ 8.55	- 7.40	+ 1.15
63	+ 8.55	- 7.40	+ 1.15
62	+ 8.55	- 7.40	+ 1.15
61	+ 8.55	- 7.40	+ 1.15
60	+ 8.55	- 7.40	+ 1.15
59	+ 5.55	- 5.40	+ 0.15
58	+ 2.55	- 3.40	- 0.85
57	- 0.45	- 1.40	- 1.85
56	- 3.45	+ 0.60	- 2.85
55	- 6.45	+ 2.60	- 3.85
54	- 9.45	+ 4.60	- 4.85
53	- 12.45	+ 6.60	- 5.85
52	- 15.45	+ 8.60	- 6.85

Ratio Calendar Spread (Put) on NDE

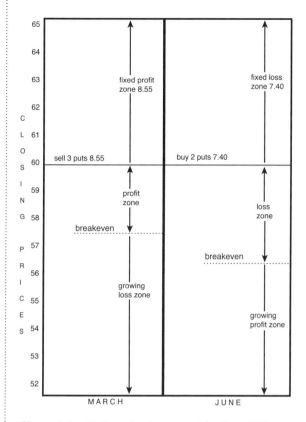

Figure 9.5   Ratio calendar spread (put) on NDE

Ratio call spread—A neutral strategy involving long calls at one strike, and a higher number of short calls at another strike, all with the same expiration. The ratio refers to the relationship between the short and long positions. For example, if you open two short calls and one long call, it is a 2:1 ratio.

Example: You open a 2:1 ratio call spread on JCN, buying one April 105 call for 8.90 and selling two April 110 calls at 6.00 each, for a total of 12.00. Your net credit is 3.10. If the underlying remains below the short call strike of 110, the short calls expire worthless. Maximum loss will increase point for point with the underlying above the 118.10 level (115 + 3.10 credit). If the price rises above the long strike of 105, the long call will be valued at its intrinsic value. And if the underlying moves above 110, the maximum loss will one point per price increase in the underlying.

Table 9.6

JCN Price at Expiration	2 Apr 110	1 Apr 105	Net
120	- 8.00	+ 6.10	- 1.90
119	- 6.00	+ 5.10	- 0.90
118	- 4.00	+ 4.10	+ 0.10
117	- 2.00	+ 3.10	+ 1.10
116	0	+ 2.10	+ 2.10
115	+ 2.00	+ 1.10	+ 3.10
114	+ 4.00	+ 0.10	+ 4.10
113	+ 6.00	- 0.90	+ 5.10
112	+ 8.00	- 1.90	+ 6.10
111	+ 10.00	- 2.90	+ 7.10
110	+ 12.00	- 3.90	+ 8.10
109	+ 12.00	- 4.90	+ 7.10
108	+ 12.00	- 5.90	+ 6.10
107	+ 12.00	- 6.90	+ 5.10
106	+ 12.00	- 7.90	+ 4.10
105	+ 12.00	- 8.90	+ 3.10
104	+ 12.00	- 8.90	+ 3.10
103	+ 12.00	- 8.90	+ 3.10
102	+ 12.00	- 8.90	+ 3.10
101	+ 12.00	- 8.90	+ 3.10
100	+ 12.00	- 8.90	+ 3.10

Ratio put spread—A strategy with a dissimilar number of long and short puts. More puts are sold at a lower strike price than are bought at the higher strike. The downside risk can be significant, but the upside profit potential is limited. The ratio is defined by the relative numbers of puts on each side. If you sell two puts and buy one at a higher strike, you have created a 2:1 ratio put spread.

Ratio Call Spread on JCN

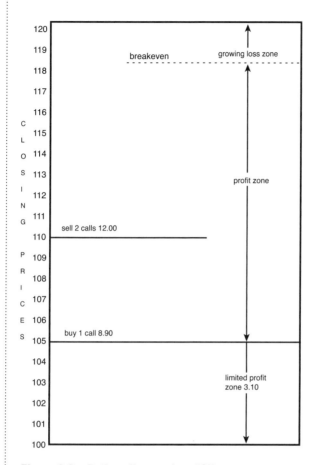

Figure 9.6 Ratio call spread on JCN

Example: You create a 2:1 ratio put spread on JCN. You buy one April 110 put for 6.90 and you sell two April 100 puts at 3.20 each, for a total of 6.40. Your net debit on this position is 0.50. This represents the maximum loss on the upside. There is a broad profit range in the middle but an increasing loss potential on the downside.

Table 9.7

JCN Price at Expiration	2 Apr 100	1 Apr 110	Net
112	+ 6.40	- 6.90	- 0.50
111	+ 6.40	- 6.90	- 0.50
110	+ 6.40	- 6.90	- 0.50
109	+ 6.40	- 5.90	+ 0.50
108	+ 6.40	- 4.90	+ 1.50
107	+ 6.40	- 3.90	+ 2.50
106	+ 6.40	- 2.90	+ 3.50
105	+ 6.40	- 1.90	+ 4.50
104	+ 6.40	- 0.90	+ 5.50
103	+ 6.40	+ 0.10	+ 6.50
102	+ 6.40	+ 1.10	+ 7.50
101	+ 6.40	+ 2.10	+ 8.50
100	+ 6.40	+ 3.10	+ 9.50
99	+ 4.40	+ 4.10	+ 8.50
98	+ 2.40	+ 5.10	+ 7.50
97	+ 0.40	+ 6.10	+ 6.50
96	- 1.60	+ 7.10	+ 5.50
95	- 3.60	+ 8.10	+ 4.50
94	- 5.60	+ 9.10	+ 3.50
93	- 7.60	+ 10.10	+ 2.50
92	- 9.60	+ 11.10	+ 1.50
91	- 11.60	+ 12.10	+ 0.50
90	- 13.60	+ 13.10	- 0.50
89	- 15.60	+ 14.10	- 1.50
88	- 17.60	+ 15.10	- 2.50
87	- 19.60	+ 16.10	- 3.50

Ratio Put Spread on JCN

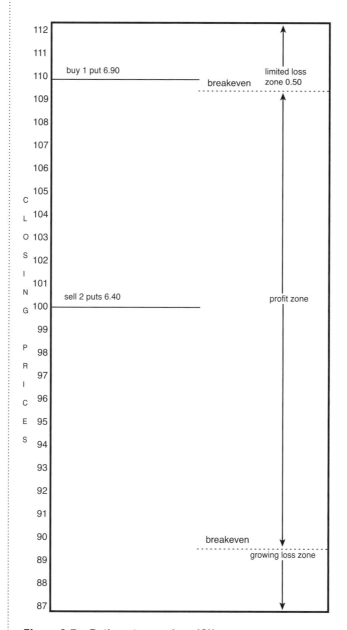

Figure 9.7 **Ratio put spread on JCN**

Ratio spread—A spread using either calls or puts, when a larger quantity of short positions are opened than long positions. Typically, the short positions are out of the money. All options in the ratio spread have the same expiration.

Ratio write—A variation of the covered call, in which a greater number of calls are written than are covered by long stock. The position consists of a series of covered calls plus one or more uncovered positions. However, it is more accurately viewed as the ratio of coverage. Because short positions can be closed to avoid losses, especially when time value declines, the risks of the ratio write are far less than for writing naked calls.

A common ratio write is a 2:1, in which two calls are written against 100 shares of stock (or four calls against 200 shares, for example). Risks are reduced, though, when the ratio is narrowed. So a 3:2 ratio write is less risky than a 2:1 ratio write.

Example: You create a 3:2 ratio write on NDE. You bought 200 shares on December 31, paying 58.91 per share; you sell three January 60 calls at 1.55 each, for a total of 4.65. In this short-term expiration, you have only three weeks to go, and the entire short position consists of time value. The return on this ratio write is 7.9 percent in only three weeks. The profit potential is immediate and considerable. The risk is that if the underlying price rises above 60, the 3:2 ratio works against the position. But it will require considerable movement in only a few weeks to offset profits. The gain in the underlying has to be brought into the equation. Profit of 1.09 per share will occur at the strike. The 4.65 credit for the short calls also provides downside protection in the stock position. Thus, a loss in the underlying of 4.65, down to 54.26, represents a breakeven based on the premium from the short calls. It would require a rise in the underlying stock price of eight points (in three weeks) to convert this into a loss position, or a decline of three points.

Table 9.8

NDE Price at Expiration	200 Shares of Stock	Three Short Jan 60 Calls	Stock and Call Net
70	+ 22.18	- 25.35	- 3.17
69	+ 20.18	- 22.35	- 2.17
68	+ 18.18	- 19.35	- 1.17
67	+ 16.18	- 16.35	- 0.17
66	+ 14.18	- 13.35	+ 0.83
65	+ 12.18	- 10.35	+ 1.83
64	+ 10.18	- 7.35	+ 2.83
63	+ 8.18	- 4.35	+ 3.83
62	+ 6.18	- 1.35	+ 4.83
61	+ 4.18	+ 1.65	+ 5.83
60	+ 2.18	+ 4.65	+ 6.83
59	+ 0.18	+ 4.65	+ 4.83
58	- 1.82	+ 4.65	+ 2.83
57	- 3.82	+ 4.65	+ 0.83
56	- 5.82	+ 4.65	- 1.17
55	- 7.82	+ 4.65	- 3.17
54	- 9.82	+ 4.65	- 5.17

Ratio Write on NDE

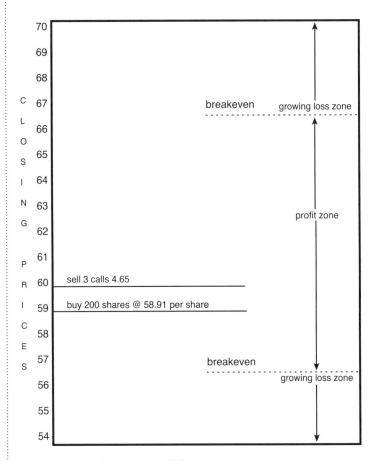

Figure 9.8   Ratio write on NDE

Reversal—A strategy combining three parts together: a short put, a long call, and short stock. For example, you shorted 100 shares of NDE on December 31 at the price of 58.91. You create a reversal by selling a March 60 put for 2.85 and buying a March 60 call for 2.40. Your net credit is 0.45. This is the locked-in profit. If the stock price rises above the 60 strike, the call matches the rise point for point, offsetting the loss on the short stock. If the price falls below the 60 strike, the loss on the short put is offset by profit in the short stock.

Reverse hedge—Also called a simulated straddle, a strategy designed to increase potential profits on shorted stock while limiting possible losses. It involves buying more calls than needed to cover the short sale. An alternative to providing the same protection and profit potential is to buy a straddle; with both a long call and a long put open, the same protection and advantages can be achieved.

Example: YPN closed on December 31 at 93.69, and you shorted 100 shares of the stock at that price. You believe the stock will decline substantially by February, but you also recognize that it could rise. So you want to open a reverse hedge to limit losses and to increase potential profits. If the stock price does decline, the shorted stock will become profitable. But if the price rises, you will have a loss. The purchase of one call would offset the rise in price; the purchase of two calls creates a reverse hedge. In the event the stock's price rises, the calls will increase two points for every point of increase in the stock. You buy two February 95 calls for 2.85 each, or a total debit of 5.70. To recapture the cost, you need the stock to decline beyond 5.7 points. If the stock's price rises 5.7 points or more, the reverse hedge produces profits.

Table 9.9

YPN Price at Expiration	100 Shares Short Stock	Two Long Feb 95 Calls	Stock and Call Net
106	- 12.31	+ 16.30	+ 3.99
105	- 11.31	+ 14.30	+ 2.99
104	- 10.31	+ 12.30	+ 1.99
103	- 9.31	+ 10.30	+ 0.99
102	- 8.31	+ 8.30	- 0.01
101	- 7.31	+ 6.30	- 1.01
100	- 6.31	+ 4.30	- 2.01
99	- 5.31	+ 2.30	- 3.01
98	- 4.31	+ 0.30	- 4.01
97	- 3.31	- 1.70	- 5.01
96	- 2.31	- 3.70	- 6.01
95	- 1.31	- 5.70	- 7.01
94	- 0.31	- 5.70	- 6.01
93	+ 0.69	- 5.70	- 5.01
92	+ 1.69	- 5.70	- 4.01
91	+ 2.69	- 5.70	- 3.01
90	+ 3.69	- 5.70	- 2.01
89	+ 4.69	- 5.70	- 1.01
88	+ 5.69	- 5.70	- 0.01
87	+ 6.69	- 5.70	+ 0.99
86	+ 7.69	- 5.70	+ 1.99
85	+ 8.69	- 5.70	+ 2.99
84	+ 9.69	- 5.70	+ 3.99

Reverse Hedge on YPN

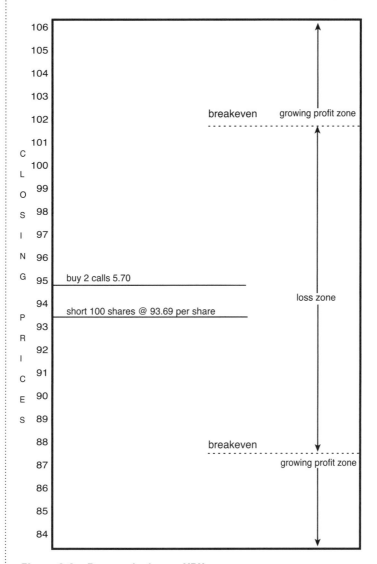

Figure 9.9 Reverse hedge on YPN

Rolling—A technique used to avoid exercise on short option positions. As the short option moves in the money, you can roll forward to a later expiration to avoid exercise. The added time value offsets the cost of closing one position for another in addition to deferring or escaping exercise. In theory, rolling can be performed indefinitely to perpetually avoid exercise. However, any time a short option is in the money, it can be exercised; but the most frequent occurrence is on the last trading day.

Traders may roll short positions as often as desired, but two disadvantages should be kept in mind. As long as the roll moves forward to a later expiration, it keeps the short position open and risk-exposed for a longer period of time. Second, the combined cost of trading between options and debits on a roll itself may ultimately erode future profits, especially if the underlying stock's trend will be likely to keep these short positions moving in the money by future expiration dates. Rolling is potentially a profitable exercise avoidance strategy, but it should be used cautiously.

Four possible forms of rolling are the following:

1. *Rolling forward with the same strike.* The horizontal roll simply replaces the current strike with a later one. If time value is high enough, this roll creates a net credit between the buy to close and the new sell to open trades. The roll forward is applied to either short calls or short puts. The theory in support of the forward roll relies on two aspects to option trading. First, later expiration creates greater time value, which is an advantage to the seller. Second, the majority of exercise occurs at or near expiration, so rolling forward avoids exercise in most situations.

2. *Rolling forward with a higher strike.* This diagonal roll is applied to short calls. It replaces the current in-the-money strike with a later-expiring, out-of-the-money strike. This is possible to achieve with a small debit or, in some cases, with a net credit on the roll. The advantage is that it takes the short position out of the money and sets up the potential for later exercise at a higher strike.

3. *Rolling forward with a lower strike.* This diagonal roll is applied to short puts. It replaces an in-the-money put with a later-expiring out-of-the-money put. In the event of exercise, the strike is lowered, creating a lower cost for future stock. It may be accomplished for little or no debit and possibly for a small credit on the exchange of positions.

4. *Rolling from one strike to another with the same expiration.* In some instances, it is advantageous to replace the strike but leave the expiration the same through a vertical roll. When the difference in premium is lower

than the distance between strikes, and exercise is certain (as in the case of a deep in-the-money short position), the loss on either call or put is reduced by that difference. For example, a covered call on JCN written originally at a strike of 100 and expiring in January is valued at 9.10. The stock as of December 31 was worth 108.10 per share, so exercise is virtually certain within three weeks. A vertical roll to the 105 strike, valued at 4.90, sets up two advantages. First, the net cost is 4.20. If the short call is exercised, it will occur at a strike five points higher, so a net gain of 0.80 results (stock will be called away at 105 instead of 100, of $500 higher, but the cost of the vertical roll is only 4.20). The second advantage is in the possibility that the underlying will move below the strike, and the short position may expire worthless. At the higher strike, the underlying is only 3.10 points in the money. A small downward move before expiration is possible, whereas a move of 8.10 points (required to move the 100 strike out of the money) is far less likely in only three weeks.

Short call—An open option contract in which the right to buy 100 shares of the underlying stock has been sold. An uncovered short call is a high-risk position, and a covered short call is very conservative (because you own the 100 shares that can be used to satisfy assignment). In comparison, a long call is one in which the holder owns the right to buy 100 shares of the underlying; and a short put grants the right to someone else to put 100 shares of stock to the trader at the fixed strike price.

Short calls are employed by traders in numerous ways, as follows:

1. *Swing trading.* If you own shares of stock as a long-term investment, you will not want to sell when prices rise or fall. However, when prices rise, selling covered calls is one way to swing trade on the temporary price movement. Once the price retreats, the short call can be closed at a profit.

2. *Simple speculation.* Short calls can be used to earn short-term profits. If these are covered calls, risk is minimal because 100 shares are owned. If uncovered, short calls are quite risky. This risk can be mitigated with the use of a ratio write. For example, you own 200 shares and you sell three calls.

3. *To insure a long stock position.* The short call is used by stock investors as one form of insurance against the stock's price decline. The open short call premium reduces potential losses if and when the price declines.

4. *As part of a straddle or spread.* The combination strategies involving two or more sides require the use of offsetting positions. Short calls offset short puts or long calls.

Short call butterfly—A neutral strategy used in anticipation of higher than average volatility in the underlying. It combines a bull spread with a bear spread like the long call butterfly and provides limited profit with limited risk. However, while the long call butterfly contains two short positions in between a high and a low strike, the short call butterfly is the opposite: It includes a high and low strike short with two long positions at a strike in between, all with the same expiration.

Table 9.10

NDE Price at Expiration	1 Jun 65	Profit or Loss 2 Jun 60	1 Jun 55	Total
70	- 7.40	+ 12.00	- 3.10	+ 1.50
69	- 6.40	+ 10.00	- 2.10	+ 1.50
68	- 5.40	+ 8.00	- 1.10	+ 1.50
67	- 4.40	+ 6.00	- 0.10	+ 1.50
66	- 3.40	+ 4.00	+ 0.90	+ 1.50
65	- 2.40	+ 2.00	+ 1.90	+ 1.50
64	- 1.40	0	+ 1.90	+ 0.50
63	- 0.40	- 2.00	+ 1.90	- 0.50
62	+ 0.60	- 4.00	+ 1.90	- 1.50
61	+ 1.60	- 6.00	+ 1.90	- 2.50
60	+ 2.60	- 8.00	+ 1.90	- 3.50
58	+ 3.60	- 8.00	+ 1.90	- 2.50
58	+ 4.60	- 8.00	+ 1.90	- 1.50
57	+ 5.60	- 8.00	+ 1.90	- 0.50
56	+ 6.60	- 8.00	+ 1.90	+ 0.50
55	+ 7.60	- 8.00	+ 1.90	+ 1.50
54	+ 7.60	- 8.00	+ 1.90	+ 1.50
53	+ 7.60	- 8.00	+ 1.90	+ 1.50
52	+ 7.60	- 8.00	+ 1.90	+ 1.50
51	+ 7.60	- 8.00	+ 1.90	+ 1.50
50	+ 7.60	- 8.00	+ 1.90	+ 1.50

Example: You construct a short call butterfly on NDE. It includes June strikes of 55, 60, and 65. You sell one 55 call at 7.60 and one 65 call at 1.90. You buy two 60 calls at 4.00 each, for a total of 8.00. Your net credit is 1.50. The position results in a fixed profit equal to this credit on the high and low sides, with a limited loss zone in between.

Short Call Butterfly on NDE

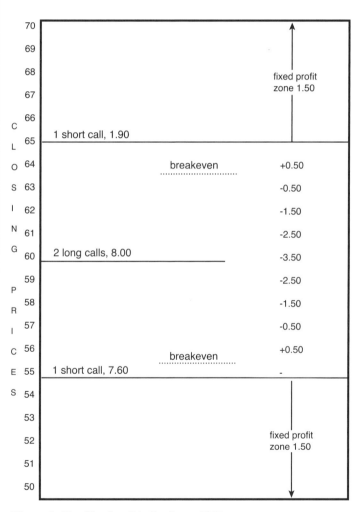

Figure 9.10   Short call butterfly on NDE

Short call condor—A neutral strategy that, like the short call butterfly, combines limited profit with limited risk. Profit results from price movement in the underlying in either direction beyond the middle price zone. The two middle calls have different strikes, whereas the butterfly is confined to one. The result is that the short call condor involves four separate strikes with the same expiration. The high and low consist of short calls and the two middle strikes consist of long calls.

Example: You open a condor on JCN by buying two middle-strike calls and protecting that position with one higher-strike and one lower-strike long call. The long positions are July 105 (11.00) and 110 (8.30), and the short positions are July 100 (15.80) and 115 (6.10). Your net credit is 2.60.

Table 9.11

JCN Price at Expiration	Jul 100	Jul 105	Jul 110	Jul 115	Total
123	- 7.20	+ 7.00	+ 4.70	- 1.90	+ 2.60
122	- 6.20	+ 6.00	+ 3.70	- 0.90	+ 2.60
121	- 5.20	+ 5.00	+ 2.70	+ 0.10	+ 2.60
120	- 4.20	+ 4.00	+ 1.70	+ 1.10	+ 2.60
119	- 3.20	+ 3.00	+ 0.70	+ 2.10	+ 2.60
118	- 2.20	+ 2.00	- 0.30	+ 3.10	+ 2.60
117	- 1.20	+ 1.00	- 1.30	+ 4.10	+ 2.60
116	- 0.20	0	- 2.30	+ 5.10	+ 2.60
115	+ 0.80	- 1.00	- 3.30	+ 6.10	+ 2.60
114	+ 1.80	- 2.00	- 4.30	+ 6.10	+ 1.60
113	+ 2.80	- 3.00	- 5.30	+ 6.10	+ 0.60
112	+ 3.80	- 4.00	- 6.30	+ 6.10	- 0.40
111	+ 4.80	- 5.00	- 7.30	+ 6.10	- 1.40
110	+ 5.80	- 6.00	- 8.30	+ 6.10	- 2.40
109	+ 6.80	- 7.00	- 8.30	+ 6.10	- 2.40
108	+ 7.80	- 8.00	- 8.30	+ 6.10	- 2.40
107	+ 8.80	- 9.00	- 8.30	+ 6.10	- 2.40
106	+ 9.80	- 10.00	- 8.30	+ 6.10	- 2.40
105	+ 10.80	- 11.00	- 8.30	+ 6.10	- 2.40
104	+ 11.80	- 11.00	- 8.30	+ 6.10	- 1.40
103	+ 12.80	- 11.00	- 8.30	+ 6.10	- 0.40
102	+ 13.80	- 11.00	- 8.30	+ 6.10	+ 0.60
101	+ 14.80	- 11.00	- 8.30	+ 6.10	+ 1.60
100	+ 15.80	- 11.00	- 8.30	+ 6.10	+ 2.60
99	+ 15.80	- 11.00	- 8.30	+ 6.10	+ 2.60
98	+ 15.80	- 11.00	- 8.30	+ 6.10	+ 2.60

Short Call Condor on JCN

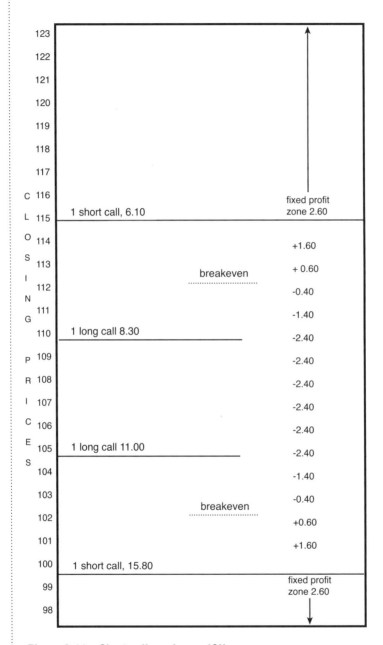

Figure 9.11   Short call condor on JCN

Short combo—A strategy based on short options, including the following:

1. Synthetic short stock comprised of a short call and a long put with the same strike.

2. Any grouping that is designed to minimize risk employing short options with offsetting protective positions (those may consist of open stock holdings, or of other long or short options that hedge the short position).

3. Straddles or spreads using short positions rather than long positions.

Short iron butterfly—Also called reverse iron butterfly, this strategy limits profits and risks and is designed to be profitable when the underlying moves significantly above or below a mid-range price. It involves both calls and puts, with the middle strike containing one long call and one long put with the same strike; the higher and lower strikes are short. The higher strike has a short call, and the lower strike is a short put. All options have the same expiration unless the strategy is constructed as a diagonal.

Example: You construct a short iron butterfly on YPN. Using February options, the long positions include a 95 call (2.85) and a 95 put (4.00). The short positions are a 100 call (1.05) and a 90 put (1.85). The net debit on this position is 3.95. The profit zone is quite narrow in this strategy. However, with the analysis constructed assuming all parts are left open until expiration, the strategy might actually become more profitable if and when short legs are closed early.

Table 9.12

YPN Price at Expiration	Profit or Loss				
	Short 90 Put	Long 95 Put	Long 95 Call	Short 100 Call	Total
105	+ 1.85	- 4.00	+ 7.15	- 3.95	+ 1.05
104	+ 1.85	- 4.00	+ 6.15	- 2.95	+ 1.05
103	+ 1.85	- 4.00	+ 5.15	- 1.95	+ 1.05
102	+ 1.85	- 4.00	+ 4.15	- 0.95	+ 1.05
101	+ 1.85	- 4.00	+ 3.15	+ 0.05	+ 1.05
100	+ 1.85	- 4.00	+ 2.15	+ 1.05	+ 1.05
99	+ 1.85	- 4.00	+ 1.15	+ 1.05	+ 0.05
98	+ 1.85	- 4.00	+ 0.15	+ 1.05	- 0.95
97	+ 1.85	- 4.00	- 0.85	+ 1.05	- 1.95
96	+ 1.85	- 4.00	- 1.85	+ 1.05	- 2.95
95	+ 1.85	- 4.00	- 2.85	+ 1.05	- 3.95
94	+ 1.85	- 3.00	- 2.85	+ 1.05	- 2.95
93	+ 1.85	- 2.00	- 2.85	+ 1.05	- 1.95
92	+ 1.85	- 1.00	- 2.85	+ 1.05	- 0.95
91	+ 1.85	0	- 2.85	+ 1.05	+ 0.05
90	+ 1.85	+1.00	- 2.85	+ 1.05	+ 1.05
89	+ 0.85	+2.00	- 2.85	+ 1.05	+ 1.05
88	- 1.15	+3.00	- 2.85	+ 1.05	+ 1.05
87	- 2.15	+5.00	- 2.85	+ 1.05	+ 1.05
86	- 3.15	+6.00	- 2.85	+ 1.05	+ 1.05
85	- 4.15	+7.00	- 2.85	+ 1.05	+ 1.05

Short Iron Butterfly on YPN

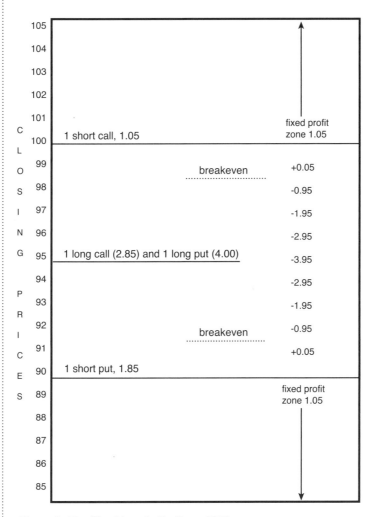

Figure 9.12   Short iron butterfly on YPN

Short put—Any put option sold and in an open position. The put seller grants the buyer the right to put 100 shares to the seller at a fixed strike price. If the underlying price falls below the strike price, the put is exercised. The short put holder agrees to pay the strike even though current market value of the underlying is lower at the time.

The short put risk is limited. Unlike the short call, which can theoretically include unlimited risk (because the underlying value could rise indefinitely), the short put risk is finite. The maximum loss is between strike price and zero; however, a more realistic risk is between strike price and tangible book value per share (or liquidation value). It would be unlikely for the market value of the underlying to decline below this level.

Short puts may be used in many strategic varieties, including the following:

1. Speculation on the change in the underlying market value.

2. As part of a swing trading strategy, when the underlying price has dropped and the trader anticipates a short-term bounce.

3. As a form of contingent purchase when the trader is willing to acquire shares at the strike price.

4. Within a spread or straddle employing short puts in conjunction with other options, either calls or puts and either long or short.

Short put butterfly—A neutral strategy combining a bull spread and a bear spread, using puts. It provides limited profit and limited risk. Three strikes are used with the same expiration, including one high and one low short put and two middle-strike long puts.

Example: You construct a short put butterfly on NDE based on June puts. This consists of a short 65 put at 6.60, two long puts at 60 for 3.70 each (7.40 total), and one short 55 put at 2.10. Net credit is 1.30, which is also the maximum profit.

Table 9.13

NDE	Profit or Loss			
Price at Expiration	1 Jun 65	2 Jun 60	1 Jun 55	Total
70	+ 6.60	- 7.40	+ 2.10	+ 1.30
69	+ 6.60	- 7.40	+ 2.10	+ 1.30
68	+ 6.60	- 7.40	+ 2.10	+ 1.30
67	+ 6.60	- 7.40	+ 2.10	+ 1.30
66	+ 6.60	- 7.40	+ 2.10	+ 1.30
65	+ 6.60	- 7.40	+ 2.10	+ 1.30
64	+ 5.60	- 7.40	+ 2.10	+ 0.30
63	+ 4.60	- 7.40	+ 2.10	- 0.70
62	+ 3.60	- 7.40	+ 2.10	- 1.70
61	+ 2.60	- 7.40	+ 2.10	- 2.70
60	+ 1.60	- 7.40	+ 2.10	- 3.70
59	+ 0.60	- 5.40	+ 2.10	- 2.70
58	- 0.40	- 3.40	+ 2.10	- 1.70
57	- 1.40	- 1.40	+ 2.10	- 0.70
56	- 2.40	+ 0.60	+ 2.10	+ 0.30
55	- 3.40	+ 2.60	+ 2.10	+ 1.30
54	- 4.40	+ 4.60	+ 1.10	+ 1.30
53	- 5.40	+ 6.60	+ 0.10	+ 1.30
52	- 6.40	+ 8.60	- 0.90	+ 1.30
51	- 7.40	+ 10.60	- 1.90	+ 1.30
50	- 8.40	+ 12.60	- 2.90	+ 1.30

Short Put Butterfly on NDE

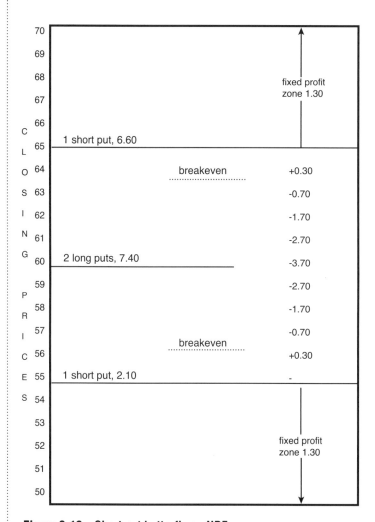

Figure 9.13   Short put butterfly on NDE

Short put condor—An expansion of the short put butterfly in which the middle puts are spread between two strikes rather than one. As a result, there are four strikes in the position instead of three, with the two short positions at highest and lowest and the two long positions in the two middle-range strikes.

Example: You construct a short put condor on NDE, with four strikes, all
with June expirations. This consists of a short 65 put at 6.60, a long 62.50 put
at 4.90, a long 60 put at 3.70, and a short 55 put at 2.10. Net credit is 0.10.
Maximum profit on the upside is 0.10 and on the downside 2.60 (the 2.5 point
difference is due to the use of the 62.50 put in between the other strikes).

Table 9.14

NDE Price at Expiration	1 Jun 65	Profit or Loss 1 Jun 62.50	1 Jun 60	1 Jun 55	Total
70	+ 6.60	- 4.90	- 3.70	+ 2.10	+ 0.10
69	+ 6.60	- 4.90	- 3.70	+ 2.10	+ 0.10
68	+ 6.60	- 4.90	- 3.70	+ 2.10	+ 0.10
67	+ 6.60	- 4.90	- 3.70	+ 2.10	+ 0.10
66	+ 6.60	- 4.90	- 3.70	+ 2.10	+ 0.10
65	+ 6.60	- 4.90	- 3.70	+ 2.10	+ 0.10
64	+ 5.60	- 4.90	- 3.70	+ 2.10	- 0.90
63	+ 4.60	- 4.90	- 3.70	+ 2.10	- 1.90
62	+ 3.60	- 4.40	- 3.70	+ 2.10	- 2.40
61	+ 2.60	- 3.40	- 3.70	+ 2.10	- 2.40
60	+ 1.60	- 2.40	- 3.70	+ 2.10	- 2.40
59	+ 0.60	- 1.40	- 2.70	+ 2.10	- 1.40
58	- 0.40	- 0.40	- 1.70	+ 2.10	- 0.40
57	- 1.40	+ 0.60	- 0.70	+ 2.10	+ 0.60
56	- 2.40	+ 1.60	+ 0.30	+ 2.10	+ 1.60
55	- 3.40	+ 2.60	+ 1.30	+ 2.10	+ 2.60
54	- 4.40	+ 3.60	+ 2.30	+ 1.10	+ 2.60
53	- 5.40	+ 4.60	+ 3.30	+ 0.10	+ 2.60
52	- 6.40	+ 5.60	+ 4.30	- 0.90	+ 2.60
51	- 7.40	+ 6.60	+ 5.30	- 1.90	+ 2.60
50	- 8.40	+ 7.60	+ 6.30	- 2.90	+ 2.60

Short Put Condor on NDE

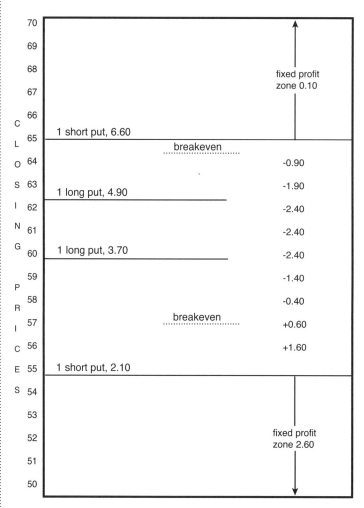

Figure 9.14   Short put condor on NDE

Short stock (synthetic)—A position involving options that sets up the same profit and risk potential as that of a short sale of stock. This involves selling a call and buying a put with the same strike and expiration. The risk is less and profit potential greater than with simply shorting stock. With the synthetic strategy, you do not need to borrow stock and pay interest on it.

Example: You set up a short stock (synthetic) position on JCN. The stock closed December 31 at 108.10. You sell a February 105 call for 6.30 and buy a February 105 put for 2.95. Your net credit is 3.35. The short call is 3.10 in the money, so the credit received for the synthetic position covers the short in-the-money gap. If the stock falls below this strike, the long put gains value. The position mirrors closely what will occur if stock were shorted (assuming underlying is valued at 108.10 at the time a short is opened):

Underlying Price	Shorted Stock	Synthetic Strategy Call	Put	Net
120	- 11.90	- 8.70	- 2.95	-11.65
115	- 6.90	- 3.70	- 2.95	- 6.65
110	- 1.90	+ 1.30	- 2.95	- 1.65
105	+ 3.10	+ 6.30	- 2.95	+ 3.35
100	+ 8.10	+ 6.30	+ 2.05	+ 8.35
95	+13.10	+ 6.30	+ 7.05	+13.35

A comparison between the value of shorted stock and the net value of the synthetic strategy demonstrates that the prices remain constant on upside and downside. The chances of exercise of the short call above the 105 strike add risk that short selling does not contain; however, modification of this strategy by covering the call mitigates this risk. The short call can be covered by owning 100 shares of stock. In this case, the synthetic strategy provides downside protection for the long position and provides coverage for the call in the event of exercise. **Short straddle (covered)**—The combined ownership of 100 shares of the underlying, with a short straddle (selling a call and selling a put). This strategy can be viewed as a covered call plus a naked put. Because both options are short, either can be closed before expiration of the position, in which case you end up with either a straight covered call or a naked put. It is likely that the out-of-the-money side would be closed, leaving a short option in the money. However, this does not necessarily lead to exercise; a decline in time value of both option positions may enable you to close both sides profitably.

Example: You open a short straddle (covered) on YPN, which closed December 31 at 93.69. You sell an April 95 call for 4.90 and an April 95 put for 5.50. Your total credit is 10.40, a range of over 20 points of profit range (10.4 points above *and* below the strike of 95).

Table 9.15

YPN Price at Expiration	Call	Profit or Loss Put	Total
110	- 10.10	+ 5.50	- 4.60
109	- 9.10	+ 5.50	- 3.60
108	- 8.10	+ 5.50	- 2.60
107	- 7.10	+ 5.50	- 1.60
106	- 6.10	+ 5.50	- 0.60
105	- 5.10	+ 5.50	+ 0.40
104	- 4.10	+ 5.50	+ 1.40
103	- 3.10	+ 5.50	+ 2.40
102	- 2.10	+ 5.50	+ 3.40
101	- 1.10	+ 5.50	+ 4.40
100	- 0.10	+ 5.50	+ 5.40
99	+ 0.90	+ 5.50	+ 6.40
98	+ 1.90	+ 5.50	+ 7.40
97	+ 2.90	+ 5.50	+ 8.40
96	+ 3.90	+ 5.50	+ 9.40
95	+ 4.90	+ 5.50	+10.40
94	+ 4.90	+ 4.50	+ 9.40
93	+ 4.90	+ 3.50	+ 8.40
92	+ 4.90	+ 2.50	+ 7.40
91	+ 4.90	+ 1.50	+ 6.40
90	+ 4.90	+ 0.50	+ 5.40
89	+ 4.90	- 0.50	+ 4.40
88	+ 4.90	- 1.50	+ 3.40
87	+ 4.90	- 2.50	+ 2.40
86	+ 4.90	- 3.50	+ 1.40
85	+ 4.90	- 4.50	+ 0.40
84	+ 4.90	- 5.50	- 0.60

| YPN | | Profit or Loss | |
Price at Expiration	Call	Put	Total
83	+ 4.90	- 6.50	- 1.60
82	+ 4.90	- 7.50	- 2.60
81	+ 4.90	- 8.50	- 3.60
80	+ 4.90	- 9.50	- 4.60

Short Straddle (Covered) on YPN

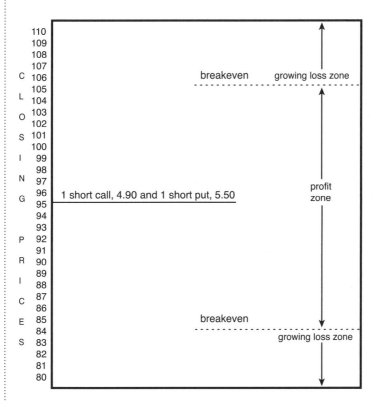

Figure 9.15   Short straddle (covered) on YPN

Short straddle (naked)—A straddle very similar to the short straddle (covered) with the distinction that shares of the underlying are not owned. As a consequence, the call is naked as well as the put. The covered version of this may be considered relatively safe as demonstrated in Figure 9.15. Note the wide profit zone, remembering as well that either short option can be closed profitably even in the money due to evaporation of time value.

The naked version contains greater risks because the call is not covered. However, given the same facts as in the previous example, the risks are not as severe as they would be for a single naked call. This is due to the two-option credit received when the position is opened. In the example for the covered version of this strategy, you gain a 20-point profit range resulting from the 10.4 points above and below the strike. The fact that you receive an overall credit by writing two options makes the point: Even with a strong move in the underlying, the evaporation of time value makes this naked straddle potentially profitable with relatively small risk.

Short strangle—Also called a strangle write, this involves both puts and calls with the same expiration but different strikes. A popular approach is to sell both options out of the money and about equal distance from the price of the underlying at the time the position is opened.

Example: JCN closed on December 31 at 108.10. You open a short strangle by selling two options with April expirations. The 115 call is sold for 3.90, and the 105 put is sold for 4.55. Your total credit is 8.45. The advantage to this position is that both sides of the short strangle are out of the money. Either or both may be closed when time value declines, regardless of the movement in the underlying. The 8.45 credit provides a profit range equal to that value both above the call strike and below the put strike, for a total of 26.9 points (10 points between the strikes, plus 8.45 above 115, plus 8.45 below 105).

Table 9.16

JCN Price at Expiration	Call	Profit or Loss Put	Total
130	- 11.10	+ 4.55	- 6.55
129	- 10.10	+ 4.55	- 5.55
128	- 9.10	+ 4.55	- 4.55
127	- 8.10	+ 4.55	- 3.55
126	- 7.10	+ 4.55	- 2.55
125	- 6.10	+ 4.55	- 1.55
124	- 5.10	+ 4.55	- 0.55
123	- 4.10	+ 4.55	+ 0.45
122	- 3.10	+ 4.55	+ 1.45
121	- 2.10	+ 4.55	+ 2.45
120	- 1.10	+ 4.55	+ 3.45
119	- 0.10	+ 4.55	+ 4.45
118	+ 0.90	+ 4.55	+ 5.45
117	+ 1.90	+ 4.55	+ 6.45
116	+ 2.90	+ 4.55	+ 7.45
115	+ 3.90	+ 4.55	+ 8.45
114	+ 3.90	+ 4.55	+ 8.45
113	+ 3.90	+ 4.55	+ 8.45
112	+ 3.90	+ 4.55	+ 8.45
111	+ 3.90	4.55	+ 8.45
110	+ 3.90	+ 4.55	+ 8.45
109	+ 3.90	+ 4.55	+ 8.45
108	+ 3.90	+ 4.55	+ 8.45
107	+ 3.90	+ 4.55	+ 8.45
106	+ 3.90	+ 4.55	+ 8.45
105	+ 3.90	+ 4.55	+ 8.45
104	+ 3.90	+ 3.55	+ 7.45

Table 9.16   continued

JCN Price at Expiration	Call	Profit or Loss Put	Total
103	+ 3.90	+ 2.55	+ 6.45
102	+ 3.90	+ 1.55	+ 5.45
101	+ 3.90	+ 0.55	+ 4.45
100	+ 3.90	- 0.45	+ 3.45
99	+ 3.90	- 1.45	+ 2.45
98	+ 3.90	- 2.45	+ 1.45
97	+ 3.90	- 3.45	+ 0.45
96	+ 3.90	- 4.45	- 0.55
95	+ 3.90	- 5.45	- 1.55
94	+ 3.90	- 6.45	- 2.55
93	+ 3.90	- 7.45	- 3.55
92	+ 3.90	- 8.45	- 4.55
91	+ 3.90	- 9.45	- 5.55
90	+ 3.90	- 10.45	- 6.55

Short Strangle on JCN

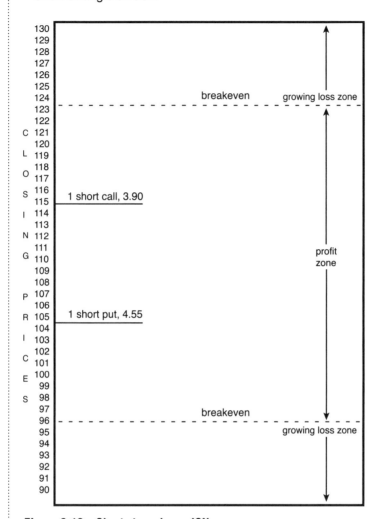

Figure 9.16   Short strangle on JCN

Simulated straddle—*See* reverse hedge.

Spread—Any combination of two option positions, one long and one short, with different terms. The spread enables a trader to reduce the risk on a short position with an offsetting long position. As long as the long position has the same expiration or a later expiration, the short position is covered.

Spreads may be vertical, horizontal, or diagonal (refer to Figure 8.10 in Chapter 8, "Option Strategies D–P"). A vertical spread consists of the same expiration but different strikes. Horizontal refers to a spread with the same strikes but different expirations. A diagonal spread has different strikes and expirations in the option positions.

Spreads may consist of calls, puts, or both. They may also be bullish, bearish, or neutral. A bull spread is going to produce the greatest profits when the underlying rises in price. Bear spreads are the opposite. A neutral spread will produce profits when price does not change significantly and is characterized by a middle profit zone with limited loss zones above and below.

Another distinction focuses on the time of expiration. The calendar spread (also called a time spread) involves the sale of one option and the purchase of another that expires later. The short position is covered by the long position in this manner. The strategy assumes that time value will evaporate in the short position so that it can be closed at a profit, but time value will tend to be more resilient in the longer-term long position. This allows for a smaller erosion and, possibly, for profit from the underlying stock's price change. Calendar spreads may be bullish, bearish, or neutral like other spreads.

The spread may be more exotic than the simple inclusion of single long and short positions. The variations include the butterfly spread, ratio spread, ratio calendar spread, reverse calendar spread, calendar combination, backspread, and condor.

Straddle—A strategy involving the opening of a put and a call with identical terms. They have the same strike price and expiration and are opened on the same underlying stock. In a long straddle, price movement of the underlying has to be great enough in either direction to offset the cost of buying the options. In a short straddle, the trader hopes that the underlying price will remain within the profit zone created by the credit for selling the options.

The straddle can be varied in several ways. For example, a strangle involves two options with the same expiration but with different strikes. A straddle may also be covered, at least partially. If you own 100 shares of the underlying and you write a short straddle, it consists of a covered call and a naked put. If you do not own 100 shares of the underlying, the short straddle is uncovered.

Strangle—A variation on the straddle, in which expiration is the same for each side, but the strike price is different. Strangles are often used in short positions in place of the straddle, as they reduce the chances of exercise. In a short straddle, one side or the other is always in the money unless the strike is exactly equal to the underlying stock's current market value. The strangle is usually built with both short positions both out of the money, one on each side of the current underlying price. For example, if the stock is selling at 93.69 per share, a strangle might include a short call at 95 and a short put at 90. The total credit received for opening a short strangle creates a profit zone equal to the points in that credit. The profit zone extends above the call strike and below the put strike. So a credit of 7.00 creates a 19-point profit zone when the strikes are five points apart: $7 + 7 + 5 = 19$.

A long strangle is based on the assumption that the underlying stock's price will be quite volatile, but the direction of movement is unknown. It requires considerable price movement to create a profit, considering the entire debit paid for put and call is time value. Just as the short straddle creates a wide profit range, the long straddle fixed just as broad a loss range, requiring the stock's price to exceed that range above or below.

A short strangle is more likely to be profitable due to the breadth of its profit range. In addition, either side can be closed at a profit when time value declines, especially for the side that remains out of the money. In a short strangle, one side of the transaction is always out of the money. This is a primary advantage of the short strangle over the short straddle.

Strap—A variation on the straddle, in which more calls than puts are opened. This adds a directional bias upward to the long straddle.

Example: You create a strap on NDE, which closed at 58.91 per share on December 31. You buy two March 60 calls at 2.40 each, for a total of 4.80, and you buy one March 60 put at 2.85. Your total debit is 7.65. In order for this position to become profitable, the underlying price must move enough in either direction to overcome the debit. Because the number of calls are doubled up, the upward movement produces a profit more quickly.

Table 9.17

| NDE Price | Profit or Loss | | |
at Expiration	Two Calls	Put	Total
70	+15.20	- 2.85	+12.35
69	+13.20	- 2.85	+10.35
68	+11.20	- 2.85	+ 8.35

Table 9.17   continued

NDE Price at Expiration	Two Calls	Profit or Loss Put	Total
67	+ 9.20	- 2.85	+ 6.35
66	+ 7.20	- 2.85	+ 4.35
65	+ 5.20	- 2.85	+ 2.35
64	+ 3.20	- 2.85	+ 0.35
63	+ 1.20	- 2.85	- 1.65
62	- 0.80	- 2.85	- 3.65
61	- 2.80	- 2.85	- 5.65
60	- 4.80	- 2.85	- 7.65
59	- 4.80	- 1.85	- 6.65
58	- 4.80	- 0.85	- 5.65
57	- 4.80	+ 0.15	- 4.65
56	- 4.80	+ 1.15	- 3.65
55	- 4.80	+ 2.15	- 2.65
54	- 4.80	+ 3.15	- 1.65
53	- 4.80	+ 4.15	- 0.65
52	- 4.80	+ 5.15	+ 0.35
51	- 4.80	+ 6.15	+ 1.35
50	- 4.80	+ 7.15	+ 2.35
49	- 4.80	+ 8.15	+ 3.35
48	- 4.80	+ 9.15	+ 4.35
47	- 4.80	+10.15	+ 5.35
46	- 4.80	+11.15	+ 6.35
45	- 4.80	+12.15	+ 7.35
45	- 4.80	+13.15	+ 8.35
45	- 4.80	+14.15	+ 9.35
45	- 4.80	+15.15	+10.35

Strap on NDE

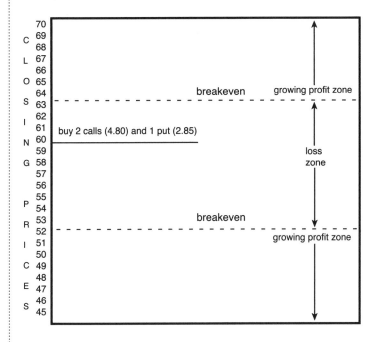

Figure 9.17   Strap on NDE

Strip—A bearish variation on the straddle, in which more puts are opened than calls. As the opposite of the strap, profit will occur more rapidly if the underlying price moves downward; however, profits will be created if and when the underlying price moves far enough above or below the debit.

Example: You create a strip on YPN, which closed on December 31 at 93.69. You buy one February 90 call for 5.90 and two February 90 puts for 1.85 each, or a total of 3.70. Your total debit is 9.60.

Table 9.18

YPN Price at Expiration	Call	Profit or Loss Two Puts	Total
110	+14.10	- 3.70	+10.40
109	+13.10	- 3.70	+ 9.40
108	+12.10	- 3.70	+ 8.40
107	+11.10	- 3.70	+ 7.40
106	+10.10	- 3.70	+ 6.40

Table 9.18   continued

YPN Price at Expiration	Call	Profit or Loss Two Puts	Total
105	+ 9.10	- 3.70	+ 5.40
104	+ 8.10	- 3.70	+ 4.40
103	+ 7.10	- 3.70	+ 3.40
102	+ 6.10	- 3.70	+ 2.40
101	+ 5.10	- 3.70	+ 1.40
100	+ 4.10	- 3.70	+ 0.40
99	+ 3.10	- 3.70	- 0.60
98	+ 2.10	- 3.70	- 1.60
97	+ 1.10	- 3.70	- 2.60
96	+ 0.10	- 3.70	- 3.60
95	- 0.90	- 3.70	- 4.60
94	- 1.90	- 3.70	- 5.60
93	- 2.90	- 3.70	- 6.60
92	- 3.90	- 3.70	- 7.60
91	- 4.90	- 3.70	- 8.60
90	- 5.90	- 3.70	- 9.60
89	- 5.90	- 1.70	- 7.60
88	- 5.90	+ 0.30	- 5.60
87	- 5.90	+ 3.30	- 2.60
86	- 5.90	+ 5.30	- 0.60
85	- 5.90	+ 7.30	+ 1.40
84	- 5.90	+ 9.30	+ 3.40
83	- 5.90	+11.30	+ 5.40
82	- 5.90	+13.30	+ 7.40
81	- 5.90	+15.30	+ 9.40
80	- 5.90	+17.30	+11.40

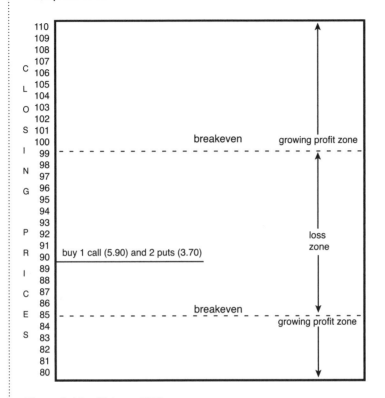

Figure 9.18   Strip on YPN

Synthetic long call—*See* married put.

Synthetic long stock—*See* long stock (synthetic).

Synthetic put—Also called a protected short sale, the purchase of a call when short on 100 shares of the underlying stock. This limits the short stock risk. If the stock price rises, the call offsets that rise with point for point increase in intrinsic value. Maximum risk is equal to the strike price of the long call, plus the call premium, minus the stock price. For example, if you pay $50 for the stock and buy a 55 call for 2, maximum risk is 55 + 2 – 50, or 7.

Synthetic short call—The combination of 100 shares of short stock and a short put. This position has the same profit potential as a short call.

Synthetic short put—The combined long position in 100 shares of the under-lying stock and a short call. The profit potential is the same as that of a short put. A well-known example of a synthetic short put is the covered call.

Synthetic straddle (long call)—A position combining 100 shares of short stock and two long calls at the money. For the cost of the long calls, the position is protected while creating profit potential. If the underlying price falls, the stock becomes profitable. If the underlying price rises, the short stock loses value, but the long calls grow 2-for-1 in intrinsic value over the short stock loss.

Synthetic straddle (long put)—A position combining 100 shares of long stock and two at-the-money puts. If the stock price rises, it becomes profitable, but the puts lose value. If the stock price declines below the put strike, the puts gain two points of intrinsic value for every point lost in the stock.

Synthetic straddle (short call)—A variation on the previous strategy, involving 100 shares of long stock and two at-the-money short calls. If the stock value declines, the short calls decline as well, providing a degree of downside protection. If the stock price rises, the overall position loses 2-for-1 of short calls over long stock. This is a form of 2:1 ratio write, with the risk on the upside.

Synthetic straddle (short put)—In this position, the trader owns 100 shares of stock and sells a call. The covered call is a well-known example (also *see* synthetic short put).

Tax put—The combination of stock sold at a loss and the sale of a put. The put premium offsets the loss on the stock. If the put is exercised, stock is reacquired at the put's strike. However, if the put is exercised within 30 days of the date the stock is sold, it is treated as a wash sale, meaning the loss on sale of stock cannot be deducted; the two sides of the transaction are treated as a single event, and tax profit or loss is netted.

Time spread—*See* calendar spread.

Uncovered option—*See* naked option.

Vertical spread—A spread consisting of options with different strikes but the same expirations (see Figure 8.1 in the previous chapter). For example, opening option positions (either both calls or both puts) in the same expiration month, but with different strikes, is a vertical spread. If this is reversed and the strikes are the same but expirations are different, it becomes a horizontal spread; when both strike and expiration are dissimilar, it is a diagonal spread.

chapter 10

Online Resources

The Internet offers a vast array of free, low-cost and subscription-based services every options trader can use to improve knowledge and trading capability. Many associations, exchanges, and regulatory agencies also provide you with valuable information about trading rules, restrictions, and consumer protection controls. Following are some of the specific sites you will find useful. For more detailed information, search on the word or phrase of interest; however, always remember that online services often come at a price. Never give out personal information and make sure you are dealing with reputable services, especially if you are asked to provide credit card information.

American Stock Exchange (AMEX)

www.amex.com

AMEX is one of the largest options exchanges in the world, and trades listed options as well as exchange-traded funds (ETFs).

Boston Stock Exchange

www.bostonoptions.com

BOX was originated in 2004 and lists index options as well as offering online classes. The Exchange employs an electronic auction process (PIP) for competitive bidding.

Chicago Board Options Exchange (CBOE)

www.cboe.com

The CBOE was founded 1973 and is the authoritative source for options information. The organization is the primary options exchange and also offers a bookstore, free quotes, paper trading, historical and current options trading data, classes, trading directory, trade symbol guide, and explanations of strategies.

International Securities Exchange (ISE)

www.ise.com

The International Securities Exchange operates a family of fully electronic trading platforms. It provides both a stock exchange and the world's largest equity options exchange, with over 6,000 different products. ISE is the only fully electronic exchange, owned by Eurex, a derivatives exchange and part of the Deutsche Börse Group.

NASDAQ

www.nasdaqtrader.com

NASDAQ provides two alternatives for options trading: its own OTC exchange and the Philadelphia OMX Exchange (the PHLX is owned by NASDAQ).

New York Stock Exchange (NYSE)

www.nyse.com and xxx.euronet.com
The New York Stock Exchange has been in existence since 1792, when 24 New York City stockbrokers and merchants signed the Buttonwood Agreement. NYSE Euronext, a holding company, was launched on April 4, 2007, and operates the world's largest and most liquid exchange group. NYSE Euronext trades in cash equities, equity and interest rate derivatives, and bonds.

Options Clearing Corporation (OCC)

www.optionsclearing.com
The Options Clearing Corporation (OCC), founded in 1973, is the world's largest equity derivatives clearing organization. Acting as guarantor for all options trades, OCC ensures that the obligations of the contracts it clears are fulfilled. In addition to its role as the industry clearing house, OCC is also a globally recognized entity for clearing of many additional products, including put and call options on common stocks and other equity issues, stock indexes, foreign currencies, interest rate composites and single-stock futures. It also provides clearing and settlement for transactions in futures and options on futures. OCC is also publisher of *Characteristics and Risks of Standardized Options* (free download at http://www.optionsclearing.com/publications/risks/ riskstoc.pdf) and many other valuable publications, such as *Taxes and Investing* (free download at http://www.optionseducation.org/resources/literature/files/ taxes_and_investing.pdf).

Options Industry Council

www.888options.com
Online classes and quotes; free DVD about options trading
The OIC was formed in 1992 to educate investors, traders, and financial professionals about exchange-traded options. This organization offers free classes, quotations, and a free DVD about options trading.

chapter 11

Option Print Resources

Many books are in print on the topics of options, strategies, and methods. Some are better than others, and it is often true that you can only tell which provide real value by purchasing and reading them. Following is a selection of published books you might find valuable as part of your personal options library. Also check options-related magazines and online resources for additional education.

Allaire, Marc and **Kearney, Marty**, *Understanding LEAPS*, McGraw-Hill.

Angell, George, *Sure-Thing Options Trading*, Plume.

Ansbacher, Max, *The New Options Market*, John Wiley & Sons.

Augen, Jeff, *The Option Trader's Workbook*, Financial Times/Prentice Hall.
   The Volatility Edge in Options Trading, Financial Times/Prentice Hall.

Baird, Allen, *Option Market Making*, John Wiley & Sons.

Bittman, James, *Options for the Stock Investor*, McGraw-Hill.
   Trading Index Options, McGraw-Hill.
   Trading Options as a Professional, McGraw-Hill.

Boer, F. Peter, *The Real Options Solution*, John Wiley & Sons.

Chriss, Neils A. and **Kawaller, Ira**, *Black-Scholes and Beyond*, McGraw-Hill.

Cofnas, Abe, *The Forex Options Course*, John Wiley & Sons.

Cohen, Guy, *Options Made Easy*, Financial Times/Prentice Hall.
   The Bible of Option Strategies, Financial Times/Prentice Hall.

Cohen, Jeffrey, *Put Options*, McGraw-Hill.

Colburn, James T., *Trading in Options on Futures*, New York Institute of Finance.

Connolly, Kevin B., *Buying and Selling Volatility*, John Wiley & Sons.

Cordier, James and **Gross, Michael**, *The Complete Guide to Option Selling*, McGraw-Hill.

Curtis, Carol E., *Pay Me in Stock Options*, John Wiley & Sons.

DeMark, Tom Jr., *DeMark on Day Trading Options*, McGraw-Hill.

DeRosa, David F., *Currency Derivatives*, John Wiley & Sons.
  Options on Foreign Exchange, John Wiley & Sons.

Elias, Samir, *Generate Thousands in Cash on Your Stocks Before Buying or Selling Them*, Leathers Publishing.

Fontanills, George A., *The Options Course*, John Wiley & Sons.
  Trade Options Online, John Wiley & Sons.

Friedentag, Harvey C., *Stocks for Options Trading*, Amacom Books.

Funk, David, *Option Writing Strategies for Extraordinary Returns*, McGraw-Hill.

Gidel, Susan Abbott, *Stock Index Futures and Options*, John Wiley & Sons.

Graham, Jim and Lentz, Steve, *Option Trading Success*, Marketplace Books.

Gross, Leroy, *The Conservative Investor's Guide to Trading Options*, John Wiley & Sons.

Haug, Espen Gaarder, *Option Pricing Formulas*, McGraw-Hill.

Hexton, Richard, *Technical Analysis in the Options Market*, John Wiley & Sons.

Jabbour, George and Budwick, Philip, *The Option Trader Handbook*, John Wiley & Sons.

Johnson, Bill, *Option Trading 101*, Morgan James Publishing.

Johnston, S.A., *Trading Options to Win*, John Wiley & Sons.

Jordan, Lenny, *Options Plain and Simple*, Financial Times/Prentice Hall.

Kaeppel, Jay, *The Four Biggest Mistakes in Option Trading*, Marketplace Books.
  The Option Trader's Guide to Probability, Volatility, and Timing, John Wiley & Sons.

Kolb, Robert W. and Overdahl, James A., *Financial Derivatives*, John Wiley & Sons.
  Financial Options and Swaps, Wiley-Blackwell.
  Understanding Options, John Wiley & Sons.

Kraus, Kevin, *How to Start Trading Options*, McGraw-Hill.

Marlow, Jerry, *Option Pricing*, John Wiley & Sons.

McMillan, Lawrence G., *McMillan on Options*, John Wiley & Sons.
  Options as a Strategic Investment, New York Institute of Finance.
  Profit with Options, John Wiley & Sons.

Morris, Virginia B., *An Investor's Guide to Trading Options*, Lightbulb Press.

Najarian, John, *How I Trade Options*, John Wiley & Sons.

Nassar, David S., *Ordinary People, Extraordinary Profits*, John Wiley & Sons.

Natenberg, Sheldon, *Option Volatility and Pricing*, McGraw-Hill.
  Option Volatility Trading Strategies, Marketplace Books.

O'Connell, Martin, *The Business of Options*, John Wiley & Sons.

Ohmstead, W. Edward, *Options for the Beginner and Beyond*, Financial Times/Prentice Hall.

Options Institute, *Options: Essential Concepts*, McGraw-Hill.

Overby, Brian, *The Options Playbook*, TradeKing.

Passarelli, Dan, *Trading Option Greeks*, Bloomberg Press.

Reehl, C.B., *The Mathematics of Options Trading*, McGraw-Hill.

Saliba, Anthony J., *Option Strategies for Directionless Markets*, Bloomberg Press.

Schaeffer, Bernie, *The Option Advisor*, John Wiley & Sons.

Schiller, Jon, *The 100% Return Options Trading Strategy*, Windsor Books.

Sincere, Michael, *Understanding Options*, McGraw-Hill.

Sinclair, Euan, *Volatility Trading*, John Wiley & Sons.

Smith, Courtney, *Option Strategies: Profit-Making Techniques for Stock, Stock Index, and Commodity Options*, John Wiley & Sons.

Spears, Larry D., *7 Steps to Success Trading Options Online*, Marketplace Books.
Commodity Options: Spectacular Profits with Limited Risk, Marketplace Books.

Summa, John F., *Trading Against the Crowd*, John Wiley & Sons.

Thomsett, Michael C., *Getting Started in Options*, John Wiley & Sons.
Options Trading for the Conservative Investor, Financial Times/Prentice Hall.
The LEAPS Strategist, Marketplace Books.
Winning with Options, Amacom Books.

Trester, Kenneth R., *101 Option Trading Secrets*, Institute for Options Research.

Veale, Stuart R., *Stocks Bonds Options Futures*, Prentice Hall Press.

Velez, Oliver, *Option Trading Tactics*, Marketplace Books.

Vine, Simon, *Options: Trading Strategy and Risk Management*, John Wiley & Sons.

Weert, Frans de, *An Introduction to Options Trading*, John Wiley & Sons.
Exotic Option Trading, John Wiley & Sons.

Williams, Michael and Hoffman, Amy, *Fundamentals of the Options Market*, McGraw-Hill.

Wolfinger, Mark D., *Create Your Own Hedge Fund*, John Wiley & Sons.
The Rookie's Guide to Options, W & A Publishing.
The Short Book on Options, 1st Book Library.

Wolpert, Edward M., *A Conservative Approach to Trading Options*, Oconee.

Wong, M. Anthony, *Trading and Investing in Bond Options*, John Wiley & Sons.

Yates, Leonard, *High Performance Options Trading*, John Wiley & Sons.

Young, Jeanette Schwarz, *The Options Doctor*, John Wiley & Sons.

chapter 12

Option Glossary

A glossary is never complete as long as it excludes the one term you are seeking. This glossary is intended as a comprehensive series of definitions that you as an options trader will find valuable. Strategies, which are explained in detail in Chapters 7, 8, and 9, are cross-referenced here to avoid unnecessary duplication.

To find terms not included here, also check www.cboe.com, which has a complete options glossary; www.investopedia.com; and www.investorwords.com. These sources, as well as online searches, should provide you with all the definitions you need.

Abandoned option—Status of any option not closed or exercised, but allowed to expire worthless.

Abnormal return—Any outcome from a trade or investment either above or below the expected rate of return.

Absolute breadth index (ABI)—A technical indicator used to track volatility without regard for price direction. The difference between advancing and declining issues is the key factor in ABI, on the theory that larger gaps between the advance/decline imply greater volatility in near-future prices.

Accumulation—(a) Holdings in securities positions, including reinvested capital gains and dividends; (b) large purchases of stock by institutional investors; or (c) retention of net profits from operations to expand markets, versus paying out dividends.

Accumulation/distribution—Technical indicator tracking momentum to determine whether buyers or sellers are dominant. Formula:

$$\big(\, (\text{close} - \text{low}) - (\text{high} - \text{close}) \, \big) \div \text{volume}$$

Accumulation area—Technical indicator descriptive of the price range in which prices do not drop, anticipating near-term increased buyer activity.

Acid test—Alternate term for the quick assets ratio; the current ratio excluding inventory. Formula:

$$(\text{current assets} - \text{inventory}) \div \text{current liabilities}$$

Active market—A market experiencing higher than average levels of volume.

Actuals—Commodities underlying specific futures contracts or options on futures.

Adjusted basis—The basis in stock, reduced by profits or increased by losses in covered call trades.

Adjustments—Changes in value, such as stock splits or stock dividends, requiring adjustment in option valuation.

Advance/decline index—The accumulated advance/decline line's value.

Advance/decline line (AD)—A technical indicator summarizing the difference between advancing and declining issues and accumulating the trend. Formula:

$$(\text{advances} - \text{declines}) + \text{previous AD value}$$

After-tax breakeven point—Net profit after deducting tax liabilities, including federal and state income taxes applicable to investment profits.

Against actual—The exchange of futures for cash, arranged between two hedgers.

All or none (AON)—A multi-contract option order specifying that the entire transaction has to be filled and that no partial orders are acceptable.

Alligator spread—*See* Chapter 7.

Alpha/beta trend channel—The creation of a channel or band consisting of two trend lines, one above and one below a moving average; this provides an averaging of price ranges, used in technical analysis.

Alternative order—The adding together of two or more orders on the same underlying security or option position, in which one position offsets or cancels the other.

American Stock Exchange (AMEX)—Also known as "the curb," acquired by NASDAQ and located at 86 Trinity Place, New York NY 10006 (www.amex.com).

American-style option—An option that may be closed or exercised at any time between the time a position is opened and the expiration date. *See also* European-style option.

Amex Rule 411—*See* know your customer.

Amortization—(a) Payment of a debt over a period of months or years; (b) reduction of asset value to reflect deferred expense over two or more tax years; or (c) payments on a loan over a specified period of years.

Annual report—A publication issued by corporations to shareholders, summarizing financial results and explaining markets, conditions, and planned expansion. The report is part disclosure by way of financial statements and footnotes and part public relations.

Annualized basis—The net profit from a trade, adjusted to reflect the return if the asset had been held for exactly one year. Formula:

$(N \div H) \times 12$
where
N = The net return
H = The holding period in months

Annualized yield—The percentage of yield or profit, when reflected on an annualized basis.

Anti-straddle rules—Federal tax rules designed to prevent options traders from mismatching gains and losses in related positions (that is, claiming a loss in the current year while deferring an offsetting straddle gain on the remaining straddle segment until the following year). In such cases, traders might be required to defer claiming the capital loss on the sold portion of a straddle.

The rules apply in some aspects to covered calls in addition to actual straddles. For example, when a covered call is closed at a net loss but the stock is still owned on the first day of the following tax year, the stock must be held an additional 30 days in order for the covered call to be treated as a *qualified covered call* (one in which the related stock profit may be treated as a long-term capital gain). The applicable 30-day period must be a period during which no covered call positions are open.

For example, a trader owns stock that has been held for many years. It was purchased at $23 per share and this year is worth $49. The trader sells a 50 call but closes it before the end of the year to avoid exercise, creating a net loss. Under the anti-straddle rules, if the stock is owned on the first day of the new year and sold before 30 days have passed, the status of stock upon sale will be short-term; the trader would lose long-term capital gains treatment under this scenario. Even if 30 days pass but the trader had replaced the previous short call with another (that is, a roll forward and up, for example), the 30-day count is tolled until the stock has been held for 30 days without an offsetting short call.

Appreciation—(a) The growth of value in a capital asset. Although assets are depreciated and report declining value, they may appreciate over time so that market value is greater than net book value; or (b) increased value in an investment asset or trade, resulting from greater demand; for example, stock market value or option premium may appreciate during a holding period, creating profits for long positions or losses for short positions.

Approved delivery facility—In the futures market, any location in which contract deliveries are approved.

Arbitrage—A strategy in which the same or equivalent stocks or options are bought and sold on different exchanges, creating a net profit due to price differences.

Asian option—A specific type of option for which profits rely on the average price of the underlying stock, versus value at expiration date; also known as an average option.

Ask price—The price a seller offers for options or shares of stock.

Asset allocation—A form of advanced diversification, involving spreading a portfolio among major asset classes, including equities, debt, real estate, and cash or cash equivalents.

Asset ratios—Fundamental tests comparing values between assets or from assets to other financial results (liabilities or sales, for example).

Assignable contract—In the futures market, a condition allowing the holder to transfer rights or obligations to another person.

Assignment—(a) Reference to notification of exercise by the Options Clearing Corporation (OCC); or (b) the act of obliging an option seller of the requirement to sell stock (when a call was sold) or to buy stock (when a put was sold), either at a contractual strike price.

At the close—A market or limit order that is to be executed at or right before a session's close, or canceled if execution does not occur.

At the money (ATM)—Condition of an option when the strike price is equal to current market value of the underlying stock.

At the opening order (OPG)—An order requiring execution at the market open or, if that is not possible, to be canceled.

Auction market—Any market allowing buyers and sellers to make competitive bids, with matching prices paired together for order execution. In comparison, over-the-counter markets involve negotiated prices rather than auction bidding.

Automatic exercise—The act of exercising options on the part of the Options Clearing Corporation (OCC), occurring automatically at expiration and based on in-the-money price levels.

Automatic reinvestment—Selection by investors, notably in mutual funds, to have all profits reinvested in the purchase of additional partial shares, creating compound rates of return on shares.

Average down—A systematic approach to buying securities when prices are falling, reducing average costs.

Average option—*See* Asian option.

Average price option—An exotic option with a payoff at zero or formulated based on the amount an average price is greater than the strike (average price call) or lower than the strike (average price put).

Average up—The act of buying stock or options as prices rise.

Averages—General reference to indices used to track markets, including the DJIA and S&P 500.

Average true range—In technical analysis, the greater of (a) the current day's high to the previous day's low; (b) the current day's high to the previous day's close; or (c) the current day's low to the previous day's close. The third variation applies only if and when the previous close is outside the range of the current's day's trades.

Back fee—In a compound option, the premium changed in the second phase of trading, which is either at the close of the position or upon exercise.

Back months—The farthest-out expiration months or delivery dates for futures contracts on a specific commodity, the equivalent of expiration dates in option cycles.

Backpricing—A system for pricing futures contracts after positions have been taken in those contracts.

Backspread—An options spread when the trader has opened more long positions than short positions. This provides the potential for greater profits from rising prices in the underlying when using calls, or from falling prices in the underlying when using puts.

Backwardation—A theory that as expiration approaches, futures contracts trade at higher prices than those with more time until expiration.

Balance sheet ratios—Any ratios comparing values found on the balance sheet, including current ratio and debt ratio as two of the primary balance sheet ratios.

Bar chart—A pricing chart showing the full day's trading range in a single vertical line, the opening price represented by a small horizontal line emerging from the left side of the range line, and the closing price represented by a small horizontal line emerging from the right side of the range line; *see also* OHLC chart.

Barrier option—A variation on the option contract specifying payoff only if the underlying stock reaches or passes a specified price level.

Barron's Confidence Index—An indicator implying investor sentiment. As the ratio increases, it indicates demand for lower yield premium. It is calculated by dividing average high-grade bond yield by average intermediate-grade bond yield.

Basis—(a) The purchase price of stock, adjusted for transaction fees and option income, also known as cost basis; or (b) in the futures market, the difference between the spot price and relative commodity price for a related contract with the shortest current delivery.

Basis grade—The minimum standard for a deliverable futures contract, also called par grade or contract grade. Because actuals may vary in quality, basis grade sets the standard to maintain uniformity in the market.

Basket option—An option not in one underlying security, but in a basket of securities or futures contracts.

Bear market—Condition when prices are broadly declining in the market, compared with a bull market.

Bear call spread—*See* Chapter 7.

Bear put ladder—*See* Chapter 7.

Bear put spread—*See* Chapter 7.

Bear spread—*See* Chapter 7.

Bearish—A pessimistic outlook; the belief that prices are falling or about to fall.

Bermuda option—A hybrid of American and European style options, allowing exercise only on a specific series of dates, often only once per month.

Bermuda swaption—An option on a swap with specified limits on timing of exercise.

Beta—A measurement of how a stock's price moves relative to movement in the broader market, quantifying volatility in the stock's price.

Bid—The current price a buyer is willing to pay to acquire stock or options.

Bid wanted (BW)—Notice that a stock or option is available for sale; the initial step to finding a buyer without specifying the price.

Bid-ask spread—The difference between ask price and current bid; the difference between the highest price buyers are willing to pay, and the lowest price sellers are willing to accept.

Big board—Slang name for the New York Stock Exchange (NYSE).

Black-Scholes—A modeling equation used to measure option pricing volatility, based on outcome if an option were held to expiration, thus appropriate more for *European-style* options than for *American-style*. The model is applied to American-style options, however, particularly on those stocks that do not pay dividends, based on the assumption that it is not advantageous to exercise an option prior to expiration in such cases. This conclusion is theoretical and not always practiced.

This model has become a standard within the industry and was originally introduced in 1973 by Fischer Black and Myron Scholes in "The Pricing of Options and Corporate Liabilities" (*Journal of Political Economy*, 1973; 81, 637–654).

It is cited as means for quantifying option premium value in absolute terms given its underlying assumptions. As a basic theory of value, Black-Scholes is a useful tool for study. However, on a practical level, most traders will not be able to make practical use of this model, and might find more useful tools in simple calculations and valid comparative studies of options that exclude calculation of interest rates; statistical normal distribution; or underlying stock volatility. As far as volatility is concerned, the basic analysis of stocks should serve as a starting point for an options strategy. Prudent options assumptions should be premised on the belief that the trader has predetermined the stocks suitable for specific volatility-based risk tolerance.

The formula for the Black-Scholes option model is as follows:

$$c = SN(d_1) - Xe^{-rT}(d_2)$$
$$p = Xe^{-rT}N(-d_2) = SN(-d_1)$$

where

$$d_1 = \frac{\ln(S/X) + (r + \sigma^2/2)T}{\sigma\sqrt{T}}$$

$$d_2 = \frac{\ln(S/X) + (r - \sigma-2/2)T}{\sigma\sqrt{T}} = d_1 - \Sigma\sqrt{T}$$

c = Call (European style)
p = Put (European style)
S = Stock price
X = Strike price of the option
r = Risk-free interest rate
T = Time to expiration (in years)
σ = Volatility of the relative price change of the underlying stock price
$N(x)$ = The cumulative normal distribution function

Block—Stock traded in large quantity, 10,000 shares or more.

Blow off top—A rapid run-up in a stock's price, followed immediately by a rapid decline; a price spike.

Blue chip—Term for stock of large, established corporations with long-established earnings and dividend growth; or, in general, descriptive of any investment of high value and quality.

Board broker—A commodities exchange member authorized to execute and match orders, issue price quotations, and ensure order in trading.

Boiler room—A high-pressure sales operation in which potential investors are called from a list (the "sucker list"). Boiler rooms are known for promoting questionable products and in many cases fraudulent products.

Bollinger bands—A technical system for plotting moving averages and showing trading range trends. Three bands are used. The middle band is a 20-day simple moving average, and upper and lower bands are calculated as standard deviations of closing prices above and below that average; developed by John Bollinger in the 1980s.

Bond—A debt instrument issued by government entities or corporations, providing fixed contractual interest and used to finance growth and expansion. Bonds are either secured by corporate assets (or guaranteed by the issuing government) or unsecured (corporate debentures).

Bond ratio—A ratio comparing bonds as a percentage of total capitalization, similar to the better-known debt ratio. The bond ratio analyzes bonds only, whereas the debt ratio includes all long-term liabilities.

Book value—(a) The net value of a corporation, calculated as the difference between total assets and total liabilities. Most commonly used is *tangible* book value, which also excludes intangible assets like goodwill; or (b) the net value of a capital asset listed on a company's books, consisting of gross purchase price minus accumulated depreciation.

Box spread (debit *and* credit)—*See* Chapter 7.

Breadth indicator—An indicator based on analysis of advancing and declining issues to track price trends in the market.

Breadth of the market theory—In technical analysis, the belief that trend strength can be tracked and anticipated by watching the number of advancing and declining issues.

Break—An unexpected or sudden movement in price, in either direction.

Breakaway gap—The difference between closing price one day and opening price on the next day, accompanied by high volume and price movement above or below established trading range or consolidation area.

Breakeven point—(a) The price required for an option position to have neither a profit or a loss; or (b) the percentage yield required to break even after allowing for both inflation and taxes. Formula:

$$\text{rate of inflation} \div (100 - \text{effective tax rate})$$

Breakout—Price movement above resistance or below support.

Broad based—A trend or price movement involving a large number of stocks or industry sectors.

Broadening formation—In technical analysis, a trading range with widening breadth (a diverging trend line), often used to confirm trend reversal patterns.

Broker—An individual representing others in market trades.

Bulge—A rapid increase in commodities prices.

Bull—An individual who believes that market prices are going to rise in the immediate future.

Bull call ladder—*See* Chapter 7.

Bull call spread—*See* Chapter 7.

Bullish—An optimistic attitude, the belief that prices are going to rise in the immediate future.

Bull market—A market characterized by rising prices, usually as part of a long-term, or primary trend.

Bull put ladder—*See* Chapter 7.

Bull put spread—*See* Chapter 7.

Bull spread—*See* Chapter 7.

Bureau of Labor Statistics (BLS)—An agency of the Department of Labor that compiles and publishes data on wages, inflation, productivity, and demographics. Web address: www.bls.gov.

Business cycle—A predictable pattern of growth and decline, applied to individual companies or sectors, or to the economy as a whole.

Butterfly spread—*See* Chapter 7.

Buy limit order—An order to be executed only at or below a predetermined price.

Buy minus—An order to be executed at a predetermined price below the current market price.

Buy on close—An order to be executed at or near the close of the trading day at a specified price or, if not, to be canceled.

Buy on open—An order to be executed immediately upon the opening of the market at a specified price or, if not, to be canceled.

Buy stop—An order to execute a purchase above the current price, which goes into effect only when price moves through a predetermined price level.

Buy the book—An order to buy all available shares at the current price, used by institutional traders.

Buy-write—*See* Chapter 7.

Buyer—An individual who opens a trade in stock or options on the long side; or a short seller entering a "buy to close" order to close out a short position.

Buying climax—A peak at the end of a long bullish period, when prices level out and then begin to retreat.

Buying hedge—Alternative name for any long hedge, entered to protect against unexpected price increases that would adversely affect the value of another position.

Buying power—Funds available to invest or, when applied to a margin account, the total of cash plus maximum available margin.

Buy-to-close—An order placed against a short position to close it out.

Buy-to-open—An order establishing a long position in stock or options.

CAC 40 index—*Cotation Assistée en Continu* (Continuous Assisted Quotation), an index of 40 stocks on the Paris Bourse, used as a benchmark for the broader market.

Calendar effect—A belief, expressed through various theories, that the market acts in a predictable manner on certain days on in certain months. These include the Monday effect and the October effect.

Calendar spread—*See* Chapter 7.

Call—One of two types of options (along with the put); the call grants its buyer the right, but not the obligation, to purchase 100 shares of a specific underlying stock, at a fixed strike price, and at any time prior to a stated expiration date. A call buyer has three possible courses of action. First is *exercise*, in which 100 shares are purchased under the call's contractual terms at the strike price. Second is *sale*, or the closing of the call position at the prevailing market price. Third is *expiration*, or allowing the call to expire worthless.

The call can be used for a variety of reasons. A long position is entered to speculate on the price movement of the underlying security, as a swing trading mechanism, or to take advantage of unexpected declines in the underlying security's market value. A short seller might purchase a call to reduce the risk of price increase in the short stock as a hedging strategy. The call also serves as one segment of a multi-option strategy involving combinations (long and short calls, or long/short variations of calls with puts).

Call premium—(a) The current market value of a call, paid by a call buyer or received by a call seller; or (b) the amount above par value of a callable bond, paid to bond holders when the bond is called by the issuer.

Call price—Also called redemption price, the price at which a bond or shares of preferred stocks may be redeemed by the issuer.

Call ratio backspread—A strategy combining options into a spread with little or no risk but some profit potential. This involves combining short low-strike calls with a larger number of long higher-strike calls, or combining short high-strike puts with a larger number of lower-strike puts.

Call warrant—A warrant including the right to buy shares of the underlying stock on or before a specified date and at a fixed amount, beyond the other rights granted under the warrant.

Called away—The exercise of stock under an option contract. A call seller has an obligation to deliver 100 shares of stock at the strike price, for each short option if and when the call is exercised.

Cancellation—A notice issued by a brokerage firm, advising a customer that a trade was entered in error and has been reversed or corrected.

Candlestick chart—A type of stock chart revealing price movement via a rectangular box and vertical lines extending above and below. The distance between the extent of the vertical lines represent the trading range for the day. The top and bottom of the rectangle represent open/close or close/open prices for the day. The rectangle is white on an upward-moving day and black on a downward-moving day.

Capital gain or loss—The net outcome of an investment. A *realized* capital gain or loss is taxed at capital gains rates if the holding period exceeds one year. Capital gains or losses with holding periods of less than one year are taxed at ordinary rates.

Capitalization—(a) The total sources of funds used by corporations, consisting of both equity and debt. Equity capital includes all classes of stock and retained earnings. Debt capital includes bonds and notes listed as liabilities on the balance sheet; or (b) the entire market value of a corporation, also known as market capitalization or "market cap." The formula for market cap is as follows:

shares outstanding × price per share

Capitalization ratios—In fundamental analysis, ratios reflecting degrees of capitalization derived from various sources. These include total long-term debt (debt ratio), long-term bonds only (bond ratio), preferred stock (preferred stock ratio), and common stock (common stock ratio). Capitalization ratios are usually expressed as percentages of total capitalization.

Capitalization-weighted index—Any index based on a selection of stocks, in which actual weighting within the total index is based on market cap.

Capped-style option—Any option with a cap on either profit or price. A cap price is equal to the strike price plus a cap interval (for a call) or the strike price less a cap interval (for a put). Capped-style options are exercised automatically when in the money.

Capping—(a) Placing of selling pressure on a stock to prevent the market price from rising; or (b) selling large blocks of stock near an option's expiration date to prevent the price from rising and moving into an in-the-money price range.

Carrying charge—The cost of holding securities or physically storing stock certificates or commodities.

Carrying cost—Interest charged on funds borrowed on margin.

Carry-over capital losses—The excess loss above annual loss limitations for federal tax purposes, which must be applied to future periods. Annual limitation is $3,000 maximum loss. Carry-over is applied to offset future capital gains or is absorbed at the annual maximum levels until used up.

Cash-based—Settlement in cash upon exercise or assignment, without any physical delivery of the underlying security.

Cash commodity—The physical commodity to be delivered at delivery date, as opposed to a futures contract on the same commodity; also called actuals.

Cash flow—(a) In fundamental analysis, the study of how cash moves in and out of the company and the level of working capital available, expressed through ratios such as the current ratio; (b) the summary of cash movement in the financial statement called "Statement of Cash Flows," which adjusts operations results on a cash basis and accounts for how cash is derived and applied during a year.

Cash market—Any market in which commodities are traded for cash in exchange for immediate delivery; also called spot market.

Cash ratio—A measure of a corporation's ability to liquidate assets and cover current liabilities, also called the liquidity ratio. Formula:

$$(\text{cash} + \text{marketable securities}) \div \text{current liabilities}$$

Cash settlement contract—A system for meeting obligations under an option contract, involving the transfer of cash equal to the in-the-money value, rather than by delivery of the underlying stock.

Cash-on-cash return—A return on investment based on annual cash income, divided by the initial cash investment.

Cash-or-nothing option—An option with payoff set at a fixed price if and when the underlying is below the strike; if this does not occur, payoff is zero. This option is usually European style.

Cemetery spread—A spread involving so many segments that the trader is "buried" by transaction costs.

Chartist—A technician who relies primarily on price and volume charts as the means for anticipating near-term price movement of stock.

Chicago Board of Trade (CBT)—A commodities exchange established in 1848; focused on more than 50 types of futures including grains, gold, and Treasury securities, as well as options on futures. Volume is greater than 675 million contracts per year. Web address: www.cbot.com. Address: 141 West Jackson Blvd., Chicago IL 60604.

Chicago Board Options Exchange (CBOE)—The national exchange for trading listed options, equity LEAPS, and index options. In 2007, CBOE volume reached an all-time high with over 944 million contracts, 40% above the previous year. Web address: www.cboe.com. Address: 400 South LaSalle Street, Chicago IL 60605.

Chicago Mercantile Exchange (CME)—The "Merc," an exchange for trading in financial and currency futures and options. The CME invented the financial futures contract in May 1972 with the introduction of seven currency contracts. In 2006, CME traded over 1.4 billion contracts valued over $800 trillion. Web address: www.cmegroup.com. Address: 10 South Wacker Street, Chicago IL 60606.

Chooser option—An exotic option in which the trader selects either a call or a put at a specified point in the contractual period.

Christmas tree—Also known as a ladder, a strategy involving the purchase and sale of calls at varying strike prices. The strike of the long positions resides below the strikes of short positions. As a variation of the ratio spread, it is entered assuming the underlying stock's price will rise. The profit from the long position will be profitable to a point; however, a substantial price rise would create losses due to a higher number of uncovered short positions. Variations include covering the short positions with stock ownership, or creating a bear inverse Christmas tree with long and short puts.

Churning—The practice of high-volume trading in customer accounts to increase a broker's commission income; also called "churn and burn."

Circuit breaker—A measure or series of measures put into place by stock exchanges when large sell-offs are underway to prevent larger drops in value. These include halts in trading or limitations on program trading.

Class of options—Groupings of call and put options associated with the same underlying stock.

Clearing house—An agency of a futures exchange or corporation allowed by the exchange to execute futures trades, collect and pay funds, maintain margin accounts, and execute delivery; facilitators of futures trading, serving as buyers to every seller and as sellers to every buyer.

Climax—The farthest extent of a price trend, after which a reversal or consolidation period follows. Although usually associated with a market top, a bottom climax also may occur.

Close—The final step in a trade. A long position is closed with a sell order, and a short position is closed with a buy order.

Closed position—Status after a closing order has been executed.

Closing order—An order to close out a position. A long position is closed with a "sell to close" order, and a short position is closed with a "buy to close" order.

Closing price—The actual price at which a trade was executed.

Closing purchase—The closing trade of a short position, also called a "buy to close" order.

Closing sale—The closing trade of a long position, also called a "sell to close" order.

Closing transaction—A trade that closes a position, consisting of a sell order for a long position, or a buy order for a short position.

Coffee, Sugar, and Cocoa Exchange (CSCE)—Originally called the Coffee Exchange when initiated in 1882, and today a subsidiary of the New York Board of Trade (NYBOT), which itself became a wholly owned subsidiary the Intercontinental Exchange (ICE). CSCE trades futures and options on coffee, sugar, cocoa, and the S&P Commodity Index.

Collar—*See* Chapter 7.

Collateral—Any asset placed as security for loans or for trading in margin accounts; in trading, the loan value of total marginable securities and cash.

Combination—*See* Chapter 7.

Commission—Payment to a salesperson or broker for executing a trade in behalf of an investor or trader, or for offering investment advice.

Commitment—A fee assessed by lenders for lines of credit or for credit to be used in the future; or an agreement for performance under a contract.

Commodity—A physical good serving as the basis for futures trading, including agricultural products, previous metals, cattle, market indices, and financial instruments (currencies and interest rates). The origin of the commodity-based futures contract was to fix a future price for agricultural products over the span of an entire season, to ensure that farmers would have a ready market upon harvest.

Commodity Exchange of New York (COMEX)—Founded in 1933, a leading exchange for gold futures and options, as well as other futures and options contracts. Today, COMEX is a division of the New York Mercantile Exchange (NYMEX). Web address: www.nymex.com. Address: One North End Avenue, New York NY 10282.

Commodity Futures Trading Commission (CFTC)—The federal regulatory agency for the futures industry, created in 1974. Web address: www.cftc.gov. Address: 1155 21st Street NW, Washington DC 20581.

Common gap—A common minor price gap between one day's closing price and the next day's opening price.

Common stock—Shares with voting rights and, when applicable, qualification for receipt of dividends. Common stock has lower priority when compared to preferred stock and bonds in the event of liquidation; also known as junior equity.

Common stock equivalent—An instrument convertible to common stock but traded like an equity, usually preferred stock or a bond.

Common stock ratio—A capitalization test, distinguishing the portion of total capitalization represented by common stock. Formula:

dollar value of common stock ÷ total capitalization

Compliance—Process of ensuring a financial service company, investing banking operation, or securities broker/dealer is operating properly under federal and state law, especially law and regulation enforced by the Securities and Exchange Commission (SEC).

Composite index—A collection of stocks, commodities, currencies, or geographical interests, used as a benchmark for market performance or for performance of a segment of a larger market.

Compound option—Any option related to another option rather than to an underlying stock or future. Because compound options involve two derivatives, there are also two strike prices and two exercise dates. The four types of compound options are calls on calls, calls on puts, puts on calls, and puts on puts.

Condor spread—*See* Chapter 7.

Confirmation—(a) Similar movement in an index or sector that verifies implied significance of the same movement elsewhere; or (b) a document or communication produced by a brokerage firm providing the details of an executed trade.

Congestion—(a) A trading pattern in which no specific price trend is established, or (b) differences between supply and demand for shares of stock or derivative contracts.

Constant dollar plan—Also called dollar cost averaging, a system for investing a fixed amount of capital into the market each month or at other intervals, regardless of changes in price levels, most often employed by those buying shares in mutual funds.

Constant ratio plan—A method for maintaining a predetermined level of asset allocation, in which periodic investments are made based on increases or decreases in portfolio value in each allocated class.

Constructive sales—In tax law, a situation treated as a taxable event even though a specific sale was not executed. Examples include offsetting positions involving stock and options, or advanced offsetting option positions. IRC Code Section 1259 explains the rules and transactions to which these rules apply.

Consumer Price Index (CPI)—An indicator used to measure inflation, which tracks products and services and changes in their price levels each month. Included are housing, utilities, food, transportation, and other products and services.

Contango—A situation occurring when a futures price is higher than the expected future spot price; the opposite of backwardation.

Contingent order—An order that is to be executed only if and when a related event takes place. For example, this order might specify an options trade if the underlying stock's price moves above or below a specified price level.

Continuation pattern—In technical analysis, price movement that will eventually lead to a continuation of a previously established trend; a false reversal or accumulation pattern.

Contract month—The month when a futures contract will expire; also called delivery month, the month delivery will occur unless open contracts are closed.

Contract size—The value of the underlying stock in an option; for listed options, 100 shares of the underlying stock for each open option contract (adjustable in the event of a stock split or stock dividend).

Contract unit—The dollar value of the physical commodity underlying each futures contract.

Contrarian investing—A strategy of investing that intentionally moves in a direction opposite of the majority opinion, based on the observation that the majority is more often wrong than right.

Convergence—Movement in two or more prices, or between moving averages and the current price.

Conversion—*See* Chapter 7.

Conversion arbitrage—A three-part riskless transaction involving the purchase of 100 shares of stock, one long put, and one short call.

Converted put—*See* synthetic put.

Convertible security—Any product that is convertible into another product; a bond or preferred stock that are structured to include a call feature, exchangeable for a specified number of common shares of stock.

Cookie jar accounting—The practice of deferring revenue during exceptionally profitable years, to use in future periods; a means of smoothing out reported operations results by distorting year-to-year actual revenues.

Core earnings—The earnings of a company derived from its recurring and primary business activity, as distinguished from non-recurring sources of income or expense.

Corner—(a) The act of gaining control over a security in order to control its market price; or (b) in the commodities market, a situation in which commitments of delivery quantities exceed the available underlying commodity.

Correction—A change in the direction of a price trend, usually downward after a strong bullish trend; usually a temporary price decline that is resolved in a return to the established trend's direction.

Cost of carry—The costs of assuming positions, including interest on margin accounts, transaction fees, or load fees, and the costs associated with committing capital and possibly losing other investment opportunities.

Cost of tender—Charges for the delivery of commodities arising from fulfillment of a futures contract.

Cover—Closing of a short position; buying stock or options to offset previously sold shorts.

Covered—Status of a short call when offset by a long position in 100 share of the underlying stock. When traders have shorted 100 shares of stock, it can also be covered by a long call or a short put on the same underlying. Options cover one another as well, when combinations consist of offsetting long and short positions on the same underlying.

Covered call—*See* Chapter 7.

Covered combination—*See* Chapter 7.

Covered put—*See* Chapter 7.

Covered short straddle—*See* Chapter 7.

Credit—A sum of money on account or received or, in bookkeeping, a right-side transaction offset by a debit of equal value.

Credit spread—*See* Chapter 7.

Cross hedging—A form of hedge in a different product with similar or identical price tendencies.

Cum dividend—Literally "with dividend," the situation when a dividend has been declared but not yet paid. The time between declaration and ex-dividend date is described as trading cum dividend.

Cum rights—Entitlement to dividend income based on ownership on the date of declaration, whether or not shares are still owned on the dividend payment date.

Cumulative volume index—A technical indicator tracking volume trends and adding together the net differences between advancing and declining issues.

Cup-and-handle pattern—A price pattern with a two-part shape. A "U" shape (the cup) is followed by a down-trending or down-drifting price (the handle).

Currency swap—A swap between different currencies; a foreign exchange swap.

Current delivery—A requirement for delivery in a futures contract, either in the current month or the month following.

Current market value (CMV)—Valuation of any asset based on the market price or equivalent, rather than on original cost; the value adjustment made to securities held as collateral in a margin account to ensure continued compliance with margin requirements.

Current ratio—A balance sheet ratio quantifying working capital. The formula is as follows:

current assets ÷ current liabilities

Curvature—Change in an option's delta, a comparison of differences in the movement of option value compared with changes in the price of the underlying stock.

Cushion—The protection sometimes built into a callable bond, when they are not callable for a predetermined number of months.

Cycle—The expiration months for series' of listed options. All options begin with expirations in the next two months, plus expirations in the next two months of one of the three cycles. Expirations on these cycles occur in (a) January/April/July/October (JAJO); (b) February/May/August/November (FMAN): and (c) March/June/September/December (MJSD). Longer-term options (LEAPS) expire in January in each year and may extend as far as 30 months out.

Day order—An order to be filled on the day placed or if any part is not filled, to be cancelled.

Day trade—Any trade opened and closed within a single trading session.

Dealer—The person who buys for his own account.

Dealer option—An option written with a commodity as the underlying rather than stock.

Debit—(a) Payment paid from an account, or (b) an option that reduces the trader's cash balance.

Debit spread—*See* Chapter 8.

Debt instrument—A bond, note, or money market instrument issued with a contractual obligation to pay interest and to repay principal with specific terms.

Debt ratio—A balance sheet ratio distinguishing the level of debt as a percentage of total assets; a test of corporate leverage employing debt. Formula:

total debt ÷ total assets

Debt/equity ratio—The primary capitalization ratio, which may be computed in two ways. As a comparison between debt and equity, the formula is as follows: total debt ÷ common shareholders' equity.

The debt/equity ratio as a measurement of how corporations capitalize operations between debt and equity involves a comparison between long-term debt and total capitalization:

long-term debt ÷ (long-term debt + total shareholders' equity)

Decay—The reduction in value in option premium over time; the course of change in time value as expiration approaches.

Decimalization system—The pricing of securities in dollars and cents, the replacement of the historical system based on eighths or sixteenths.

Deep discount broker—A brokerage firm charging low trading fees and offering no investment advice, usually involving a flat fee per trade regardless of the dollar value or share value of the trade.

Deep in the money (DITM)—Any option five points or more in the money based on current market price. A call is deep in the money when current market value of the underlying stock is at least five points above strike price; and a put is deep in the money when the current market value of the underlying stock is at least five points below strike price.

Deep out of the money (DOTM)—The opposite of deep in the money; this condition exists for a call when the underlying stock is at least five points below the strike price; and for a put when the underlying stock is at least five points above the strike price.

Delivery—The transfer of stock or options upon completion of a transaction or when an option has been assigned.

Delta—A comparison between changes in an option's market value and changes in the value of the underlying stock; a measurement of variations in non-intrinsic value of the option and both option and stock volatility.

Delta hedge—*See* Chapter 8.

Delta spread—*See* Chapter 8.

Depository Trust Corporation (DTC)—A corporation created to hold registered securities and to guarantee delivery if and when options are assigned against securities held by the DTC.

Derivative—Any security with value based on the value of an underlying security, including options and futures.

Diagonal spread—*See* Chapter 8.

Digital option—An option with a provision that the payout amount is fixed if and when the underlying stock exceeds a threshold price level; also known as a binary option.

Diluted earnings per share—A calculated of earnings per share if all convertible securities were to be exercised, including convertible preferred shares, debentures, employee stock options, and warrants.

Discount—Condition when an option is trading below intrinsic value.

Discount arbitrage—The simultaneous transaction of a discount option and an opposite position (long versus short or vice versa) in the underlying stock.

Discount broker—A broker executing trades at very low commissions while offering no investment advice.

Discount yield—The yield on any security that was transacted at a discount.

Discounted cash flow—The present value of future cash flow, an analytical method used to compare investment opportunities when current terms are not identical.

Discretion—Permission granted by an investor to a floor broker or account executive, to execute orders without first consulting with then account holder. Discretion may be limited to a range of points or order type.

Distribution—(a) Condition when volume exceeds volume of the previous day, but with little or no price change; (b) payments from an account to the account holder, especially in a tax-deferred retirement account; (c) payments from mutual fund accounts for capital gains, dividends, or interest.

Divergence—Condition when stock or option prices move away from an index or moving average, used in technical analysis as a signal of impending price action.

Diversification—The spreading of risk to avoid a large loss. This is achieved by investing in different stocks, different sectors, or dissimilar markets (allocation); and by avoiding issues subject to the same market and economic forces.

Dividend—Payment to stockholders for a portion of earnings upon approval by the board of directors. Payment occurs in cash or additional stock.

Dividend payout ratio—Earnings paid in dividends, expressed as a percentage. Formula:

annual dividend per share ÷ earnings per share

Dividend reinvestment plans (DRIPS)—A system allowing stockholders to have dividends reinvested in shares or fractional shares of stock. This creates a compound rate of return in dividend income.

Dividend yield—The return from dividend income, based on a comparison of the dollar amount of dividends paid per year, and the market value of stock. Formula:

annual dividends per share ÷ current price per share

Divisor—The number used to calculate relative value of stock as part of an index, adjusted for stock splits in a price-weighted index, or for additional issues of shares in a capitalization-weighted index.

Do not increase (DNI)—Condition attached to an order, to not increase the number of shares to be traded in case of a stock dividend or split.

Do not reduce (DNR)—Condition attached to an order to not decrease the limit price on the cash dividend record date.

Dollar cost averaging—The buying of a fixed dollar amount every month no matter how the share price changes; this technique can be applied to stock but is more popular as a method of investing in mutual funds; also called constant dollar plan.

Don't know (DK)—Description of a trade when unexplained discrepancies are outstanding.

Double barrier option—An option containing two separate price triggers. In order for the trader to receive a payout, the price must first reach or pass a range limit, or the price has to avoid reaching a specified limit (or limits).

Double bottom—In technical analysis, a pattern where price levels fall, rebound, and fall again to approximately the same level; believed to anticipate an upward price movement.

Double top—In technical analysis, a pattern with two price peaks and a decline in between, anticipating a downward trending price movement.

Double witching—The expiration of two classes of options or futures on the same day (any two of the three: listed options, index options, or index futures).

Doubling option—The right held by a bond issuer to redeem twice the debt level when repurchasing and closing out callable bonds.

Dow Jones Industrial Average (DJIA)—The most popular market-tracking index, also known as "the Dow," based on market observations of Charles Dow in the 1890s. The DJIA is price-weighted and includes 30 industrial stocks traded on the New York Stock Exchange and NASDAQ.

Dow Jones Transportation Average (DJTA)—A price-weighted average of 20 transportation stocks.

Dow Jones Utility Average (DJUA)—A price-weighted average of 15 utility stocks, the third of three Dow Jones Averages, initiated in 1929.

Dow Theory—A technical market theory based on the Dow Averages; identification of primary uptrends or downtrends based on advances in one average and confirmation in another.

Down-and-in option—An option with payout to occur only if the price of the underlying stock drops to a specified price level (the barrier price). If the barrier price is not reached, the option can be exercised at the strike value.

Down-and-out option—An option with payout to occur only if the price of the underlying stock rises to a specified price level (the barrier price). If the barrier price is not reached, the option can be exercised at the strike value.

Downside protection—A feature describing covered calls, in which the premium received is viewed as a cushion to protect against potential price declines in the underlying stock. For example, a covered call sold at 4 ($400) provides a four-point downside protection by reducing the net basis in the underlying stock.

Downside risk—The risk of losses resulting from price declines.

Downtick—The price immediately below a security's previous price level.

Dual listing—A listing on two or more exchanges.

Due diligence—Reasonable care on the part of a company or investor to ensure full understanding of an investment's features and risks.

Dynamic analysis—A form of analysis while positions are open and changing over time, versus post-closing analysis of a transaction.

Early exercise—Assignment of an option before expiration.

Earnings growth—A fundamental trend reflecting changes in annual net income from year to year, reported as dollar value, percentage of increase or decrease, or in earnings per share (EPS).

Earnings per share (EPS)—Total earnings reflected on a per-share basis, a popular fundamental indicator. To accurately report this value, the *average* number of outstanding common shares has to be calculated from beginning to end of the fiscal year. EPS formula:

total earnings ÷ average outstanding shares

Earnings report—A quarterly or annual summary of operations, provided to investors and to regulators.

Efficient market theory—A technical theory premised on the belief that the market cannot be beaten because all available and known information has been factored into stock prices at all times.

Efficient portfolio—A portfolio structured to provided maximum expected returns for a specified risk level; also called optimal portfolio.

Elliott wave theory—A technical theory based on the belief that a specific number of upward and downward waves occur in price trends. This involves the analysis of patterns, time, and ratios. The legs of a predictable price wave pattern decline as the pattern develops.

Embedded option—An option whose price movement is tied permanently to another instrument, which cannot be removed. In comparison, a normal option trades separately from its underlying security.

Employee stock option (ESO)—A call granted as an employee benefit or as a form of non-cash compensation. These options can be exercised at a fixed price and by or before a specific expiration deadline. Contracts often require passage of a vesting period before stock options can be exercised.

End of day—An order requiring execution at a specified price or better, which remains in effect only until the end of the current trading day. If the price is not reached or passed, the order expires.

Equilibrium price—A price when there is a match between supply and demand, seen in periods of sideways movement in a stock or index.

Equity—(a) A margin account's net difference between securities owned and loans outstanding, or net account equity; or (b) in fundamental analysis, the value of a corporation calculated as the difference between assets and liabilities.

Equity investment—Ownership, a form of investment in the stock of a corporation, as opposed to a debt investment such as a bond.

Equity options—Any options with equity (stock) as the underlying security, or options on exchange-traded funds (ETFs).

Equity swap—A swap involving approximately equal cash flow, usually between stock and fixed-income securities, usually entered to hedge other positions.

Equivalent positions—Two or more strategies with identical or similar risks and profit potential. An example: A long vertical call spread is approximately equivalent to a short put vertical spread, although one creates a debit, and the other creates a debit.

Escrow receipt—A document assuring that an option writer has placed the underlying stock on deposit and that it is available for delivery if and when the option is exercised.

European-style option—A type of option that can be exercised only at expiration or during a brief period immediately prior to expiration.

Even lot—A benchmark value of commodities to be used in quoting futures prices.

Exchange—The marketplace for trading of stocks, bonds, commodities, or derivatives, where an orderly market is maintained and current price information is published and announced; and where member or listed company activities are monitored and regulated in accordance with exchange rules.

Exchange rate—A currency price relative to the currency of another country.

Exchange-traded funds (ETFs)—Mutual funds first created in 1993 and traded on public exchanges rather than directly with a fund's management. These are as liquid as stocks because transactions are executed at any time rather than based on prices at the end of the trading day. Each ETF consists of a pre-identified basket of stocks associated together in some manner (sector, country, or commodity, for example). Many ETFs allow options trading, expanding the range of underlying securities.

Exchange-traded options—Any option traded over an exchange based on that exchange's standardized terms (advance knowledge of underlying stock, quantity per option, expiration, and strike price); also known as listed options.

Ex-dividend—Reduction of a stock's price at the time dividends are applied.

Ex-dividend date—The day prior to the date that investors must own shares of stock to qualify for dividend payments; also called ex-date.

Execution—Successful completion of a buy or sell order.

Exercise—The process of buying stock under the terms of a long call, or selling stock under the terms of a long put. At exercise, the transaction is completed at the fixed strike price regardless of current market value of the underlying stock.

Exercise by exception processing—A rule applied by the Options Clearing Corporation (OCC) for clearing members. A member is assumed to have placed exercise notices that are in the money, protecting option owners from the loss of intrinsic value. Unless instructed not to do so, all expiring options that are in the money will be exercised if they have reached predetermined threshold values.

Exercise limit—A limit on the number of options any individual owner is allowed to exercise within a specified period of time. This restriction prevents attempts to corner a market in the underlying security.

Exercise notice—A notice to an option seller, also known as an assignment, advising that 100 shares are required to be sold for each short call, or that 100 shares must be bought for each short put, when those options have been exercised.

Exercise price—The strike price; the price at which an underlying security is to be bought under terms of a call or sold under terms of a put if and when exercised.

Exercise settlement amount—The net difference between exercise price and settlement value of the related index, on the day of exercise.

Exhaustion gap—A type of gap taking place following a strong uptrend or downtrend in a stock's price, signaling that the trend is coming to an end.

Exotic option—A complex option trading over the counter and not in conformity with the terms of listed options, including options on other options or containing terms and conditions not common to listed options.

Expected return—The return investors or traders expect to make based on statistical distribution analysis of historical returns.

Expiration—The end of an option's life, after which it becomes worthless.

Expiration cycle—The months during which options expire. All options have expiration dates in the next two months. In addition, there are four specific cycles. For listed options, three of these apply. In addition to the immediate two-month expiration months, expirations will also occur in the first two months of a four-month cycle: January, April, July, October (JAJO); February, May, August, November (FMAN); and March, June, September, December (MJSD). The fourth cycle applies only to LEAPS options (long-term equity anticipation securities). These have expirations in the immediate two months, as well as in every January up to the third year out (maximum lifespan is 30 months).

Expiration date—For listed options, the Saturday immediately after the third Friday of the expiration month.

Expiration Friday—The last trading day before expiration; the third Friday of each expiration month. (If a holiday, the expiration day is moved to the last trading day preceding expiration Friday.)

Expiration month—The month when options are scheduled to expire.

Expiration time—The precise time of day when expiration notices are given out on actual expiration day. The expiration time is 5:00 p.m. EST; however, holders of options must make notification by 5:30 p.m. EST on expiration Friday.

Exponential moving average (EMA)—A method of calculating moving average to add weight to the latest entry in the field. The formula is based on the use of a multiplier, for which the formula is as follows:

$$multiplier = 2 \div (1 + n)$$

In this formula, "n" is the number of fields being averaged. For example, if there are eight periods, the multiplier is: 2 ÷ (1 + 8), or .222. Using the multiplier, the formula for EMA is as follows:

$$\big((E-P) \times M \big) + P$$

where E = The current, latest entry
P = Previous EMA
M = Multiplier

Extraordinary item—In accounting, any item outside of the core business, which will not recur in future years.

Extrinsic value—The portion of an option's premium value excluding intrinsic value.

Facilitation—Provision of a market in securities.

Fail to deliver—An order in which one side did not meet its requirements. In the options market, this means a seller did not have shares to meet a call, or cash/margin to accept a put; or a buyer did not have adequate funds or margin value to pay for the purchase.

Fair market value (FMV)—The current market price or value of securities or property, based on current trading levels *and* on the assumption that an adequate time period is allowed to complete a transaction.

Fair value—The value of an option contract, often used to describe only the intrinsic value portion of premium.

Far option—The segment in a spread with a later expiration date.

Fast market—Description of a market experiencing heavy trading, especially when accompanied by high volatility in price levels.

February-May-August-November (FMAN)—One of the three listed option cycles. In this cycle, options will have expirations in the next two months, plus the first two of the four indicated months.

Fence—A strategy involving a short call and a long put when the underlying stock is also held. The fence enables the trader to protect paper profits by building in downside protection. For short positions, a long call and short put provides protection in the event the underlying stock's price rises, which is a reverse fence position.

Fibonacci retracement series—Named for Leonardo Fibonacci, a twelfth-century mathematician who observed a repetitive sequence of numerical values in nature. Each successive number is added to the previous total to arrive at the sequence:

$$1 + 2 = 3; 2 + 3 = 5; 3 + 5 = 8; 8 + 5 = 13$$

Each new number is approximately 1.618 times higher than the previous total. Technicians employ this sequence to predict price patterns in charting.

Fifty-two week high and low—The range of highest and lowest price a stock reached during the previous 52 weeks.

Fill—Completion of an order or satisfaction of transaction requirements.

Fill or kill (FOK)—An order requiring complete execution or cancellation. Similar to an all-or-none, the FOK is to be canceled immediately if all segments cannot be executed. The FOK cannot be employed in a GTC order due to this requirement.

Financial Accounting Standards Board (FASB)—An independent board of accounting professionals designed to develop and publish accounting and auditing standards in the U.S., as a major segment of the GAAP system. Web address: www.fasb.org. Address: P.O. Box 5116, Norwalk CT 06856.

Financial futures—Any futures contracts based on underlying financial instruments rather than physical commodities. These include Treasury securities, currencies, and indices.

Financial plan—A systematic evaluation of financial assets and income, risk tolerance, and specific long-term goals, with the intention of identifying and selecting investment strategies to meet future goals while protecting current portfolio, investment, and personal assets.

Financial statement—A report subject to independent audit and published by listed corporations, summarizing the year-end values of all assets, liabilities, and stockholders' equity (the balance sheet); the past year's operations including revenue, cost of sales, expenses, and net profit (the income statement); and an analysis of the sources and uses of cash during the year (the cash flows statement). Financial statements are filed quarterly and annually with the Securities and Exchange Commission (SEC) and are also included, with extensive footnotes and explanations, in the company's annual report.

Firm order—An order within a brokerage firm's own account or a discretionary order executed by a broker in behalf of a client.

Firm quote—A guaranteed quote provided by a dealer or market maker.

First notice day—The earliest day that a notice of intent to deliver a commodity may be forwarded to a buyer to satisfy the terms of a futures contract.

Fiscal year—A 12-month period used by a company for accounting purposes, calculation and payment of income taxes, and annual audit.

Flag—A pattern in a technical price chart, often called a pennant, in which the trading range is broadening or narrowing, used as a signal to anticipate short-term price direction.

Flat market—The condition when no specific trend is apparent.

Flexible exchange option (FLEX option)—An exchange-traded index option enabling a trader to specify exercise price and date, within limits.

Float—The number of currently outstanding common shares for a company.

Floating security stock or other securities held in street name, in anticipation of a short holding period and quick sale.

Floor broker—A broker in an exchange responsible for execution of orders for customers.

Floor traders—Members of the exchange who buy and sell for their own accounts.

Follow-up action—Trading after establishing an open option positive, to reduce risk exposure or limit losses. An example includes buying shares to cover the position in an uncovered call write.

Forced conversion—Exercise of an issuer's contractual right to convert a security, when investors to not favor the conversion.

Forced liquidation—Brokerage action to sell securities in a customer's account when that customer is delinquent or to meet a margin call.

Formula investing—Any system for placing money into securities based on a formula rather than on changing market conditions, including dollar cost averaging or asset allocation investing.

Forward contract—A variation of the futures contract involving a cash transaction, when delivery is deferred until the contract is made. In this arrangement, price is set on the original trade date rather than upon delivery.

Forward market—The market for over-the-counter futures trading.

Forward price—The set delivery price as part of a futures contract.

Forward P/E—The price/earnings ratio based on a forecast of future earnings per share (EPS) rather than on reported past earnings. Normally applied to a 12-month period, the formula is as follows:

market price per share ÷ expected EPS

Free market price—The price of a security estimated by current supply and demand, based on a belief in the efficiency of the market.

Front fee—A premium assessed when a trader opens a compound option.

Frozen account—A brokerage account in which no transactions are allowed, due to the account holder's failure to make timely payments or to meet margin requirements.

Full disclosure—A requirement by the Securities and Exchange Commission (SEC) that all regulated public companies provide investors and markets with all information concerning on-going business operations, especially to the extent that the information may affect investment value in the company's stock.

Full-service broker—Also accurately called a full-commission broker, a firm charging full commissions for trades, while offering investment advice, research, and planning.

Fully diluted earnings per share—A company's EPS, calculated if all stock options and warrants were exercised, and all convertible bonds and preferred stock were converted.

Fundamental analysis—A form of analysis based on financial statements and other operational information. Although there might be no direct relationship between current stock price and financial results, most analysts agree that long-term price trends are affected by the company's revenue and earnings trends.

Fundamental volatility—A tendency for variation in year-to-year reported results of operations. A low-volatility report reflects steady and consistent revenue, costs, expenses, and profits; a high-volatility report is erratic and unpredictable.

Fungibility—The result of setting standardized terms on options; descriptive of listed options, whose terms are clearly distinguished and serve as part of the option contract.

Futures contract—An agreement for delivery of a stated amount of an underlying commodity, at a specific date in the future, the value of which is set as part of the contract regardless of changes in market value. Such changes make existing futures contracts more valuable or less valuable in the same way that option values change due to price changes in the underlying stock.

Futures equivalent—A comparative value between futures and options; the number of futures contracts equal to an option position.

Futures market—A market for the buying and selling of futures contracts, operating as an open outcry auction market.

Futures option—An option with a futures contract as the underlying security.

Futures price—The agreed-upon price between buyer and seller for a futures transaction at a later settlement date.

Futures spread—A position involving the buying on one exchange and selling on another of the same futures contract; a futures arbitrage strategy.

Gamma—The rate of change in an option's delta; one of the "Greeks" applied to option analysis.

Gap—Any space between a closing price on one trading day and opening price on the following day. Some gaps are viewed as strong technical signals based on current price movement, volume, and proximity of the gap to resistance or support; other gaps recur as a normal part of trading and are not technically important.

Generally accepted accounting principles (GAAP)—The accounting rules for interpreting and reporting financial transactions, based on standards published by accounting boards, AICPA or FASB opinions, published accounting material, and government regulation.

Gilt-edged bond—A bond issued by a blue-chip corporation; a high-grade bond with little risk of default.

Globex—A trading exchange operated entirely on an electronic basis, which runs 24 hours per day and operates internationally. Globex was introduced by Reuters in 1992.

Going concern value—The value of a company with established assets enabling it to continue operations; a distinction used to identify companies unlikely to be able to continue as a going concern due to excessive debt or declining market share.

Good delivery—Condition when a trade is in proper form and title.

Good till cancelled order (GTC)—A type of limit order that remains open as long as required to be executed (filled) or later canceled by the originator.

Greeks—Descriptive of various types of risk in option positions. The name comes from the use of Greek letters to distinguish them from one another (delta, gamma, theta, and rho). Vega is included with the Greeks, although not part of the Greek alphabet.

Greenshoe option—A provision in some underwriting agreements for new issues of stock, allowing the underwriter to sell more shares than the issuer intended; used when demand for shares is greater than anticipated and also called an over-allotment option.

Growth stock—Any stock with earnings estimates greater than market averages.

Gut spread—A spread involving short positions in calls and puts that are both in the money.

Haircut—(a) The reduction in reported value of one or more assets for the purpose of calculating capital requirements or collateral levels; or (b) the spread between buy and sell prices for market makers.

Hardening—Condition when futures price volatility is declining, or when market prices are rising gradually.

Head-and-shoulders pattern—A popular technical chart signal characterized by three price tops. The first and third (shoulders) are not as high as the middle top (the head). It is believed to signal a downward move resulting from a failed attempt to move through resistance. A reverse, or invested, head-and-shoulders involves three price bottoms. The first and third (shoulders) are not as high as the middle bottom (the head). This reverse head-and-shoulders pattern is usually viewed as bullish, anticipating rising prices after a failed attempt for price to decline below support.

Heavy—A futures market tending toward declining prices.

Hedge—*See* Chapter 8.

Hedge ratio—*See* Chapter 8.

High-low index (H/L)—A technical moving average consisting of a comparison and accumulation of stocks reaching new high prices, versus those reaching new low price levels. Technicians use H/L to measure strength or weakness in the market.

Historic volatility—Stock price movement over a period of time.

Historical yield—Actual yield earned and reported in a mutual fund over a stated number of months or years.

Holder—The owner of an open option contract.

Holder of record—The individual listed as registered owner of a security.

Holding period—The time an investment position remains open.

Horizontal spread—*See* Chapter 8.

Hot issue—An IPO selling above its original offering price on its first trading day.

House rules—Internal rules mandating how customer accounts are handled in a brokerage firm.

Hypothecation—The rights held by a lender regarding collateral for the loan, including liquidation of securities without advance notice to satisfy a margin call.

Immediate or cancel (IOC)—A type of order allowing cancellation of part of the transaction or complete cancellation if not filled right away; the IOC cannot be attached to a GTC order. Unlike the AON or FOK order, the IOC can be partially filled.

Implied volatility—In the options market, volatility in the underlying stock based on current option pricing rather than on the stock's historical volatility.

In and out—A fast trade opening and then closing a position, often within the same day (a day trade), as opposed to employing a buy-and-hold strategy.

In the money (ITM)—Condition when the underlying security's current market value is higher than a call's strike price or lower than a put's strike price. The number of points an option is in the money is equal to the option's intrinsic value.

Incentive stock option—An employee benefit, as a form of compensation, in which no income tax is payable by the employer at the time it is granted. Tax is deferred until the employee exercises the option *and* sells the stock. This type of stock option cannot be issued at a strike price lower than current market value of the company stock.

Incremental return—A covered call writing strategy intended to create higher returns on stock intended for eventual sale.

Index—A grouping of stocks reported together as a single value, based on an average that may or may not be weighted (by price or by capitalization). An index serves as a benchmark for investing or as a tracking device for the overall market.

Index arbitrage—Simultaneous buying and selling on an index future and stock, to profit from the net differences.

Index fund—A mutual fund with a portfolio consisting of or matching a market index, to provide broader market-wide returns with relatively low operating expenses.

Index futures—Any futures contracts with a financial index, currency, or interest rate as the underlying security.

Index option—Any option with an index as the underlying security.

Indicated yield—The yield on stock based on dividends paid during the past year, and assuming the same dividend will be paid in the coming year. It is expressed as a percentage. The indicated dividend is compared to current price per share. Formula:

indicated dividend ÷ price per share

Individual volatility—The volatility in option premium based on a pricing model and using the five pricing factors: time to expiration, strike price, underlying stock price, dividend, and assumed interest rate.

Inflation risk—Type of risk associated with investments based on the rate of inflation. For example, if a rate of return after taxes is lower than inflation, an investment loses purchasing power.

Initial margin—The required cash or securities that have to be on deposit before an investor is allowed to trade on margin. Federal Reserve Board Regulation T requires 50% initial margin; some brokerage firms require higher minimum initial margin levels.

Initial public offering (IPO)—The first public sale of corporate stock to the public.

Inside day—A formation in candlestick charting in which a day's trading range is within the trading range of the previous day.

Inside market—The range of highest (bid) and lowest (ask) prices made by market makers for their own accounts.

Insider information—Any material information about a company or its stock that is not available to the public.

Insider trading—Illegal trading by insiders and based on knowledge not available to the general public.

Institutional investor—A mutual fund, pension plan, insurance company, or other financial institution actively trading in the market.

Intangible asset—An asset listed on a company's balance sheet but lacking physical value. The distinction is critical in applying certain ratios, such as tangible book value per share (in which intangible assets are excluded). Intangibles include goodwill, brand, patents, covenants, trademarks, and franchise values.

Interest—(a) A basic return, usually expressed as a percentage, on a debt investment. Basic formula:

> dollar value of interest ÷ amount invested

To ensure accuracy, holding periods of varying times should be annualized so that expressions of interest income are truly comparable. Formula for annualizing return:

> (yield ÷ months owned) × 12

(b) Fee for borrowed money, charged by a lender, expressed as an annual percentage as well as an annual rate based on compounding and additional fees charged; or (c) the holdings by an investor in an asset, as in a partial interest represented by stock or partnership equity.

Interest coverage—A company's financial capability to make scheduled interest payments on its outstanding debts. The lower the percentage of interest coverage, the greater the debt burden. Formula:

> earnings before interest and taxes ÷ interest expense

Interest rate option—An obligation with a debt obligation as the underlying security.

Interest rate—The rate lenders charge for borrowed money or, for debt investors, the rate earned on a bond or money market instrument.

Interim report—Any financial report issued during the fiscal year, normally on a quarterly basis for quarters one, two, and three, reporting results of operations for the partial months from the beginning of the year until that time.

Intermarket spread—A simultaneous purchase and sale of options or futures contracts on different exchanges, to take advantage of price differences.

Intermediate trend—A trend of less time than a primary trend but more time than a short-term trend, most often used to describe Dow Theory status, notably for reverse price direction within the primary trend.

Internal rate of return (IRR)—A discounted rate of return based on the present value of future cash flow and assuming a fixed interest rate.

Internet broker—Any brokerage firm offering services to clients via the Internet rather than in person.

International Securities Exchange (ISE)—A fully electronic exchange, including both stock and options trading. Website: www.ise.com. Address: 60 Broad Street, New York NY 10004.

Intrasector spread—A yield spread between two fixed-income securities in the same market sector and with an identical maturity date.

Intrinsic value—The portion of option premium equal to the number of points in the money. This occurs when the current market price of stock is higher than a call's strike price, or lower than a put's strike price.

Inverse head-and-shoulders—A head-and-shoulders pattern turned upside down, showing three price lows. The first and third (shoulders) are not as low as the second (head). Because this pattern is a failed attempt at price moving lower, it anticipates an upward price movement.

Inverted market—The futures market when the nearest-expiring contracts are set at higher prices than later-expiring contracts.

Investment grade bond—A safe bond, issued by a company with the higher levels of credit rating, generally BBB or above.

Iron butterfly (long *and* short)—*See* Chapter 8.

Island reversal—In technical analysis, a pattern involving a price gap, a period of trading in the newly established range, and then a gap returning price levels to the previously established trading range.

January-April-July-October (JAJO)—One of the three listed option cycles. In this cycle, options will have expirations in the next two months, plus the first two of the four indicated months.

Japanese candlesticks—Alternate name for the candlestick charting system, which originated in seventeenth- and eighteenth-century Japan for use in trading of rice contracts.

Kansas City Board of Trade (KCBT)—Founded in 1856 and chartered in 1876, a primary exchange for grain futures. Website: www.kcbt.com. Address: 4800 Main Street, # 303, Kansas City MO 64112.

Kappa—One of the Greeks, a measurement of option value based on assumptions of current and future volatility.

Knock-in option—An option that gains intrinsic value only if and when a specified price is reached or passed.

Knock-out option—An option that becomes worthless if and when a predetermined price level is reached or crossed.

Know your customer—A basic rule of the National Association of Securities Dealers (NASD), known as Conduct Rule 2310(b), and similar to New York Stock Exchange (NYSE) Rule 405(1) and American Stock Exchange (AMEX) Rule 411. Also known as the suitability rule, a duty is placed on brokers to understand every customer's knowledge level, financial limitations, and risk tolerance as requirements for entering into investment positions.

Ladder option—An option with locked-in profits that go into effect if the underlying security reached predefined levels, effective even if the underlying prices retreat or the option expires.

Lambda—One of the Greeks estimating a change in option values compared to changes in the volatility levels of the underlying security.

Lapsed option—An option that expires without being exercised.

Last trading day—The third Friday in an option's expiration month; the day immediately prior to expiration day.

LEAPS—Long-term equity anticipation securities, long-term (or long-dated) options. Expirations occur in the immediate two months from a current date, plus the next two years, in January.

Leg—A two-sided option transaction entered at different times. The first leg is opened with the idea that it will close profitably on its own, or seeking a more favorable price for the second leg at a later date. If this does not occur, the position is hedged by opening the second, offsetting leg.

Leg in / leg out—*See* Chapter 8.

Letter of guarantee—Notification from a brokerage firm or bank stating that a customer with a short option position either owns the underlying stock, or guaranteeing delivery if and when the position is exercised.

Leverage—(a) The use of capital to control additional, borrowed funds to take trading or investment positions, as through a margin account; or (b) use of any product enabling control over an underlying security for a smaller amount of capital; for example, options limit capital risk by requiring relatively small investment, while providing control over 100 shares of the underlying stock.

LIFFE—The London International Financial Futures and Options Exchange.

Limit move—The greatest price movement allowed for a futures contract within a single trading day, set by the futures exchange.

Limit order—An order to either buy at or below a stated price, or to sell at or above a stated price. A limit order with discretion allows a broker to determine whether to buy or sell beyond the limit if necessary to fill the entire order.

Limit price—The specified price attached to a limit order.

Limited risk—An attribute of an investment, usually a long position and associated with the initial amount invested. A long option position's limited risk is the premium cost. An uncovered call has no limited risk because the price of the underlying stock could rise indefinitely.

Limit-on-close order—A limit order to be executed only if and when a closing price is more advantageous than the specified limit price, expanding on the market-on-close order.

Limit-on-open order—A limit order to be executed only if and when an opening price is more advantageous than the specified limit price, good only for the day's opening price.

Linkage—The opening of a position on one exchange and simultaneous sale of the same security on another exchange.

Liquid market—A market with a high volume of trading or volatility.

Liquidation—(a) Closing of a business by selling its assets and paying its liabilities, with any remaining capital paid to shareholders; or (b) a trade that eliminates an offsetting position (long versus short or vice versa).

Liquidation value—The quick-sale value of a company, or the current tangible book value per share on the basis of selling all assets and paying off all liabilities.

Liquidity—(a) On the markets, a trading situation with high volume and narrow big/ask spreads; (b) for investments, the ability to match buyers and sellers easily or via the auction market; or (c) for companies, availability of cash adequate to pay current debts and fund on-going operations.

Liquidity ratios—Financial tests used in fundamental analysis to compare and track a company's management of working capital and ability to pay its current debts. These include the current ratio, quick assets ratio, and other tests of operating cash flow. The trend in debt ratio also affects long-term liquidity.

Liquidity risk—Any risk associated with how readily a position can be traded in the market. Highly liquid assets such as listed stock or options are more desirable than less liquid assets such as units of limited partnerships.

Listed company—A corporation whose stock is traded on a public exchange.

Listed option—An option traded on the public exchanges, with standardized terms, versus over-the-counter options, for which the terms are individually negotiated.

Listed stock—The stock of listed corporations, traded over public stock exchanges.

Local traders—Futures traders who buy and sell on their own accounts.

Locked in—Problem faced when closing a position would create a tax liability the trader or investor wants to avoid.

Lognormal distribution—A statistical analysis of price movement based on the shape of a bell curve, in which most likely outcomes occur in a top range of prices.

London International Financial Futures and Options Exchange (LIFFE)—An exchange for futures and options and part of the NYSE Euronext Group, including over two trillion Euros in derivatives trading each day. Web address: www.euronext.com. Address: Cannon Bridge House, 1 Cousin Lane, London EC4R 3XX.

Long—Any position involving ownership in a stock, option, or futures product. The sequence of events in a long position is buy-hold-sell (compared to the sequence of a short position, which is sell-hold-buy).

Long call—*See* Chapter 8.

Long call butterfly—*See* Chapter 8.

Long call condor—*See* Chapter 8.

Long combination—*See* Chapter 8.

Long iron butterfly—*See* Chapter 8.

Long jelly roll—A time value spread including offsetting call *and* put positions. It usually consists of two separate spreads. First is a long put with a short call with identical strike and expiration. The second consists of a short put and a long call with the same strikes (but different than the previous spread) and later expirations than those of the first spread.

Long market value (LMV)—The total value of securities based on the previous day's closing prices.

Long option position—Ownership in an open option entitling the owner to buy the underlying stock at a fixed price (in the case of a call) or to sell the underlying stock at a fixed price (in the case of a put). The amount of underlying is equal to 100 shares per option, and each must be exercised or closed before expiration date, or it expires worthless.

Long-dated options—Alternate name for LEAPS, long-term options.

Long put—*See* Chapter 8.

Long put butterfly—*See* Chapter 8.

Long put condor—*See* Chapter 8.

Long stock (synthetic)—*See* Chapter 8.

Long straddle—*See* Chapter 8.

Long stock position—Ownership of stock.

Long-term capital gains—Profits from investments or other capital assets that were held longer than one full year. These are taxed at lower rates than short-term gains, which are taxed at the same rate as ordinary income.

Long-term equity anticipation securities (LEAPS)—Options with expiration longer than one year. Time erosion takes longer than for shorter-term expiring options, but these also tend to be less responsive to price changes in the underlying stock as long as expiration is far off. Expirations occur in the next two months and in the next two Januarys.

Lookback option—A variation on the option contract enabling traders to exercise based on the best possible prices of the underlying stock. A *fixed* lookback refers the option price, which is fixed upon purchase. Exercise can be made based on the underlying stock's highest price (for a lookback call) or lowest price (for a put). A *floating* lookback fixes the strike price at maturity. The call strike is the lowest price reached by the option and for a put it is fixed at the highest option price.

Loss zone—The price zone of an underlying stock at which an option position will produce a loss.

Lost opportunity risk—(a) The risk that by having capital invested in one position, other, better positions will be lost, or (b) in the case of covered calls, the lost profits in a rising underlying stock that are lost because of requirement to cover the short call position.

Maintenance margin—The lowest allowable value of cash and securities that has to be kept in a margin account when margin positions are open; also called minimum maintenance.

Manipulation—The practice of artificial adjustments in market value of a security for the purpose of profiting from current positions at the expense of other investors.

March-June-September-December (MJSD)—One of the three listed option cycles. In this cycle, options will have expirations in the next two months, plus the first two of the four indicated months.

Margin—(a) Transacting in the market with a combination of cash and securities owned, and funds borrowed from a brokerage firm; (b) an account set up by a brokerage firm to enable investors to borrow money for the trading of securities; (c) an account in which investment activity may include borrowing funds from the brokerage firm; (d) a demand for payment to settle margin debt, or to increase holdings to meet minimum requirements within the margin account; (e) the level of debt in a trader's margin account, subject to interest, or at times a reference to the total of all margin debt on an exchange; (f) the requirement for dollar value of securities and cash that must be held in a margin account in order to borrow money; or (g) a minimum dollar amount required for uncovered option writers to leave on deposit, subject to daily adjustments as market values change.

Market basket—A collection or portfolio of stocks sharing attributes, which simulate an index's performance.

Market capitalization—The overall market value of a listed company, used to distinguish size in terms of capitalization (versus total revenue or earnings). Formula:

common shares outstanding × price per share

Market if touched (MIT)—A conditional order that converts to a market order if and when a specified price is reached (a price below current price for a buy order or above current price for a sell order).

Market maker—A member of an exchange who trades for his or her own account and maintains an orderly market by entering bids and offers for a stock or range of stocks and their related options.

Market not held order—A type of market order for which the floor broker has discretion as to the timing of execution.

Market on close (MOC)—An order to be executed at or near the day's close of business.

Market on open (MOO)—An order to be executed at or near the day's opening.

Market order—An order asking for execution at the best available price.

Market quote—The current price or bid/ask for a stock or option, either in real-time, delayed, or after-hours.

Market risk—The actual risk from changes in the prices of stocks or options, also called systemic risk.

Market value—(a) The current value of shares of stock or options; or (b) in fundamental analysis, a company's total capitalization including equity and long-term debt.

Marketability—The degree to which a security can be traded. In an active, ready market, securities are easily traded, and in this respect, marketability is the same as liquidity.

Marketable securities—Current assets held by companies that can be converted to cash easily and quickly.

Mark to market—Adjustment in the valuation of options in an account based on the prior trading day's closing market prices or latest quotes, settlement set by the Options Clearing Corporation (OCC).

Married put—*See* Chapter 8.

Matching orders—Offsetting buy and sell orders, creating an illusion of trading at greater volume than is actually taking place.

Matrix trading—A bond swap involving varying yields from bonds with dissimilar ratings.

Maturity date—The date when a loan or debt security is repayable in full.

Max pain—The time of option expiration, based on the observation that many long options traders will hold their options until they expire.

Member—(a) A broker who belongs to the exchange and is authorized to enter trades for their clients; (b) a person or firm who owns a seat on the NYSE; or (c) a broker-dealer member of the NASD.

Members' short sale ratio—Short sales opened in member accounts on the NYSE as a percentage of total short sales. In technical analysis, a high percentage is viewed as bearish and a lower percentage of shorts as bullish.

Minimum price contract—A forward contract including guaranteed minimum delivery price.

Minimum price fluctuation—A tick; the smallest allowed price movement in a security.

Minneapolis Grain Exchange (MGEX)—The major market for hard red spring wheat (and other agricultural) futures contracts, founded in 1881. The exchange also structures index-based contracts, as well as options on various agricultural futures. Web address: www.mgex.com. Address: 130 Grain Exchange Building, Minneapolis MN 55415.

Minus tick—A downtick, a trade taking place at the smallest allowable increment below the previous price.

Misery index—An economic indicator begun in the 1970s to describe current economic opinions among the general public. Formula:

unemployment rate + inflation rate

Mixed account—Any account with a combination of both long and short positions in stocks, options, or both.

Model—A formula used to price options based on a series of known values and variables, including the price of the underlying stock, the strike price, time to expiration, dividends, and an assumed interest rate. The best-known of these is the Black-Scholes model.

Momentum—A technical method for analyzing price trends based on the rate of movement rather than simple price change. This is used to identify overbought or oversold situations to time trades.

Momentum indicator—A mathematical calculation of price or volume rates of change.

Momentum trading—A technical strategy employing momentum indicator trends to time entry or exit, including the study of price and volume.

Money flow—A technical system in which the high, low, and closing prices are added and then multiplied by daily volume, compared to the previous day's money flow, and quantified as either positive or negative.

Money flow index (MFI)—A momentum indicator that compares daily price and volume levels, similar to the relative strength index (RSI).

Money management—A range of activities including portfolio diversification, savings, budgeting, and long-term planning, to ensure availability of cash and liquidity levels, often part of a formal financial plan or investment strategy.

Monte Carlo Simulation—A probability analysis system using random variables, so-called because games of chance (such as gambling in Monte Carlo) involve random outcomes in a way similar to investing and trading.

Most active issue—The stock with the highest trading volume during a trading day, driven by buyers or sellers.

Moving average—A technique used in charting, to smooth out volatility. In addition to tracking daily high, low, opening, and closing prices, moving averages are shown as a line moving along with price trend. Popular time periods include 14-day, 20-day, and 200-day MAs. These may also be weighted, giving more importance to the most recent price information. Calculation of weighted moving average is performed in many ways, the best-known being exponential moving average (EMA).

Moving average chart—A price chart focusing on the moving average rather than current price levels or trends.

Moving average convergence divergence (MACD)—A technical indicator used to identify overbought or oversold conditions. As two different moving averages move closer (converge) to current price or farther away (diverge), trend reversal signals appear.

Multiple listed options—Those options listed and traded on more than one exchange.

Mutual fund—A pooled investment company, in which many investors contribute capital to create a managed portfolio of stocks, bonds, or both. Management identifies a specific investment and risk level for each fund. One variation, the exchange-traded fund (ETF), identifies a basket of securities in advance so that management decisions are removed from the equation. ETF shares are traded during a trading day like stocks rather than based on a fund's closing net asset value (NAV). Many ETFs also allow options trading on the basket of securities.

Mutual funds cash/assets ratio—A measure of a mutual fund's investment posture, comparing cash to the total value of the fund. Funds generally maintain approximately 5% of total assets in cash to settle redemptions. However, when the cash ratio rises, it indicates a bearish opinion among the fund's management. Formula:

cash on hand ÷ total fund assets

Naked option—*See* Chapter 8.

Naked strategy—Any option strategy involving selling options without underlying stock as cover; a high-risk strategy.

Naked writer—The trader holding an uncovered option.

Narrow-based—An index made up of a relatively small number of stocks or other securities, as opposed to broad-based.

National Association of Securities Dealers (NASD)—The self-regulatory agency of the broker/dealer industry, which sets standards and enforces rules, audits members, and publishes opinions for compliance and due diligence, consolidated with the Financial Industry Regulatory Authority (FINRA) in 2007. Web address: www.finra.org.

National Association of Securities Dealers Automated Quotations (NASDAQ)—The largest electronic exchange in the United States. Founded in 1971 when all other exchanges were floor-based, NASDAQ pioneered electronic trading. Web address: www.nasdaq.com. Address: One Liberty Plaza, 165 Broadway, New York NY 10006.

National Futures Association (NFA)—The self-regulatory association of the futures industry. Website: www.nfa.futures.org. Address: 300 S. Riverside Plaza, # 1800, Chicago IL 60606.

Near option—The portion of a multi-option position that expires the soonest.

Near term—Short-term, meaning about to expire (options) or payable very soon (liability).

Negotiated market—Unlike an auction market, one in which security prices are negotiated between buyer and seller.

Net book value per share (NBV)—The value of a corporation (assets minus liabilities) excluding intangible assets, divided by outstanding common shares. Formula:

$$\Big(\,(\,\text{total assets} - \text{intangible assets}\,) - \text{total liabilities}\,\Big) \div \text{outstanding common shares}$$

Net change—The price difference between the current day's closing price and the previous day's closing price, the most common financial indicator reported for individual stocks in the financial press.

Net earnings—Revenue minus all costs and expenses, a key financial indicator.

Net proceeds—The amount received from the sale of securities or other property after deducting all costs or liens.

Net transaction—Any transaction not involving fees or commissions.

Neutral—An opinion about a security or the market as a whole, which does not favor either a rise or a decline in price.

Neutral hedge ratio—See Chapter 8.

Neutral position—See Chapter 8.

Neutral strategy—Any trading or investing strategy based on a neutral opinion about market direction.

New high/new low ratio—A technical indicator, comparing new 52-week highs to new 52-week lows. As the rate changes, technicians see the ratio as bullish (number of new highs rising) or bearish (number of new lows rising).

New York Mercantile Exchange (NYMEX)—The largest futures exchange in the world, focusing on energy and precious metals futures trading. NYMEX initiated energy futures and options in 1978. Web address: www.nymex.com. Address: World Financial Center, One North End Avenue, New York NY 10282.

New York Stock Exchange (NYSE)—The largest stock exchange in the world, with total capitalization value among listed companies over $27 trillion as of 2007. The exchange originated in 1792 with the signing of the Buttonwood Agreement in New York. Web site: www.nyse.com. Address: 11 Wall Street, New York NY 10005.

Ninety-ten (90/10) strategy—A strategy combining 90% of a portfolio in Treasury securities and 10% in long calls or puts.

Nominal yield—The rate earned on a bond based on face value, which is paid by the issuer, regardless of the current premium or discount value of that bond; the coupon rate.

Non-equity option—An option with an underlying security other than stock, usually based on an index, commodity, debt security or financial future.

Nonqualified stock option—An employee stock option subject to income tax, to be based on the difference between grant price and exercise price and taxed at ordinary rates.

Non-statutory stock option—An employee stock option that creates a tax liability upon exercise; also called non-qualified stock option.

Not held (NH)—An order giving discretion to the floor broker in fulfillment.

Note—A debt obligation maturing between one and 10 years. A *bill* usually matures in under one year, and a *bond* usually matures beyond 10 years from issue date.

Notice period—The time during which a futures buyer may be asked to accept delivery, usually between three and six weeks before delivery date.

Number of advancing or declining issues—A basic technical indicator comparing issues rising in price to those declining in price during a single trading session.

NYSE Composite Index—A widely used market indicator tracking movement in four other indices: industrials, transportations, utilities, and financials. Price per share is multiplied by the total number of shares listed to arrive at changes in the index each day.

NYSE rule 405—*See* know your customer.

Odd lot—An amount traded other than the normal trading unit, usually referring to stock transactions of less than 100 shares.

Odd lot theory—A technical indicator based on the belief that odd lot traders are usually wrong. Thus, when odd lot sales rise, it is seen as a strong indicator to buy; and vice versa.

Offer—(a) The price a buyer is willing to pay for an asset; or (b) placing an asset for sale and stating the price.

Offering circular—A short-form prospectus for a new listing, disclosing the basic attributes and risk features.

Offset—Eliminating an open position with its opposite (long versus short or short versus long) to reduce exercise obligation.

Offsetting transaction—A transaction that closes another open position or eliminates its risk. For example, a naked call seller may either buy the call in an offsetting transaction or buy 100 shares of stock to satisfy assignment if it occurs.

OHLC chart—A chart showing open, high, low, and close price levels; *see also* bar chart.

On balance volume (OBV)—A technical indicator entered onto a price chart as a means of identifying when the stock is being accumulated or distributed; a confirmation of price trends based on volume analysis.

One-cancels-other (OCO)—An option order treating different transactions as a combination, when execution of one side will reduce the number of contracts to be executed in the other.

On close—A market or limit order to be executed immediately before the trading session's close; also called at the close.

Open—(a) The beginning of the trading day; (b) status when a placed order has not yet been executed or canceled; (c) the first price in a security in a trading day; or (d) the process of starting (opening) a customer account with a brokerage firm or bank.

Open interest—The current number of open option contracts within a specific series.

Open order—An order that has not yet been filled.

Open outcry—A method of trading in which market makers or floor brokers interact in person rather than electronically, employing voice or hand signals for placing orders.

Opening purchase transaction—Creation of a long position.

Opening sale transaction—Creation of a short position.

Opening transaction—A trade creating new positions, either long or short.

Opportunity cost—(a) The cost of deciding upon one investment over another; or (b) differences in yield from a selected investment or strategy versus another.

Option—A contract granting its owner the right, but not the obligation, to buy (via call) or to sell (via a put) 100 shares of a specified underlying security, at a fixed price and by or before a specified expiration date. An option seller grants the same rights to a buyer and might be required to sell 100 shares (via a short call) or to buy 100 shares (via a short put) under the specific contract's terms.

Option account—A brokerage account that includes approval for options trading.

Option agreement—(a) The agreement signed by an investor with the brokerage firm, laying out conditions and acknowledging risks in trading options; or (b) reference to the overall terms in every option contract to buy or sell shares of the underlying stock.

Option chain—The collective options available on an underlying security, listed in order by strike price and expiration date.

Option contract—*See* option agreement.

Option cycle—The distinctive expiration months for all options. Listed options have expirations in the next two months and in the following two months in one of three cycles: January, April, July, October; February, May, August, November; and March, June, September, December. LEAPS expire in the next two months as well as in the next two Januarys.

Option exchange—Any physical or electronic exchange accepting options trades.

Option margin—The requirement stated under Federal Reserve Regulation T for the amount of cash and securities that must be maintained in an option account, which changes as the degree in the money changes.

Option period—The span of time between the opening of an option position and expiration.

Option premium—The current price of an option contract, reported in dollars and cents per share of the underlying security. For example, an option currently valued at 2.60 has a premium of $2.60 per share, or a total of $260 (since each option is tied to 100 shares of the underlying stock).

Option pricing curve—A chart of the projected option price between the current date and expiration, based on predictable decline in time value and estimated price of the underlying stock.

Option pricing model—A mathematical estimation of an option's value, based on its attributes and assumed interest rates. The best-known model is Black-Scholes.

Option series—A grouping of calls or puts on the same underlying stock and with the same strike price and expiration date.

Option writer—A seller of options, either calls or puts.

Optionable stock—Any stock allowing trading of listed options.

Optionee—The trader currently holding open options.

Options Clearing Corporation (OCC)—The clearing agency for all option contracts traded on U.S. exchanges, which acts as buyer to every seller and as seller to every buyer. Website: www.optionsclearing.com. Address: One North Wacker Drive, Suite 500, Chicago IL 60606.

Options Price Reporting Authority (OPRA)—Provider of listing information and latest quotations on option contracts. Website: www.opradata.com. Address: 400 South LaSalle Street, Chicago IL 60605.

Or better—Condition attached to an order to achieve a minimum price or lower as part of a buy order, or a minimum price or higher as part of a sell order.

Order—An instruction to buy or to sell securities.

Order book official—An employee of an exchange responsible for tracking orders placed by the public.

Original issue discount (OID)—A bond discount at the time of issue; the difference between par value and issue price.

Oscillator—In technical analysis, a trend indicator showing price variations and potential overbought or oversold conditions.

OTC option—Over-the-counter, an option traded without standardized terms, negotiated between buyer and seller.

Out of the money (OTM)—Status of an option when strike price of a call is higher than current market value of the underlying stock, or when strike price of a put is lower than current market value of the underlying stock; an option with no intrinsic value.

Outside day—A candlestick charting pattern in which the current day's trading range extends above *and* below the range of the previous day.

Over the counter (OTC)—A market in which trading occurs electronically rather than on a physical exchange.

Overbought—A price resulting from excess demand for a security; price levels greater than those justified by technical indicators.

Overreaction hypothesis—An observation that investors and traders tend to create excessive priced movements by overreacting to current news, leading to price corrections in subsequent trading.

Oversold—A price resulting from reduced demand for a security; price levels lower than those justified by technical indicators.

Overvalued—Status of securities trading above price levels justified through analysis.

Owner—The holder of an open long position in stock or options.

P/E ratio—One the best-known analytical tools, combining technical (price) with fundamental (price) indicators. A measure of valuation, the formula is expressed on a per-share basis. The current market value is the latest market price per share. Total dollar value of earnings is divided by the average common shares outstanding. The formula is as follows:

current market value per share ÷ (earnings ÷ outstanding common shares)

Pairs trading—Matching up a long and short position in two different stocks within the same market sector. This hedges the sector, as well as the overall market. The strategy usually is applied to stocks, but the use of options also creates an equivalent position.

Paper profit or loss—Any unrealized profit or loss, which is the current outcome if open positions were to be closed.

Paper trading—The practice of tracking trade decisions without actually investing or risking capital. The purpose is to check strategies in a real-time environment but without the risks.

Par—The maturity value of a bond; face value. This is normally $1,000 for corporate bonds. During their existences, bonds may trade at a premium above par or at a discount below par. These variations occur due to changing market interest rates because the rates contractually attached to bonds are fixed.

Parity—For options, condition when current premium consists entirely of intrinsic value so that it is said to be trading at parity.

Participate but do not initiate (PNI)—An order including instructions to trade in a security only after trading has been started by others but restricting initiation of a position.

Payback—The time required to recapture the initial cost of investments, calculated on cash income. The overall cost is divided by yearly cash received to calculate the time; this might be adjusted to include interest cost on the original investment.

Payoff diagram—An options-based chart used to calculate profits or losses before execution of a position or combination strategy. It includes profit and loss zones as a means for estimating overall risk and opportunity.

Pennant—A technical charting price pattern including converging trend lines that form a pennant or flag-like shape, often anticipating a price breakout.

Perfect hedge—The elimination of all risk in a position or portfolio.

Phantom option plan—Employee compensation equaling a specific number of shares, with the added feature that those shares can be sold later including any subsequent price appreciation.

Philadelphia Stock Exchange (PHLX)—The oldest U.S. stock exchange. Web address: www.phlx.com. Address: 1900 Market Street, Philadelphia PA 10103.

Physical option—An option written against an actual amount of a commodity rather than on futures contracts or shares of stock as the underlying security.

Pin risk—The risk that the expiration-date price of underlying stock will exactly equal the strike price of a short option. The risk arises in the contingency of exercise and subsequent price movement in the underlying stock.

Pinning the strike—A tendency for the price of the underlying stock to move close to the strike price of options being traded heavily immediately prior to expiration.

Pit—The location on an exchange's trading floor where trading occurs in a specific stock, options, or range of securities.

Pivot—Price set in technical analysis, which becomes significant if and when the trend moves beyond that level.

Plus tick—An uptick; trading one increment above the previous trading level.

Point-and-figure chart—A type of price chart consisting of "X" and "O" entries. X is used for continuation patterns in an upward movement, and O is used for decreases. Both are stacked vertically to show the duration of the trend.

Portfolio—A collection of securities held by an investor in an account, including stocks, options, mutual funds, and debt securities; and both long and short positions.

Portfolio insurance—(a) A hedging system involving long positions in stocks with short selling index futures; (b) insurance for brokerage accounts provided by the SIPC; or (c) a system of using options to protect positions in stocks to avoid losing paper profits.

Position—Status of holdings in a portfolio, such as long or short.

Position limit—The greatest maximum number of calls or puts an individual is allowed to have open at any given time.

Positive carry—Holding of two offsetting positions when one side's inflow of cash is greater than the other side's outflow.

Positive yield curve—The yield when long-term debt instruments offer yields greater than short-term debt instruments; also called nominal yield curve.

Preliminary prospectus—The initial draft of a prospectus, published prior to the initial public offering date. This has been called a "red herring" because the SEC requires the use of red ink on a portion of the cover.

Premium—(1) An option's price including intrinsic and time value; or (2) for bonds, status when the current bond value is greater than par value.

Present value—Current worth of money or cash flow, based on an assumed rate of interest; also called discounted value.

Price limit—A range of prices that options or futures are allowed to extend in either direction during a single trading day; the daily trading limit.

Price risk—*See* market risk.

Price/book ratio—A financial ratio comparing current price per share to book value per share; specifically, the denominator is usually the tangible books value per share, which excludes goodwill, patents, trademarks, value assigned to brand names, covenants, and other intangible assets shown on a company's books. Formula:

price per share ÷ (tangible book value ÷ outstanding common shares)

Price/core earnings ratio (P/CE)—A variation of the P/E ratio, employing only core earnings, or earnings only from a company's core business and excluding non-recurring income or expense. Formula:

price per share ÷ (core earnings ÷ outstanding common shares)

Price/earnings ratio (P/E)—A comparison between current price per share and latest reported earnings per share. Formula:

current market value per share ÷ (earnings ÷ outstanding common shares)

Price/sales ratio (PSR)—A comparison between current price per share and sales reported for the most recent 12 months. Formula:

current market value per share ÷ (sales ÷ outstanding common shares)

Price-weighted index—Any index based on a computation of each price of stocks in the index, divided by a set divisor.

Primary market—The exchange where securities are traded in the highest volume, when also traded in lower volume on other exchanges.

Principal—(1) A loan's repayment amount or the amount remaining due; (2) face value of a bond, to be repaid upon maturity; (3) the amount invested, without considering earnings; (4) a legal term describing an owner of a business or of property, or a party in a contract or other transaction.

Pro forma—A Latin term meaning "for the sake of form," used for calculating financial reports, including projections or forecasts of future revenues, expenses, and earnings.

Pro forma earnings—Estimated future earnings based on assumptions, often used in business plans or budgets; reports beyond GAAP-based rules.

Producer Price Index (PPI)—A grouping of indicators used by economists to report changes in sales prices for domestic goods or services.

Profit graph—A graph reporting profit or loss from a specific investing strategy at a single moment or over a period of time, often used to summarize option strategies at various expiration dates.

Profit margin—A financial ratio comparing net profit and revenues, expressed as a percentage and used as a means for comparison between different companies in the same sector or for a single company over a period of years. Formula:

net profit ÷ revenue

Profit range—The range, or zone, in which a strategies will realize a profit, often used in combinations or situations where two separate breakeven levels and profit ranges may occur.

Profit table—A compilation of prices and profits or varying levels, reported as a table or graph.

Profit taking—Closing positions to take available profits, even when the original strategy involved a longer holding period or higher profits.

Profit zone—The profit range, or price level or levels where a strategy produces profitable results.

Program trading—Method for large-volume and large-dollar trading, involving automatic execution generated from an automated source.

Prospectus—The offering document for an initial public offering, disclosing risks and other important information required by the SEC.

protected strategy—A strategy with limited risk, such as a covered call or protected straddle write.

Prudent man rule—A requirement stating that anyone managing funds or providing investment advice should limit that advise to what a prudent or reasonable person would do.

Pullback—A reversal of prices downward from a peak or upward from the lowest point of decline; a signal of a pause in momentum of the dominant trend.

Purchasing power—(a) Credit in a margin account available for additional transactions; or (b) currency valuation in a trend influenced by inflation or lost value relative to other currencies.

Put—An option granting its owner the right, but not the obligation, to sell 100 shares of a specific underlying stock, at a fixed strike price and by or before a specific expiration date.

Put diagonal spread (bear *and* bull)—*See* Chapter 8.

Put ratio backspread—*See* Chapter 8.

Put swaption—A position providing a put buyer to enter into a swap with a floating rate.

Put warrant—A warrant including the right to sell at an agreed-upon price before a specified expiration date.

Put/call parity—The price relationship when puts and calls in the same class are static, enabling traders to create positions equivalent to stock ownership.

Put/call ratio—A technical indicator used to judge bullish or bearish sentiment, measuring the number of outstanding put contracts to the number of outstanding calls.

Pyramiding—Growing a position with the use of unrealized profits.

Qualified covered call—In federal tax rules, a covered call entitling the seller to claim long-term tax rates on the underlying stock if the call is exercised. An unqualified covered call either tolls the 12-month period or requires that it begin anew after closing the call position. Qualification is based on the degree the short call is in the money. Deep in-the-money short calls will probably be unqualified.

Quality of earnings—A distinction of earnings resulting from higher revenues accompanied by lower costs and expenses, rather than as the result of accounting restatements or gimmicks.

Quality spread—A spread between Treasury debt securities and non-Treasury debt securities with identical rates but different credit ratings.

Quanto option—An option on a specific currency, which makes payment in a different currency.

Quick assets ratio—A variation of the current assets ratio, also called the acid test. It includes current assets with the exception of inventory value. As a general rule, a quick assets ratio of 1 or better is considered acceptable (in comparison, the standard for current ratio is 2 or better). Formula:

(current assets – inventory) ÷ current liabilities

Quote—The current or latest price of a security.

Rally—Strong and sustained increases in price, either in individual issues or in the market as a whole.

Random walk hypothesis—A belief that market prices cannot be predicted or anticipated, and are independent of one another. Under this theory, past trends are not reliable indicators of future price movements.

Range—Also called trading range, the distance between support and resistance. On a day-to-day basis, the distance between highest and lowest price levels.

Rate of change—The rate of change, usually used in reference to price, which is usually expressed as a ratio between two variable factors.

Rate of return—Basic calculation of investment yield expressed as a percentage, which should be compared among dissimilar holding periods on an annualized basis. Formula for rate of return:

net gain ÷ basis

Formula for annualized yield:

(basis ÷ months owned) × 12 (months)

Ratio analysis—Any form of comparison between two or more factors, normally used as part of fundamental analysis. Comparisons are made between two current values, or between a current value and historical value.

Ratio backspread (call *and* call)—*See* Chapter 9.

Ratio calendar combination spread—*See* Chapter 9.

Ratio calendar spread (call *and* put)—*See* Chapter 9.

Ratio call spread—*See* Chapter 9.

Ratio put spread—*See* Chapter 9.

Ratio spread—*See* Chapter 9.

Ratio strategy—Any strategy involving a dissimilar number of long and short options, or covered calls greater than shares of stock (for example, four short calls against 300 shares) or less than shares of stock (for example, two short calls against 300 shares of stock); the most common strategy involves more short calls than stock, and is also called a ratio write.

Ratio write—*See* Chapter 9.

Reaction—A movement in prices opposite the prevailing direction.

Real time—Quotations system when prices are current, as opposed to lag time, commonly involving a 20-minute delay.

Realized profits—Those gains that have been taken, as opposed to paper gains (unrealized gains); a closed transaction, with the net subject to capital gains tax.

Record date—The date used to determine which investors are entitled to dividends.

Red herring—Name given to a preliminary prospectus, so called because of the required use of red ink on the cover as part of SEC-mandated disclosures.

Redemption—Return of principal adjusted for gain or loss in a security, realized upon closing of an open position.

Registered options principal (ROP)—A brokerage firm employee who has successfully passed the NASD Series 4 examination, qualified to provide investment advice concerning options trading.

Regulation T—Federal Reserve Board rule specifying the amount of cash and securities that must be maintained in a margin account and limiting credit a brokerage firm can extend; also known as initial margin, current limitation calls for a limit of 50% that can be invested on margin.

Rehypothecation—A pledge of securities held on margin, used as collateral for a loan.

Reinvestment rate—An assumed rate available from income, usually applied to fixed-income positions, which is available for reinvestment. This is used to compare investment strategies and to calculate total return.

Reinvestment risk—The risk that upon closing a position, the rate available on alternative future investments of similar risk will be lower than the rate currently being earned.

Relative strength—A measurement of price performance in relation to a sector or related index. Price performance for a stock is divided by price performance for the sector as a whole or by price performance of the index.

Relative strength index (RSI)—A momentum indicator used in technical analysis, to quantify price trends and flag overbought or oversold conditions. The RSI range, also called the RS (relative strength), moves from zero to 100. When the indicator exceeds 70, it indicates an overbought situation; and when it falls below 30, it indicates the stock is oversold. Formula:

$$100 - \left(100 \div (1 + \text{RS})\right)$$

Relative value—Any comparison in value between two or more positions. In fundamental analysis, this may involve comparative analysis of key financial ratios to determine higher-quality or safer companies.

Relative volatility—Comparison of risk levels in different instruments, or between portfolios or indices.

Reload option—A type of employee stock option providing for the grant of additional options when the employee exercises the initial positions.

Resistance level—An important technical concept, which is the highest price in the current trading range of a stock. Prices are expected to not exceed resistance; however, if and when it does, the breakout may signal a rally to the upside and eventual establishment of a new trading range (or anticipate a retreat to the previously established range).

Retail investor—An individual; anyone who trades for his or her own account, rather than acting as a broker or trading in behalf of an institution such as mutual fund, pension plan or insurance company.

Return—The net gain or loss from opening and closing security positions, expressed as a percentage. Formula:

    net profit ÷ basis

Return if exercised—The net return from a short option position that will be realized if and when the option is exercised. The calculation may include dividends earned on stock when a covered call is open or may be limited to the comparison between call premium and strike price of the underlying stock.

Return if unchanged—The return from a short option position if there is no in-the-money movement and the option expires worthless or is sold at a reduced premium.

Return on equity (ROE)—The calculation of net profit based not on revenue, but on the value of shareholders' equity, often involving calculation of average equity within the range of a complete fiscal year. Formula:

net profit ÷ shareholders' equity

Return on investment—The calculation of profit based on the initial net amount invested, often referred to simply as return. Formula:

net profit ÷ basis

Reversal—*See* Chapter 9.

Reversal arbitrage—Riskless arbitrage combining short stock with a short put or a long call, also called conversion arbitrage.

Reversal day—In swing trading, a trading day in which price direction first moves opposite the direction of the established short-term trend.

Reverse conversion—A synthetic long position (a short put with a long call) combined with a short position in the underlying stock, creating a position equivalent to owning the underlying stock.

Reverse hedge—*See* Chapter 9.

Reverse split—A stock split that reduces rather than increases the number of shares. For example, in a one-for-two split, the owner of 200 shares at $25 before the split would end up with 100 shares worth $50.

Rho—One of the Greeks used in option analysis, which measures changes in an option's theoretical values in comparison to changes in market interest rates.

Rights—The privileges associated with ownership in a security. For example, holders of shares of stock might also acquire rights to purchase additional shares at a fixed price; also called subscription rights. Option investors also acquire specific rights of exercise at a fixed strike price.

Risk—Potential losses or inconveniences associated with security positions. The best-known is market risk, or the risk that a position will lose value. Liquidity risk means that it is difficult or impossible to resell securities at market value, or that it may take time to close out positions.

Risk arbitrage—A form of arbitrage with a degree of risk.

Risk averse—Condition of an investor who wants minimum risk in a portfolio and seeks safer, more conservative investments; an individual with low risk tolerance.

Risk-free rate—An assumed interest rate that could be earned in any position that was completely riskless. Investors used the rate on the three-month Treasury Bill rate as an approximately risk-free rate.

Risk tolerance—An investor's willingness or ability to live with risk. Low risk tolerance means the individual is risk averse, and high risk tolerance means more speculative positions may be appropriate.

Risk/return tradeoff—The unavoidable relationship between the two sides to any investment: Greater returns require taking greater risks, and safer, less risky investments yield lower returns.

Rolling—*See* Chapter 9.

Rollover—(a) Movement of funds in a qualified retirement fund to a different fund, in a manner that does not create a taxable exchange; or (b) reinvestment from a maturing debt security into a new one with a later maturity date.

Rotation—Strategy in which one sector is weighted more than another, subject to readjustment later based on changing sector and market conditions; also called sector rotation.

Round lot—A normal trading unit, such as 100 shares of stock.

Round trip transaction cost—Total cost for completion of a transaction on both sides, also called a round trip.

Rules of Fair Practice—Regulations of the National Association of Securities Dealers (NASD) governing member broker-dealers in their dealings with customers.

Run—A panic; a time when large numbers of bank customers or investors in the market attempt to withdraw or sell at the same time.

Runaway gap—Type of gap occurring during periods of strong upward or downward trends, when either buying or selling activity is so strong that prices move in a rapid series.

Russian option—A type of lookback option that has no expiration date.

S&P 500—A widely used, market-weighted index of 500 widely-held stocks; one of the most popular market benchmarks.

Same-day substitution—A change in a margin account in which one asset is replaced by another within a single trading day.

Sarbanes-Oxley Act of 2002 (SOX)—Important legislation meant to curtail fraudulent accounting, conflicts of interest, and improper actions by corporate executives. The Act established a Public Accounting Oversight Board to monitor auditing firm activities; set new controls for auditors and auditing committees within the corporation; increased corporate liability for fraudulent activities including both civil and criminal remedies; set guidelines defining conflict of interest for analysts and others speaking in the media; and required stricter financial disclosures. SOX also increased the enforcement budget of the SEC and expanded its oversight authority.

Scale order—An order consisting of several incremental limit orders with either increasing (buy scale) or decreasing (sell scale) price limits.

Scalping—Strategy aimed at creating large volume of profit on small price increments.

Seat—Membership on the New York Stock Exchange (NYSE), allowing the member to trade on the exchange floor for others (floor broker) or for their own account (floor trader).

Secondary market—A market for resale of securities or assets traded in the primary market.

Sector index—An index that includes stocks within a single market sector.

Securities Act of 1933—Federal law requiring greater financial statement transparency and establishing laws to prevent fraud and misleading reports; the first federal legislation concerning publicly traded companies and markets.

Securities and Exchange Commission (SEC)—The primary federal agency that regulates the securities industry. This includes mergers and acquisitions, corporate financial reporting, and analysts operating within the public markets.

Securities Exchange Act of 1934—A law designed to oversee actions and reports among listed corporations and broker/dealers. The act also created the Securities and Exchange Commission (SEC) to enforce this law and other federal laws.

Securities Industry Association (SIA)—A trade association for the broker/dealer industry, which merged in 2006 with the Bond Market Association to form the Securities Industry and Financial Markets Association. Website: www.siaonline. org. Address: 635 Slater Lane, Suite 110, Alexandria VA 22314.

Securities Investors Protection Act of 1970—Federal law designed to protect investors in case of bankruptcy within the broker/dealer industry, which also created the SIPC.

Securities Investors Protection Corporation (SIPC)—A nonprofit corporation created by the Securities Investors Protection Act of 1970 to protect brokerage firm clients from the consequences of bankruptcy. Website: www.sipc.org. Address: 805 15th Street, N.W., Suite 800, Washington DC 20005-2215.

Security—(a) An investment, including equity (stock), debt (bond or money market instrument), or derivative (option or future contract); (b) property used as collateral for a loan or in a margin account; or (c) an investment objective aimed at protecting capital worth.

Sell limit order—An order to sell at or above a specified limit price.

Sell the book—An order placed by an institutional investor to sell the maximum amount possible of a currently held position at the current market price.

Seller—(a) One who disposes of holdings with a sell to close order or, in short selling, who opens a position with a sell to open order.

Selling hedge—A short hedge.

Selling short—The act of opening a position with a sell to open order, either in stock or options.

Sell-plus—An order requiring the sell of a position above current market price.

Senior security—Any security with seniority in the case of liquidation, usually a bond (following by preferred stock and then common stock).

Sentiment indicators—Technical tests of investor opinion within the market, or to define long-term opinion as bullish or bearish.

Serial option—An option on a futures contract in which expiration of the option will occur prior to the future contract's own expiration.

Series—The collective options of the same class (call or put), expiration date, strike price, and underlying security.

Settlement date—(1) The date executed trades must be settled, including payment by the buyer and delivery by the seller. This is normally three trading days for stocks and one trading day for options.

Settlement price—An option's final premium at the end of a trading day, set by the Options Clearing Corporation (OCC), through a process called mark to market.

Share—Ownership in a corporation or mutual fund, a portion of the total equity.

Shock absorber—A trading restriction or halt resulting from a high volume of trading and large-scale losses within the session.

Short—Any position opened with an initial sale transaction. Shorted stock involved borrowing the stock from the brokerage firm, paying interest, and holding the short position in the belief its value will fall. Shorted options may include uncovered or covered calls or uncovered puts. In the event of exercise, a short call writer is required to deliver stock at the strike price; a short put writer is required to accept delivery of stock at the strike price.

Short call—*See* Chapter 9.

Short call butterfly—*See* Chapter 9.

Short call condor—*See* Chapter 9.

Short combo—*See* Chapter 9.

Short iron butterfly—*See* Chapter 9.

Short interest—Shares sold short and currently open.

Short interest ratio—The short interest in a company's stock, divided by the average trading volume in the same company; as a technical indicator, this ratio measures the current sentiment in the market for the specific company; also called short ratio. Formula:

short interest ÷ average daily volume

Short interest theory—A belief that growth in short interest anticipates an increase in price; a contrarian indicator.

Short position—Any position in stock or options initiated with a sell order and remaining open until a buy to close order is entered.

Short put—*See* Chapter 9.

Short put butterfly—*See* Chapter 9.

Short put condor—*See* Chapter 9.

Short sale—In stock, a position opened to sell shares in the hope that share price will fall; in options, covered or uncovered sell transactions that expire worthless, are closed before expiration, or are exercised.

Short selling—The sale of securities not owned, anticipating a decline in value leading to profits at a later date.

Short squeeze—Excess demand arising from declines in supply of a security.

Short stock (synthetic)—*See* Chapter 9.

Short straddle (covered *and* naked)—*See* Chapter 9.

Short strangle—*See* Chapter 9.

Short the basis—A strategy in the futures market involving the purchase of a futures contract to offset a delivery commitment in the future.

Short-term capital gains—The profits from the sale of securities or other assets owned less than 12 months and subject to ordinary tax rates.

Simple moving average—An unadjusted average in which the values in a field are added together and then divided by the number of values (n) in the field. Each new calculation involves dropping the oldest value and adding the newest one, and recalculating the average. Formula:

(value 1 + value 2 + ... value n) ÷ n

Single option—A solitary call or put position versus combinations involving multiple contracts.

Single stock future (SSF)—A future on a stock as the underlying security in place of a commodity or financial value. Stock futures include no dividends or voting rights.

Slippage—The net difference between estimated transaction cost and actual costs incurred.

Small-cap stocks—The stocks of companies with total market capitalization smaller than mid-cap or large-cap companies.

Specialist—Exchange member allowed to both buy and sell for his or her own account and to execute public orders.

Speculator—An investor willing to accept higher than average risks in exchange for the opportunity for short-term profits (or losses), likely to trade in options and futures.

Spike—A large price movement either above or below the established trading range, which immediately retreats back to that range. For the purpose of tracking price volatility, spikes should be removed from the averaging equation.

Spin-off—Issue of shares of stock or dividends in a subsidiary corporation, or the sell of an operating segment to another company.

Split—An adjustment in the total outstanding common shares. For example, with a two-for-one split, shareholders are given twice the number of shares worth half the per-share value; thus, overall value remains unchanged. This often occurs when the market price per share becomes too expensive for small investors.

Spot commodity—A commodity trade occurring on the spot market, meaning delivery is expected; in comparison, trading in futures contracts usually does not include likely delivery of the underlying commodity.

Spot price—The price of an underlying commodity based on delivery date and time.

Spot trade—Transaction in currency or commodity on the condition that delivery takes place immediately.

Spread—*See* Chapter 9.

Spread order—An order with two or more options in a spread position. This usually includes both long and short sides of a related option strategy with the same underlying stock.

Spread strategy—An option strategy with two sides, one long and one short, on the same underlying stock.

Standard & Poor's (S&P)—A financial organization that publishes bond ratings and other financial services, and managers of the benchmark S&P 500 Index.

Standard and Poor's 500 Index—A market value weighted index containing 500 stocks and serving as a leading indicator of the large cap market.

Standard deviation—A statistical concept to measure the degree of change in a value; in technical analysis, this is applied to analysis of price movement compared to the average over time.

Standardization—A system ensuring conformity among different exchanges for all listed options. So, classes of options trading on multiple exchanges are defined by the same terms under standardization.

Static return—The return earned by options traders when the price of the underlying stock remains unchanged.

Statutory stock option—An employee stock option providing the employer with tax benefits, but that also has greater restrictions than a non-qualified stock option. These restrictions include the number of options that can be granted to an individual employee, and options must be equal to or greater than current market value at the time they are granted.

Stochastic indicator—A type of technical indicator based on observations about price behavior. As prices of stocks rise, closing price levels tend to move closer to high prices in each trading session; and as prices fall, closing prices tend to be closer to the low trading levels of the range. This observation is used to anticipate likely price levels as trends become established.

Stock—A security with the feature of equity, or ownership, in a corporation. Common stock provides the holder with voting rights, participation in shareholder meetings, and dividends, if declared. Preferred stock excludes most of these rights, but gives owners priority in the event of liquidation.

Stock dividend—A dividend to be paid in the form of additional shares rather than in cash.

Stock market—Overall, the market for buying and selling shares of stock and related derivatives, such as options or stock futures.

Stock option—A contractual right to buy 100 shares of stock (call option) or to sell 100 shares of stock (put) in a specific underlying company, at a set strike price, and at any time before a specific expiration date.

Stock option plan—A company benefit allowing employees to buy options in stock issued by the corporation. The number is normally limited within specific time frames, and rules for exercise and strike price are included in the option agreement.

Stock split—*See* split.

Stockholder of record—The registered owner of stock on a specific date, for the purpose of identifying who is entitled to dividends. Because the record date is not the same as payment date, the stockholder of record on the declaration date receives dividends even if stock is sold prior to payment date.

Stop and reverse order—A stop order that, once reached, leads to a close of the current position and an open in the opposite direction.

Stop-limit order—An order that is converted to a limit order when the security is traded at the stop-specified price. (In comparison, a stop order is converted to a market order in the same circumstances.)

Stop-loss order—An order to sell a security if and when it reaches a specified price.

Stop order—A contingent order that is converted to a market order if and when the security trades at or through the specified price. Buy stops are placed above current market value, and sell stops are placed below current market value.

Straddle—*See* Chapter 9.

Strangle—*See* Chapter 9.

Strap—*See* Chapter 9.

Strategy—A plan of investing or trading, usually including related long or short positions and actions leading to closing and taking of profits; or a means for limiting or eliminating risk through the use of options in offsetting positions with one another or with the underlying stock.

Strike price—The unchanging price per share at which calls or puts can be exercised. No matter how market price per share changes, the option owner is allowed to call stop away from a call writer or put stock to a put writer at the fixed strike price. Also called striking price, strike, or exercise price.

Strike price intervals—The incremental prices for a series of options. When the underlying stock is valued at $25 or less, intervals are usually $2.50. When underlying values are between $25 and $100, strike price intervals are usually $5; and above $100 in the underlying, intervals change to $10.

Strip—*See* Chapter 9.

Structured product—A pre-set investment plan that consists of stocks, bonds, options, futures contracts, or an allocated combination of investment types and risk levels.

Suitability—A concept stating that anyone investing or trading in a particular way should be able to tolerate the risk associated with the trading strategy.

Supply and demand—A basic economic concept recognizing that prices of any goods vary based on buyer and seller levels. Excess supply causes price reduction, and excess demand drives prices upward. This principle applies to the overall economy as well as to stock and options markets.

Support level—The opposite of resistance; the lowest price level a security is expected to fall, given current conditions. As the lowest price that sellers are willing to accept for a security, support defines the lower end of the existing trading range.

Swap—Exchange of one security for another, to extend maturity or to avoid exercise.

Swaption—An option for entry into an interest rate swap, also called a swap option. The premium is paid to acquire the right to fix an interest rate until a specified date.

Switching—The liquidation of a position for other securities.

Synthetic put—*See* Chapter 9.

Synthetic short call—*See* Chapter 9.

Synthetic short put—*See* Chapter 9.

Synthetic stock—A combination of options to create an artificial position approximating stock ownership. This usually involves a long call and a short put (synthetic long position) or a long put and a short call (synthetic short).

Synthetic straddle (long call, long put, short call *and* short put)—*See* Chapter 9.

Systematic risk—*See* market risk.

Tangible book value per share—The book value (assets less liabilities) excluding intangible assets, with the net divided by the number of outstanding shares. The number of shares is usually computed as the average of shares outstanding at the beginning and end of a fiscal year. Formula:

$$\big((\text{assets} - \text{intangible assets}) - \text{liabilities} \big) \div \text{outstanding shares}$$

Tangible asset—An asset with physical value and form, as opposed to an intangible or non-physical asset.

Tax basis—The purchase price or acquisition value of an asset or investment, reduced by trading costs and other buyer's fees. Tax basis is applied to calculation of capital gains or losses; also called cost basis or basis.

Tax loss carryover—The excess loss in a year, which cannot be deducted and must be applied to future tax years. For capital losses, the annual loss limit is $3,000, so any net losses above that amount are carried forward.

Tax put—*See* Chapter 9.

Technamental analysis—A term describing the application of both technical and fundamental analysis in combination.

Technical analysis—Market analysis focused on price and volume as well as trading patterns, all designed to anticipate upcoming price action.

Technical rally—An upward price movement immediately following a downtrend, caused by technical factors rather than by fundamental developments.

Terms—Option features, including strike price, expiration date, underlying stock, and type of option (call or put).

Theoretical value—The price estimated to be proper for an option, based on a price model rather than the actual current market value; this modeling includes analysis and comparison of strike price, time until expiration, stock volatility, and an assumed rate of interest.

Theta—A measurement of the change rate in an option's value, compared to changes in time until expiration.

Tick—The minimum incremental price change in a security.

Time decay—The erosion of value in an option's premium due to the time remaining until expiration.

Time order—An order to be executed at a specific time or, if not so executed, to be canceled or converted to either market or limit order.

Time spread—A type of option spread in which each side has the same strike price but different expiration dates, also called a horizontal spread.

Time value—The portion of an option premium outside of intrinsic value, which is associated with the time remaining until expiration.

Time value of money—A concept observing that the value of money varies based on (a) the time it remains on deposit or loaned out, (b) the interest rate in effect, and (c) the method of compounding applied.

Time-weighted rate of return—The return from investment based on compound growth rate of interest, exclusive of new transactions that follow the initial deposit.

Total return—A method of calculating return from an option and stock strategy, that includes all forms of income. Usually applied to covered call writing, this provides a means for accurate comparisons between different strategies and various outcomes. Total return includes profit from the short option write, dividends, and capital gains if and when the short call is exercised. This concept is also applicable to combined strategies involving multiple option positions, both long and short, as well as positions in the underlying stock.

Trade date—The date when a trade is executed, as opposed to settlement date.

Trader—(a) An individual who trades in the market, often in short time increments, with trading as a short-term activity opposed to longer-term investing; or (b) an exchange member conducting business on the floor of an exchange.

Trading floor—The floor of an active exchange where traders bid with one another.

Trading limit—The limit imposed by various exchanges on the number of option or futures contracts that can be bought or sold in a single trading day.

Trading pit—A trading floor location designated for trading in a particular class of stock or option.

Trading range—The price span between highest and lowest prices within the current trend, defined by resistance level on the top and support level on the bottom.

Trailing stop—A type of stop-loss order set below a long position's market price, or above a short position's market price.

Transaction costs—Fees and charges involved with trade execution, which include brokerage fees, assignment and exchange fees, and interest on outstanding margin balances, as well as penalties involved with any trade completion.

Treasury bill / option strategy—Also called 90/10, a strategy in which 90% of capital is invested in interest-bearing debt securities such as Treasury bills, with the remaining 10% used to buy options.

Treasury stock—Shares of common stock that have been repurchased on the market by the issuing corporation. Treasury stock is retired permanently, has no voting rights, and pays no dividend. It is also excluded from the calculation of outstanding shares.

Trend—Direction of price movement, usually associated with technical analysis and divided into time periods (short-, intermediate-, or long-term) or, under the Dow Theory, divided into primary and secondary market-wide trends.

Trendline—In technical analysis, a line drawn onto a chart indicating the general price direction of a stock or index.

Triangle—A pattern seen on a price chart, in which the trading range narrows due to declining tops, bottoms, or both.

TRIN indicator—*TR*aders *IN*dex, a technical indicator dividing the advance/decline spread by the net difference between advancing and declining issues.

Triple bottom—A technical chart pattern in which prices decline to support three times. The third unsuccessful attempt to break through support anticipates a price reversal to the upside.

Triple top—The opposite of a triple bottom, a pattern in which prices rise to resistance three times and, failing an upside breakout, precedes a price decline.

Triple witching day—The third Friday of a month with three expirations: stock index futures, stock index futures, and stock options. This occurs in March, June, September, and December each year.

True strength index—A momentum indicator used to identify overbought or oversold conditions. Short-term purchasing momentum is compared to the 25-day and 13-day exponential moving average of price. When current price is compared with the two EMA trends, the price status and anticipated next move are more easily interpreted.

Turnaround—Descriptive of the price of stock in a company whose performance has been poor in the past but currently is experiencing a price rally.

Type—One of the four option terms, the distinction between call or put (the other three terms being strike price, expiration, and underlying stock).

Uncovered call writing—A strategy in which calls are sold when the trader does not own 100 shares of the underlying stock. This presents theoretical unlimited risk because the stock price could rise indefinitely. In comparison, a covered call contains less risk because the writer owns 100 shares per short call; so in the event of exercise, the shares are used to satisfy the assignment.

Uncovered option—A call or put that is sold without offsetting stock position.

Uncovered put writing—A short put not offset by a position in the stock. To cover a short put, the trader would need to be short 100 shares of the underlying stock.

Underlying security—The security on which an option or future are based. In the case of options, the underlying security is stock; for futures, it is a commodity.

Undervalued—A security trading at a bargain price, or at a price below fair market value.

Underwater—Status of a call when strike price is greater than the underlying stock's market value or of a put when strike is lower than current market price of the underlying; more commonly known as being out of the money.

Unit of trade—The minimum quantity of a security in a normal trading increment. Stock unit of trade is 100 shares, and for options, it is one contract (which relates to 100 shares of the underlying stock).

Unlisted security—A stock or other security not listed on an exchange often because the company has not met listing requirements.

Unsystematic risk—Any form of risk other than market risk, or a form of risk unique to a particular sector or in various kinds of markets.

Up-and-in option—An option that cannot be exercised unless or until the underlying stock reaches or passes a predetermined price level; also known as a knock-in barrier option.

Up-and-out option—An option that expires not on a specific date, but if and when the underlying stock reaches or passes a predetermined price level; also known as a knock-out barrier option.

Upside—The profits that might be realized in the best outcome of a strategy. As applied to stock prices, this is the likely price estimated for the stock. For combined option strategies, it refers to the profit zone or maximum profit when that profit is limited by the components in the strategy.

Upside/downside ratio—A ratio of advancing issues to declining issues on the New York Stock Exchange (NYSE).

Uptick—The incremental minimum advance in the price of a security, based on how it is listed and valued; a plus-tick.

Value investing—A concept for selecting stocks currently available at bargain prices, in some cases below their tangible book value. Such stocks are also perceived as dominant in their sector, well-capitalized, and characterized by moderate or low P/E ratio or higher than average dividend yield.

Vanilla option—A listed option with no exotic features or limitations.

Variable ratio write—A strategy involving ownership of 100 shares of an underlying stock and writing of two calls with dissimilar strike prices.

Vega—A measurement of option premium movement in relation to assumed volatility.

Vertical line chart—A technical price chart including the opening and closing prices (represented by small horizontal lines) and the day's trading range (represented by a vertical line from top to bottom); an OHLC (open, high, low, close) chart.

Vertical spread—*See* Chapter 9.

Volatility—Price risk; the degree of change in price over a specified period of time. As a measurement of the breadth of a stock's trading range, volatility affects option pricing as a reflection of market risk in the underlying stock.

Volatility quote trading—Quotation system for option contracts with quotes based on implied volatility instead of prices in the underlying stock.

Volatility smile—A technical chart pattern in which a grouping of options' strike prices and volatility are plotted using the same expiration.

Volume—Shares traded on a single trading session in a particular stock or on the market as a whole, often divided into volume on advancing versus declining issues.

Warrant—A derivative similar to an option but usually associated with a debt issue, used as an inducement to attract investors. The warrant enables the debt investor to purchase additional positions at a pre-set price; also called subscription warrant.

Wash sale rule—A rule disallowing any losses on trades when closed positions are reopened within 30 days of the closing date. In such a case, the loss cannot be claimed but is rolled into the original position.

Wasting asset—Any derivative asset whose value deteriorates over time, such as options experiencing time decay.

Watered stock—Shares of stock with issue price greater than the value of corporate assets.

Wedge—A technical price pattern with converging trading range lines.

Weighted moving average—A moving average including mathematical adjustment of the latest fields to provide greater impact. The exponential moving average (EMA) is popularly used as a weighted calculation.

Whipsaw—Price pattern in which a movement in one direction is immediately followed with a reversal.

Wild card option—An option with Treasury securities as the underlying, providing for a delayed delivery for the short side of the transaction.

Wild card play—The right to deliver commodities at the last available price, even when the specific contract is no longer in effect.

Working capital—A fundamental test of a corporation's ability to pay current debts from available current assets. "Current" assets are cash and any assets convertible to cash within one year (accounts receivable, inventory, marketable securities); and "current" liabilities are all debts payable within one year, including 12 months' payments due on long-term liabilities. Expressed as a dollar amount, the formula is as follows:

current assets – current liabilities

Working capital turnover—A ratio used in fundamental analysis, comparing revenue levels to working capital, designed to estimate the use of working capital to generate income. Formula:

revenues ÷ (current assets – current liabilities)

Write—Action of selling an option; a short option position, operating on the sequence of sell-hold-buy *or* sell-hold-exercise. When a written option is exercised, the writer is required to deliver 100 shares of the underlying stock (for a short call) or to accept 100 shares (for a short put), both at the specific strike price of the option contract.

Writer—The trader who sells short one or more options.

Yield—Income from an investment consisting of interest or dividends, expressed as a percentage. Yield is distinguished from capital gains or losses that are realized upon closing positions in a security.

Yield equivalence—The rate earned on a taxable security that is equivalent to the rate earned on a tax-free security when tax liability is taken into account. Formula for the taxable yield equivalent is as follows:

tax-exempt yield ÷ (1 – effective tax rate)

Yield for the tax-exempt equivalence:

taxable yield × (1 – effective tax rate)

Zero-minus tick—A security price identical to the previous transaction price but lower than the most recent trade price.

Zero-plus tick—A price level identical to the previous transaction price but higher than the most recent trade price.

Options Listings

Options listings change every day, so using any actual examples of current stock and option values would be out of date immediately. The following tables are actual options listings based on three companies listed on the New York Stock Exchange, with end-of-year stock values and with option values as listed at the time. Names have been changed for these companies, and the year indicators have been made generic. However, the *relative* value of listings will always remain constant given proximity between stock values and strike prices, time until expiration, and volatility of both stock prices and options.

YPN   December 31 current year
Last trade 93.69

Strike	First Year Calls	Puts	Second Year Calls	Puts	Third Year Calls	Puts
Jan 35	58.50	0.05				
Jan 40	54.30	0.05	54.84	0.15	51.30	0.80
Jan 45	49.10	0.05				
Jan 50	44.80	0.05	45.30	0.40	41.80	1.35
Jan 55	39.90	0.05	39.86	0.75		
Jan 60	34.10	0.05	35.40	1.25	36.66	2.50
Jan 65	29.10	0.05	32.21	1.75	33.80	3.40
Jan 67.50	26.20	0.05				
Jan 70	23.90	0.05	26.90	2.25	30.00	4.50
Jan 72.50	21.64	0.05				
Jan 75	19.10	0.05	23.70	3.30	27.00	5.70
Jan 80	14.20	0.10	19.70	4.40	24.23	7.80
Jan 85	9.20	0.19	17.05	6.00	20.02	9.20
Jan 90	4.70	0.80	13.40	8.00	17.40	11.31
Jan 95	1.45	2.50	10.70	9.90	15.50	13.20
Jan 100	0.20	6.20	8.20	12.10	12.42	16.80
Jan 105	0.05	11.09	6.49	17.80		
Jan 110	0.05	16.11	4.80	18.30	8.72	21.90
Jan 115	0.05	23.90	3.60	25.60		
Jan 120	0.05	28.90	2.50	26.80	6.20	28.36
Jan 125	0.05	33.90	1.70	37.50		
Jan 130			1.45	39.70		
Feb 75	19.00	0.20				
Feb 80	14.50	0.45				
Feb 85	9.90	0.85				
Feb 90	5.90	1.85				

Strike	First Year Calls	Puts	Second Year Calls	Puts	Third Year Calls	Puts
Feb 95	2.85	4.00				
Feb 100	1.05	7.00				
Feb 105	0.35	10.31				
Apr 55	39.00	0.05				
Apr 60	35.20	0.15				
Apr 65	30.20	0.20				
Apr 70	24.70	0.34				
Apr 72.50	22.60	0.52				
Apr 75	20.10	0.70				
Apr 80	15.60	1.19				
Apr 85	11.50	2.05				
Apr 90	7.94	3.40				
Apr 95	4.90	5.50				
Apr 100	2.75	8.20				
Apr 105	1.45	12.00				
Apr 110	0.70	15.70				
Apr 115	0.30	26.60				
Apr 120	0.15	29.00				
Apr 125	0.10	33.10				
Apr 130	0.10	38.10				
Apr 135	0.05	44.00				
Apr 140	0.05	49.10				
Jul 60	35.50	0.45				
Jul 65	30.20	0.70				
Jul 70	26.70	1.09				
Jul 75	22.30	1.70				
Jul 80	17.60	2.50				

YPN   December 31 current year
Last trade 93.69

Strike	First Year Calls	First Year Puts	Second Year Calls	Second Year Puts	Third Year Calls	Third Year Puts
Jul 85	13.54	3.60				
Jul 90	10.10	5.10				
Jul 95	7.30	7.00				
Jul 100	5.00	9.80				
Jul 105	3.20	12.70				
Jul 110	2.10	17.20				
Jul 115	1.28	20.60				
Jul 120	0.80	29.30				

JCN   December 31 current year
Last trade 108.10

Strike	First Year Calls	Puts	Second Year Calls	Puts	Third Year Calls	Puts
Jan 55	48.90	0.05				
Jan 60	49.30	0.05	50.20	0.95		
Jan 65	45.20	0.05	47.68	1.25		
Jan 70	40.30	0.05	40.70	1.60		
Jan 75	35.00	0.05	36.20	1.95		
Jan 80	29.46	0.05	34.00	2.45		
Jan 85	24.30	0.05	26.70	3.36		
Jan 90	18.10	0.10	24.30	4.10	29.30	7.00
Jan 95	13.80	0.20	21.00	5.03		
Jan 100	9.10	0.65	17.37	7.30	21.70	10.00
Jan 105	4.90	1.70	14.70	9.10		
Jan 110	2.15	3.90	11.70	10.50	16.64	14.70
Jan 115	0.70	7.28	9.40	13.30		
Jan 120	0.20	12.10	7.30	16.90	12.30	19.36
Jan 125	0.10	15.40			11.30	24.80
Jan 130	0.05	23.20	5.30	22.50	9.30	26.20
Jan 135	0.05	27.20				
Jan 140	0.05	31.50	2.85	30.10	8.00	36.20
Jan 150			1.80	42.50	5.30	39.50
Jan 160			0.75	51.70	2.65	52.40
Jan 170			0.45	61.90		
Feb 65	43.60	0.05				
Feb 70	38.70	0.05				
Feb 75	33.70	0.10				
Feb 80	31.30	0.10				
Feb 85	23.90	0.20				

JCN   December 31 current year
Last trade 108.10

Strike	First Year Calls	Puts	Second Year Calls	Puts	Third Year Calls	Puts
Feb 90	19.00	0.35				
Feb 95	14.46	0.78				
Feb 100	10.20	1.55				
Feb 105	6.30	2.95				
Feb 110	3.63	5.00				
Feb 115	1.71	8.10				
Feb 120	0.70	11.80				
Feb 125	0.30	17.30				
Feb 130	0.10	22.20				
Feb 135	0.05	27.20				
Feb 140	0.05	32.20				
Feb 145	0.05	37.20				
Apr 65	46.40	0.10				
Apr 70	39.10	0.20				
Apr 75	36.20	0.40				
Apr 80	29.40	0.40				
Apr 85	26.80	0.75				
Apr 90	20.50	1.08				
Apr 95	17.80	2.05				
Apr 100	12.30	3.20				
Apr 105	8.90	4.55				
Apr 110	6.00	6.90				
Apr 115	3.90	9.70				
Apr 120	2.40	13.40				
Apr 125	1.30	15.70				
Apr 130	0.70	21.30				

First Year Strike	Second Year Calls	Puts	Third Year Calls	Puts	Calls	Puts
Apr 135	0.45	27.10				
Apr 140	0.20	31.80				
Apr 145	0.15	37.20				
Apr 150	0.05	40.40				
Jul 65	47.88	0.35				
Jul 70	39.70	0.55				
Jul 75	36.00	0.80				
Jul 80	30.90	1.00				
Jul 85	27.30	1.60				
Jul 90	21.70	2.30				
Jul 95	17.80	3.30				
Jul 100	15.80	4.50				
Jul 105	11.00	6.40				
Jul 110	8.30	7.70				
Jul 115	6.10	10.50				
Jul 120	4.30	14.50				
Jul 125	2.80	17.50				
Jul 130	2.00	22.80				
Jul 135	1.50	25.00				
Jul 140	0.80	30.30				
Jul 145	0.60	36.70				

NDE   December 31 current year
Last trade 58.91

Strike	First Year Calls	Puts	Second Year Calls	Puts	Third Year Calls	Puts
Jan 20	40.50	0				
Jan 25	34.20	0.05	34.10	.40		
Jan 30	29.70	0.05	30.30	0.45	32.20	0.55
Jan 35	24.90	0.05	25.50	0.65		
Jan 40	19.90	0.05	21.70	1.00	21.70	1.75
Jan 45	14.60	0.05	16.60	1.70		
Jan 47.50	12.70	0.05				
Jan 50	9.20	0.05	12.50	2.65	14.10	4.00
Jan 52.50	6.90	.15	10.82	3.30		
Jan 55	4.30	0.15	9.30	4.06		
Jan 57.50	2.15	0.55				
Jan 60	0.65	1.55	5.90	5.90	8.40	8.16
Jan 65	0.05	5.90	3.90	8.50		
Jan 70	0.05	10.30	2.05	11.60	4.30	11.50
Jan 75	0.02	13.50	1.10	17.20		
Jan 80			0.50	21.30	2.10	21.70
Jan 85			0.30	26.30		
Feb 47.50	0	0				
Feb 50	9.40	0				
Feb 52.50	7.10	0.33				
Feb 55	4.90	0.60				
Feb 57.50	3.10	1.30				
Feb 60	1.65	2.20				
Feb 62.50	0.80	3.40				
Feb 65	0.25	6.30				

First Year Strike	Second Year Calls	Puts	Third Year Calls	Puts	Calls	Puts
Feb 67.50	0.18	8.80				
Feb 70	0	11.30				
Feb 75	0	16.30				
Mar 40	20.50	0.15				
Mar 42.50	20.04	0.10				
Mar 45	14.90	0.25				
Mar 47.50	12.70	0.27				
Mar 50	10.11	0.38				
Mar 52.50	8.80	0.65				
Mar 55	5.70	1.10				
Mar 57.50	3.80	1.85				
Mar 60	2.40	2.85				
Mar 65	0.70	6.20				
Mar 70	0.15	11.20				
Jun 45	16.40	0.50				
Jun 47.50	13.30	0.75				
Jun 50	11.70	1.00				
Jun 52.50	9.00	1.45				
Jun 55	7.60	2.10				
Jun 57.50	5.50	2.85				
Jun 60	4.00	3.70				
Jun 62.50	2.80	4.90				
Jun 65	1.90	6.60				
Jun 70	0.70	9.80				
Jun 75	0.20	16.30				
Jun 80	0.10	18.37				

Index

FT Press
FINANCIAL TIMES

In an increasingly competitive world, it is quality
of thinking that gives an edge—an idea that opens new
doors, a technique that solves a problem, or an insight
that simply helps make sense of it all.

We work with leading authors in the various arenas
of business and finance to bring cutting-edge thinking
and best-learning practices to a global market.

It is our goal to create world-class print publications
and electronic products that give readers
knowledge and understanding that can then be
applied, whether studying or at work.

To find out more about our business
products, you can visit us at www.ftpress.com.